T0312736

Trading Psychology

by Roland Ullrich, CFA

A Wiley Brand

Trading Psychology For Dummies®

Published by: **John Wiley & Sons, Inc.,** 111 River Street, Hoboken, NJ 07030-5774, www.wiley.com

Copyright © 2022 by John Wiley & Sons, Inc., Hoboken, New Jersey

Published simultaneously in Canada

The German original published 2021 under the Title *Trading Psychologie fuer Dummies*

Copyright © 2021 by Wiley-VCH GmbH, Germany.

For general information on our other products and services, please contact our Customer Care Department within the U.S. at 877-762-2974, outside the U.S. at 317-572-3993, or fax 317-572-4002. For technical support, please https://hub.wiley.com/community/support/dummies.

Wiley publishes in a variety of print and electronic formats and by print-on-demand. Some material included standard print versions of this book may not be included in e-books or in print-on-demand. If this book refers to media such as a CD or DVD that is not included in the version you purchased, you may download this material http://booksupport.wiley.com. For more information about Wiley products, visit www.wiley.com.

Library of Congress Control Number: 2022941293

ISBN 978-1-119-87958-9; ISBN 978-1-119-87959-6 (ePDF); ISBN 978-1-119-87960-2 (epub)

SKY10035100_071222

Contents at a Glance

hin
se visit

ued with
efers to
l at

Table of Contents

Introduction

Trading psychology — the psychological basis of securities trading— generally isn't taken very seriously, even though experts maintain that your emotions and your mental state are actually what determine the success or failure of your trading business. Those in the know are clear on this point: Trading is 80 percent psychology and 20 percent methodology. Trading is fundamentally a matter of character.

Trading — the common term for the short-term trade in securities, currencies, and financial derivatives — has become increasingly popular recently. Discount brokers especially have been seeing record numbers since 2020. They promise they'll make stock market trading as easy as pie with the help of their various trading apps. This has a certain attraction for a younger, less experienced generation and encourages gambling. But a word to the wise: If you're looking for an adrenaline rush and you think that leveraged products will make you rich overnight, you're sure to hit the rocks sooner or later. Trading in financial instruments is a sophisticated business and requires not only lots of patience and discipline but a clear head as well. You don't stand a chance without a plan, a strategy, and processes you can rely on.

Regarding terminology, I'd like to make one thing clear from the start: When I say *traders* in this book, I'm referring to those private investors who independently invest their own money on the stock market at their own risk and on a short-term basis. The time period can be as short as a few minutes (scalping) or as long as a few weeks (position trading).

Fundamentally, trading in this sense is the opposite of a long-term investment. You're looking for calculated short-term profit. If you make regular contributions to a stock portfolio in order to prepare for retirement, you're a long-term investor, not a trader. Admittedly, you could turn a trading position into a long-term investment now and then, perhaps because you don't want to sustain a loss, so you use a bit of mental jujitsu on yourself and — *voilà* — your short-term investment is now presented as something you'd always intended as a long -term investment. (I talk more about this bias known as mental accounting later on in this book. I know: The suspense is killing you.)

The stock market is all about psychology, and trading places psychology under a magnifying glass. Limiting beliefs, self-doubt, a lack of self-control, unprocessed traumatic experiences from the past, those negative conversations you hold with yourself (*self-talk*, to use the current jargon), and harmful patterns of thought will all come to light sooner or later as you go about your work as a trader. As such, trading turns out to be quite an expensive way to work through your personality issues. After all, you're risking your own money on the markets — conceivably, money in the form of savings you worked very hard to accrue. And the numbers are against you because (according to statistics) over 90 percent of all private traders on the stock exchange don't earn any money. The vast majority close their trading account within a few months, feeling frustrated — often, after suffering a total loss. The success rate is particularly low for those operating in the short-term arena.

An old stock market proverb puts it well: If you don't know yourself, the stock market is an expensive place to figure out who you are. The traders who are successful have not only often learned some quite expensive lessons but have also experienced quite the emotional roller-coaster ride. However, they have moved beyond themselves, overcoming that which initially limited them. It's worth the effort, as experienced traders will readily acknowledge. Having finally obtained their financial freedom, independence, and self-determination, they'll refuse to give up such hard-earned gains voluntarily.

When you have dealt with the trading business long enough, you discover that it's always the very same problems that continue to drive you up the wall — coping with loss, your fear, your own greed, your lack of discipline, the loss of control, stress, being overburdened, or overconfidence. All such ills are direct consequences of the special features of financial markets you have to contend with — namely, uncertainty, volatility, hyperbolic situations, barely visible actors, and, to top it all off, automated programs and algorithms that don't care a fig whether you win or lose. Price movements are neither as predictable nor as controllable as you think, and they happen to be more random.

You won't move the markets as an individual trader. You have no influence on what is happening in the market. What you *can* do is you can work with probabilities and patterns, and you can also change your perception of the markets — your attitude and point of view, in other words. You control those things that are within your power to control: yourself. You keep a clear head. This is how mental strength is created.

Never let the markets take control of you and your trader psyche. A successful process orientation and a fixed set of rules protect you from losing control. Protecting your portfolio is your top priority.

Our evolutionary heritage weighs heavily; we are not naturally suited to trading. The human brain isn't designed to operate successfully on financial markets. The way the stock market works contradicts our naturally acquired ways of thinking and behavior. Therefore, it's even more important to internalize fixed routines and to systematize your trading so that you can protect yourself.

You'll develop as a trader when you find out what you can control, what you can change, and why. What are your trading goals? What are your expectations? What trading style matches your personality? Only then can you address the question of a) how you want to proceed and b) which methods you want to use. The challenge with trading is a psychological challenge. Trading platforms and systems are important but do not determine your success. You alone are responsible for what you earn with your trading — not the technology, not the systems, and not the markets, either.

About This Book

This book about trading psychology isn't one of those heavy theoretical tomes — I wanted it to be a practical book where I can offer advice. The idea is to provide you with multiple examples, practical tasks, and useful exercises designed to build the psychological foundations you need in order to prepare yourself for the specific requirements of trading. Beginners, in particular, underestimate the psychological stress factors involved in trading. Getting rich quick on the stock exchange is a tempting proposition but not at all realistic, as the statistics confirm. This book will save you from many painful and expensive experiences. I'll provide you with the mental armor you'll need in order to trade in a successful, brain-compatible manner.

Trading is a hard-core business that punishes mistakes and weaknesses immediately. You're playing with the top echelon right from the start. Whether you're a professional or an amateur, you're all competing in the same markets. Regardless of which market you choose to be active in, you'll be unable to move it one way or another. It's the other ones, the big professional actors, who move the markets. Let this fact teach you to be humble, but don't let it intimidate you too much. Your status as a small fish means that you're flexible; you're not subject to investment guidelines or other practical constraints. Your niche isn't competing with anyone. You're trading under the radar of the big fish, and you can profit from that fact.

This book is addressed to all market participants. Whether you're a short-term trader or a long-term investor, the psychological effects apply to you all, albeit to different extents. You'll be sure to profit when you understand how the distorted and biased way you make financial decisions affects your portfolio. Neither will it hurt to see to what extent your trading performance depends on your emotional state.

If you read this book from start to finish, you will

>> Be in a better position to know whether trading really and truly is something for you

>> Find out which character traits and core competencies are needed for trading

>> Familiarize yourself with mental self-coaching techniques and understand how to develop psychological resilience and mental strength

>> Understand that developing as a trader involves psychological development

Conventions Used in This Book

This book is written in the most practical and realistic manner possible, regarding the topic of trading psychology. I avoid complicated and extensive scientific explanations. I hope you can forgive me that my explanations about exciting discoveries in modern brain research tend to be a tad theoretical. After all, neurofinance is my passion. (If you're keeping track, most of the more theoretical paragraphs in this book sport the Technical Stuff icon.)

I am looking forward to your feedback and your opinions. I am grateful for any suggestions and corrections. Please share your experience. That will provide material for any revised editions. If the topics in this book speak to you or you realize with some embarrassment that you're not familiar with one particular corner of the trading world and you want to inform yourself, go to my website at www.roland-ullrich.com. There, you'll find a wealth of blog articles, videos, coaching materials, and workshops.

What You Don't Need to Read

This book is structured in a reader-friendly way — that means you don't need to read its 300 pages from beginning to end. Browse the book at your leisure and read the parts and chapters that interest you. The cross-references in the book provide you with more in-depth information on topics you want to know more about. The modular structure gives you the option to read individual parts of the book independently. This obviously has the consequence that you will see repetition. If you read the book from end to end, you'll know all about the fact that such repetitions are the key to stabilizing the neural circuits and synaptic connections in your brain.

You can skip the text in the sidebar boxes, if you like. Those contain further information, entertaining stories, and anecdotes that aim to loosen up the book. (Of course, feel free to read them — they may bring a smile to your face.)

Foolish Assumptions

Because you're obviously interested in the topic of trading psychology, I assume that you have some experience with the stock exchange. That means you have presumably made profits and losses with your own money. There's a slight chance you may have experienced a number of involuntary emotional outbursts. In my experience, some people will have experienced more severe losses. In any case, you should understand that psychology plays an important role in trading.

Here are some further assumptions I have made about you:

>> You want to understand what goes on in your brain when you make financial decisions.

>> You want to know what influence evolution has had on your thought and behavioral patterns.

>> Sometimes, you can't get a grip on your emotions.

>> You need support when you experience fear and stressful situations.

>> You want to learn how to make better and smarter decisions.

>> You want to be able to deal with unavoidable losses in a more sensible manner.

>> You're looking for methods to develop mental strength and psychological resilience in trading.

>> You can't find a strategy, niche, or trading style that suits you.

>> You want to know which character traits and core competencies are important in trading.

>> You want to know whether trading is truly something for you.

How This book Is Organized

This book has six parts. Its simple structure is easy to understand, and it should help you navigate the content. The structure looks like this:

Part 1: The Sovereign Trader

Does the fact that it's difficult to consistently earn money on the stock market surprise you? The explanation is as simple as it is sobering: You're human! And that means you have all the genetic dispositions associated with being a human being. The first part of this book explains the evolutionary development process and the neural structure of the human brain. When it comes to brains, everyone gets the standard model — no upgrades are available.

It turns out that your fundamental nature isn't particularly suited to trading. Don't worry, though: You can learn to be suited for it, simply because the human brain is quite capable of change and development. You can learn the mental prerequisites for brain-compatible trading. With the right mindset, you can preemptively recognize and avoid trading errors. The innovative discoveries of modern neurofinance research have revealed the necessary success factors for brain-compatible — and therefore successful — trading.

Part 2: Making a Successful Trade

Successful trading depends on how consistently you practice trading and develop your trading skills. Using a demo account makes it easier for you to test your strategies; paper trading trains the sequences and processes involved in trading until you can automatically call them up. In this part, I show you the advantages of frictionless trading processes and how you can profit from training plans. I introduce you to the secrets of explicit and implicit pattern recognition — the supreme trading discipline! You'll find out how to improve your profit opportunities while limiting your risk exposure. I show you how to get a grip on losing streaks impacting your portfolio as well as getting a grip on your psyche.

Part 3: Emotional Sovereignty

You'll get tons of very practical tips and notes in this part. The many exercises and tasks should help you develop your personality as a trader as well as help you act in an emotionally sovereign, strong-willed way. An important technical and psychological component to your development involves keeping a trading journal. It's the key to your personal development. With it, you'll be in a position to recognize and solve psychological patterns affecting your trading behavior. With all this knowledge, you'll be able to find a trading style that suits your personality.

A further important component involves self-coaching techniques. All the exercises I discuss are designed to provide you with the mental strategies you need in order to deal with losses, stress, and fear in a healthier way. You'll find out how you can work to set aside the beliefs you hold that are sabotaging your success as well as how to quiet that stream of negative self-talk that is holding you back. From this inner work, you'll gain confidence and strengthen your self-esteem.

Part 4: Making Decisions Safely

In this part, you'll lay the foundations for smart and well-thought-out trading decisions. You'll see how to deal with subconscious decision-making processes and how to better manage your susceptibility to failure. After having grasped the evolutionary development of your brain, you'll be able to preempt irrational thought and behavioral patterns and to make use of the trading rules of thumb I introduce in this section. This is how to find the correct foundation for trading decisions.

Part 5: Keeping Bad Behavior in Check

This part is all about recognizing and understanding how irrational and biased your behavior has been so far, including when trading. Behavioral finance research has made some exciting discoveries in this area. Keep in mind that systematic miscalculations, cognitive and emotional biases, and a pronounced herd mentality tend to have grave consequences. You'll find out how to recognize this kind of incorrect behavior and avoid it. You'll also see how to better deal with your ego and better understand your feelings of fear and regret.

Part 6: The Parts of Ten

Picture The Parts of Ten as a hit list of important stock exchange knowledge. It's a significant component of the *For Dummies* series. Without attempting to be exhaustive, I present ten avoidable psychological trading traps that you should always keep in mind when you're trading. Then I show you the ten secrets of success of mentally superior traders. If you take these to heart, there is practically nothing standing in your way when it comes to becoming a successful trader. Finally. I explain the ten basic rules for the perfect trading day.

Icons Used in This Book

It's part of the *For Dummies* tradition series to use icons. They're meant to catch the eye and loosen up the structure of the book. In this book, you'll find the following symbols.

The Tip icon marks bits of information you will find particularly helpful. When you're skimming the book, these tips should pop out to give you a quick grasp of the topic.

The Remember icon marks information that's important to keep in mind. Sometimes it reviews topics from earlier in the book that are relevant to the information being presented.

The Technical Stuff icon marks information of a technical nature that is more important to someone working in the field who might need to see a bit more depth.

The Warning icon points out bits of information you can use to avoid issues you might encounter.

Here you'll find examples that help get the point across.

Beyond the Book

In addition to the introduction you're reading right now, this book comes with a free, access-anywhere Cheat Sheet containing information worth remembering about the nature of trading psychology and the trading brain. To get this Cheat Sheet, simply go to www.dummies.com and type **Trading Psychology For Dummies Cheat Sheet** in the Search box.

What's Next

Now that you've had a chance to read the operating manual for this particular book, I hope you realize what you're in for. So, get going! Start wherever you want when it comes to its 300 pages. Look for topics that most interest you. Use this book as a reference book and advisor. Try out the techniques and exercises provided. They're definitely worth your while, and they will propel you further down the road of trading success.

I hope you have lots of fun with these lessons and that you have lots of success implementing them in the exciting world of trading.

1

The Sovereign Trader

IN THIS CHAPTER

» Seeing how human evolution has impacted financial decision-making processes

» Looking more closely at the trader brain

» Understanding neural circuits and biochemical processes

» Tracing the miracle of neuroplasticity

» Using process orientation for success

Chapter **1**

Brain-Compatible Trading

I n this chapter, I take you way back — *way*, way back. Across millions of years, the evolutionary selection process has made us humans what we are today. We must take that knowledge into account when we're surprised about behaviors that no longer fit in our modern time — including behaviors on the trading floor. To better understand what's going on, it pays to take a closer look at the trader brain. (I hope to convince you that this closer look will provide some answers.) Modern brain research has made some exciting discoveries about how the decision-making process actually takes place — which parts of the brain are involved and which biochemical processes occur simultaneously, for example. In fact, the research has progressed to such an extent that experts in the field are able now to predict financial decisions by the activity of specific areas of the brain.

By their very nature, your brain and its interconnections are not quite suitable for the trading business. But you can train them to overcome their inherent weaknesses. The human brain is changeable and can adapt to changing conditions. In other words, you can learn behaviors for *successful* trading — brain-compatible trading, in other words.

The key to successful trading is process orientation — what I call the *systemization* of your trading approach. You need professional rules and a proven trading strategy in order to survive in unpredictable markets. When you add that to a trading style that suits your personality, there may not be much holding you back when it comes to a successful trading career.

Recognizing the Human Barriers to Trader Success

In the last decades, science has closely investigated human behavior in the area of economic decision-making. The findings are sobering. The science tells us that humans are characterized by emotional patterns of thought and behavior that have been formed in the course of evolution. The science is also telling us that there's a good chance that these subconscious automatic behaviors are unsuitable when it comes to making wise financial decisions. In numerous studies, behavioral economists have demonstrated how irrational humans are when they're making investments. The truth is, financial decision-making behavior can be distorted by many factors, including these:

» Overestimating your abilities

» Learning from your mistakes seems beyond your power

» Letting emotions, such as fear and greed, unconsciously determine your behavior when making financial decisions

» Letting yourself get carried away by the crowd

» Being unable to objectively assess risks

» Letting the situation — rather than calculation — determine your appetite for risk

» Taking profits too early and letting losses run on

Taking a closer look at the brains of investors and traders demonstrates why the failings listed here occur and how they impact the decision-making process. Laboratory experiments within the relatively young field of neurofinance provide some exciting answers.

Using Neurofinance to Look Deep Inside the Trader Brain

Neurofinance is an interdisciplinary area of research that resulted from the combined efforts of economists, behavioral psychologists, and neuroscientists in the 1990s. Neurofinance research, by making use of modern brain research methods, focuses on analyzing financial decision-making processes. These are the central questions: How does the human brain deal with money? Which neural structures are involved in processing financial decisions? What is the importance of the biochemical processes in the brain when it comes to dealing with money? Neurofinance studies of the drivers of choice behavior pay special attention to the trading behavior of financial market actors, focusing on the central question of how behavioral and cognitive biases distort the rational decision-making of investors. Another aspect is the influence of personality traits on investor behavior.

REMEMBER

The neurobiological correlates of financial decision-making processes have been decoded. A brain scanner can display the enormous influence of emotions, cognitive biases, and archaic instincts in real time. Most of the time humans may not act rationally. Many of the phenomena described in behavioral finance research can be explained by taking a closer look at the trader brain. Today, brain researchers are able to predict and influence investor behavior.

Professor Bernd Weber, a clinical neuroscientist and dean of the Medical Faculty at the University of Bonn, has come to the conclusion that, because of their evolutionary development, humans are incapable whatsoever of rational thinking and acting. That would also suggest (quite highly, in fact) that the human brain simply isn't made to invest successfully in the stock market. The laws and functioning of financial markets contradict learned human behaviors.

THE DEVELOPMENT OF THE BRAIN SCANNER

With the help of new measuring procedures, brain research in the past 30 years learned more about the workings of the human brain than in the previous 100 years combined. Neuroscientific research tools — in particular, functional magnetic resonance imaging (FMRI) — make the activities of the brain visible and show which regions are activated when carrying out specific tasks. You can see the brain at work in real time, so to speak. This means it's possible to analyze human behavior when dealing with money from a neuroscientific perspective. Laboratory experiments explain irrational financial decisions, emotions, and the impact of evolution on human behavior on capital markets.

The neural networks in the human brain have developed over the past million years and have adapted to the respective living conditions faced by said humans. We today are the result of an evolutionary selection process, where the genetic makeup and the structure of the human brain has changed incredibly slowly. As a matter of fact, according to leading neuroscientists the human brain hasn't changed much over the last 50,000 years. In the face of the rapid developments of the world in the last centuries, evolution has been unable to keep up. Unconscious and highly automated behaviors probably arose as the best possible adaptation to prevailing environmental conditions. Automated behaviors when faced with threat situations probably kept humans alive in the Stone Age (fight-or-flight reflex), but present-day threat situations still trigger the same stimulus-response patterns.

REMEMBER

The living conditions of the human species have changed drastically, but evolution isn't that fast. The human brain comes from another time. Deeply rooted instincts still determine our behavior, especially when we are under emotional duress. These instinctual mechanisms do not suit the ways present-day financial markets function. Humans are conditioned to act, while the stock exchange often rewards patience and waiting.

Is our evolutionarily ancient brain system even suited to make sensible trading decisions? Neurofinance research has answered this question with a resounding No. We were given a brain to help us survive in a harsh environment; its nature isn't suited to making economically rational decisions in complex financial markets.

Recognizing Typically Human Behavioral Patterns

Today we understand that our brain, over the millennia, has always tried to adapt in the best possible manner to our respective living conditions. In comparison to the millions of years of our history of evolution, the past centuries are only a tiny window of time, but one with a dynamic speed of change that never occurred before this. That means the neural circuits in our brain may require a few generations until they have adapted to modern life.

Therefore, it should come as no surprise that the behavior and thought patterns of many market participants aren't always rational and therefore can be explained better within an evolutionary context.

Deeply rooted reflexes and unconscious reactions from previous epochs seem to determine our financial decisions. This applies to individual traders as well as to the majority of market participants. Strong price movements are emotionally contagious and can lead to collective herd behavior. That's why the stock exchange is, at its most fundamental level, psychology. To fully comprehend the psychological nature of the stock exchange, you must realize that the dominant emotions experienced there stem from another era and that they are characterized by irrational exaggeration in both directions. Speculative bubbles and stock market crashes repeat at regular intervals, as the history of the stock market shows.

This may sound quite sobering for traders, but it explains market realities.

REMEMBER

Don't let yourself be fooled: The neurobiological prerequisites for successful trading are not a given.

But there is hope: You can balance many human inadequacies and learn to acquire the necessary equipment for brain-compatible trading. It requires a lot of practice and training. Self-awareness and self-reflection are the first step. As a trader, you should understand and accept how your brain works. Be clear that the structure of your brain isn't suited to financial market mechanisms. You have no other option but to accept that fact. You have only one brain.

TIP

You can't change anything about your genetic makeup, but you can learn to deal more consciously with your emotions and natural reflexes. You need to do so from the position of an objective observer. When you learn to perceive your response patterns in a more conscious manner, you can avoid all sorts of evolutionary traps. You'll be in a position to adapt your behavior to markets by observing, analyzing, and following the markets in a conscious manner.

Our expert knowledge and our own analytical logical powers of thought can be called up only when we can reduce the negative impacts of emotions. This is the only way to be balanced and in full possession of our cognitive capacity — with unfiltered access to our intellect and intuition.

REMEMBER

The discoveries of modern brain research can build a bridge between the realities of human behavior and the way that financial markets function. Neurofinance can provide you with an important set of tools as you make your way down the path to becoming a successful trader.

Leveraging Neuroscientific Discoveries

Accepting the limitations of the structures of your brain initially sounds frustrating. However, modern brain research has some good news: The human brain isn't hard-wired — it's capable of change throughout our lives.

TECHNICAL STUFF

Fifty years ago, science was still convinced that human brains were fixed and incapable of change. Today, we know that the central nervous system and our brain slowly but steadily change in response to our actions and experiences over the course of our entire lives.

Neuronal (also known as *synaptic*) plasticity refers to the ability of our brain to change and optimize processes and sequences when used effectively. To simplify, one can say that the brain works like a muscle: When you don't use neuronal structures and synaptic connections, they tend to degrade over time. Networks you *do* use intensively tend to stabilize and strengthen over time. This is visible on a brain scanner and can be easily recognized.

The psychologist Donald Hebb is considered to have discovered synaptic plasticity. In 1949, he formulated the learning rule named after him (Hebb's rule) which states that learning processes take place in neural networks by means of synaptic transfer between neurons (in other words, "Neurons that fire together wire together"). Consistent repetition creates stable new connections and strengthens memory.

Neuroplasticity always works in both directions, independent of age. By that, I mean that you can

>> Lose abilities if you don't use them

>> Learn abilities if you practice them consistently

You probably use a navigational system when you're driving in an unknown area. (It's practically basic equipment for cars these days.) This leads to cognitive offloading, where the hard work of cognitive processing is shifted to somebody (or something) else. (The evidence for such cognitive offloading is quite clear, as research on brain scanners shows.) Research has proven that our natural orientation skills significantly worsen with the use of navigational systems.

The determining factor in learning any new skill is regular repetition. Practice makes perfect, as the old saying goes. We can do anything we want if we practice regularly and intensively. Abilities aren't genetic; there is no natural talent for trading. Because it's now a simple matter to open a trading account and just start trading, lots of newbies underestimate the amount of time, stamina, and practice required in order to trade successfully.

According to best-selling author Malcolm Gladwell, you can achieve anything with discipline and hard work. In *Outliers*, his book from 2008, he explains how extremely successful people — athletes and professional musicians, for example — train on the average for 10,000 hours over the course of their career. Practice is much more important for success than talent, the author claims.

Trading Success Factors

Even if current studies on the topic of peak performance in general come to the conclusion that talent is the most important factor when it comes to success, this applies to only a limited extent to the trading business. If you want to be successful in trading, you require large measures of motivation, discipline, and stamina. All three have more to do with attitude than with talent. Without the appropriate mindset, you won't achieve your goals. If you want to master your field, you need to develop constantly and train consistently. Expert status will not just fall from the sky and you certainly don't get it at birth. Training and performance are tightly linked — no doubt about it.

In looking at trading success, I've determined that there are a few basic success factors, all of which can be divided into these four main areas:

>> Processes

>> Practice

>> Personality

>> Talent

The secret to success in trading is to have clear processes and structures as well as predefined strategies and trading plans. You must train for these, until the fixed sequences become part of your flesh and blood. Routines provide you with the support and stability you need in stressful situations without having to think about them. Habits keep your head free, saving cognitive energy that you can use for more important tasks in trading. Formulated in a neuroscientific manner: Repetition builds and consolidates the neural circuits of process orientation until they can be recalled automatically. This doesn't sound particularly exciting, but it's the key to success. After all, your behavior won't change by changing your opinion. A new conviction is formed only when you have drilled the new behavior into you.

REMEMBER

Trading is a particular psychological and emotional challenge that humans aren't ready for in their natural state. Tried-and-tested processes provide you with security and prevent old reflexes from taking over in stressful situations.

Your personality as a trader plays an important role here. This is because markets will hold up an unfiltered mirror to you and will lay bare your specific strengths and weaknesses. This is why having a good mix of strong personal characteristics and competencies is so important.

Every trader has individual talents for certain trading styles and market segments or niches. With a lot of practice, you can perfect your personal abilities. In this way, you'll become an expert in your particular niche. The trick is finding the right trading environment for your personality. (For more on how to determine your trader personality and trading style, see Chapter 3.)

Using psychological testing tools to identify your personality traits and determine your fields of competency helps you discover your special strengths and develop them in the most effective way. I can assure you that this method has helped many traders achieve real breakthroughs in their development.

This is why it's in your hands — well, your head, to be exact — to create the prerequisites and the foundation for successful trading.

REMEMBER

Expertise requires many years of hard work and a lot of practice. What sets successful traders apart is goal orientation, a strong will, a lifelong desire to learn, and a willingness to always develop further. The brain of a successful trader has developed and consolidated the corresponding neural circuits because, as you have now found out, trading is first and foremost a head thing, not a market thing.

IN THIS CHAPTER

» Defining mental strength

» Aiming for self-analysis instead of market analysis

» Moving step-by-step toward your goal

» Dealing with stress

» Building mental resilience

Chapter **2**

Developing Mental Strength

Traders report that one of the biggest problems they encounter is a lack of discipline. They note that this lack of discipline sometimes leads to a loss of control as well as avoidable errors in the preparation and execution of trades. The truth is, what they lack is the mental strength necessary for the trading business. Motivation is no substitute for discipline.

The development of mental strength — the focus of this chapter — is an essential prerequisite for your success in trading. That development begins with the mental preparation of each trading day. A positive mindset promotes self–discipline and allows you to focus on the success parameters of your trading strategies. In this way, you continually learn and develop, which is always your own best strategy for avoiding stress and lessening emotional pressures. Mental strength and stress resilience are mutually dependent. In the face of incalculable and volatile markets, you need a good portion of mental resilience.

Preparing the Mind

How do you prepare for a typical trading day? You probably invest a lot of time in the analysis of fundamental data, market indicators, and charts. You read studies and carefully view the daily flood of news on various channels. You follow one or two experts and include their market assessments when you prepare your trading plans.

Viewed from the psychological point of view, these efforts serve to reduce the extent of uncertainty and give you a feeling of control. This creates self-confidence in a market environment that is always hard to predict. Therefore, some traders put a considerable amount of effort into market analysis.

Searching for the holy grail

Let's be honest: All traders are secretly looking for the perfect strategy, the much-cited holy grail (the dream of guaranteed success on the stock exchange, in other words.) That's why traders invest so much energy into sophisticated forecasting models and complicated calculation models.

TECHNICAL STUFF

The holy grail strategy originated in the United States with Linda Bradford Raschke, known the world over as one of *the* best commodities and futures traders. In the mid-1990s, she developed a set of trading *setups* — strategies that were supposed to predict the optimum entry point during clear trend movements to maximize profits and minimize risks. The defined trading signals were supposed to enable an optimum risk-reward ratio. These classic trend-following systems, however, require stable trends to work. They lose their halo in volatile sideways markets. According to the Arthurian legend, the original Holy Grail disappeared and its secret was never discovered. In the trading world, the search for the grail continues unabated. (It's a wistful goal, in my humble opinion.)

In retrospect, the holy grail has achieved notoriety by way of its name rather than its track record for producing profitable trading strategies, but that doesn't mean that Linda Raschke's holy grail strategy doesn't deserve a closer look. In my opinion, her "legendary" trading approach provides three valuable fundamental principles that are worth remembering for newbies as well as experienced traders:

>> Insisting on consistent risk minimization and loss limitation with every single trade

>> Developing systematic and structured trading processes

>> Opening a trade only if it has clearly identifiable chart patterns

Seeing why a market analysis isn't sufficient

Why would I even suggest that an in-depth analysis of the markets isn't sufficient for success? The answer is quite simple: because the human factor comes into play on the stock market. The trader's psyche is the weak link in the process chain. Technical and fundamental preparation is just as important as mental preparation for what happens on the market. Your mental constitution and your attitude determine whether you will benefit from your technical expertise. Experience shows that it's much harder to implement a tested strategy according to the rules than it is to find a new profitable strategy — apart from the fact that, unfortunately, there are no perfect consistently profitable strategies.

WARNING

Don't allow yourself to be fooled by the dubious promises of some self-appointed experts: "Guaranteed dream returns with my XYZ system" remains a pipe dream and serves only one purpose: to extract money from your pocket.

Doing self-analysis instead of market analysis

What is the correct procedure? First off, you need to shift your focus. Rather than focus exclusively on market analysis, devote more attention to self-analysis. Emotional stability, as well as the knowledge of your personal strengths and weaknesses, may offer significantly higher potential returns than crunching the numbers. In practice, there will always be more profitable strategies than profitable traders. Let me assure you: You need mental strength to implement your own strategy *consistently* — always based on your own pre-defined rules, in other words.

TIP

Self-analysis requires the willingness to engage in some introspection. You need to learn how to recognize your thought and behavior patterns as well as your emotional patterns early enough for it to be useful. Write down all anomalies immediately — because memory can deceive you after some time has passed.

REMEMBER

Experience has taught me to write down patterns of any kind in a trading journal the moment I notice them, and I strongly suggest that you do the same. Otherwise, you give your ego time to correct unpleasant truths as it sees fit. At the end of the day, you can evaluate the entries in peace and reflect on them. (See Chapter 5 for more about trading journals.) Such reflection often leads to some useful insights, such as the ability to

>> Identify harmful patterns and their impact on profitability

>> Recognize useful patterns that you were not even aware of

Adopting the position of a neutral observer who is only documenting facts can be the best way to recognize your own strengths and weaknesses. That is the prerequisite for positive change and further development.

In Chapter 3, I go into detail about the various forms of pattern recognition.

REMEMBER

The inability, or in some cases the unwillingness, to be introspective is a reason that many traders stagnate from the beginning and then give up after some time. Almost every trader has problem patterns. The art is to recognize these patterns and break through them.

With the right mindset, you can turn every trading day into a positive experience. You can't prevent loss days, and you're unlikely to make money on the stock exchange every day. It's therefore important that you refuse to identify with the losses, or you'll end up feeling like a loser.

If you focus on your strengths, implement your trading plans according to the rules, and limit your losses at an early stage, there's no reason to doubt yourself. Just continue to learn and develop your strategies.

REMEMBER

Observe your own behaviors carefully, ask the right questions, work on your trader personality, and develop mental strength rather than look for the holy grail.

Learning from experience: Small steps, big impact

As most everyone knows, no one can predict the future — you can only be prepared for certain likely developments. As a result of your thorough preparation, you're sure to regularly make good and rational decisions — decisions that, despite their goodness and rationality, will turn out to be completely wrong. The best models don't protect against wrong decisions.

According to a well-known trader adage, "If you set out to be smarter than the market, then you have already lost." The trader who can realistically assess their abilities, however, still stands a chance.

REMEMBER

The market holds up a mirror to you every single day. This may disrupt your self-image, but the market doesn't care. The market immediately punishes personal weaknesses, emotional reactions, and a lack of preparation.

It's a mental challenge to design your development as a trader in such a way that all your trading experiences — whether good or bad — take you to the next level. You'll know you're on the right track when you manage not to take personally any errors or setbacks, but rather to constructively analyze such errors and setbacks and draw the right conclusions from them. However, blaming yourself isn't constructive — it leads to you focusing on your weaknesses rather than your strengths, and can leave you feeling incompetent and cause your self-confidence to suffer. (For tips on how to build your self-confidence and boost your self-esteem, see Chapter 6.)

A good way to strengthen your self-confidence is to think in small steps. Many experienced traders report that setting many small, achievable goals has proven to be a tremendous help. Two strategies make sense here:

>> **Time frames:** Set daily, weekly, or monthly goals.

>> **Process levels:** Set task-oriented goals associated with implementation strategies, trading setups, and trading plans.

TIP

If you decide to keep a trading journal (see Chapter 5), expand your focus beyond your weaknesses and errors. Watch out for balance. Successful setups and successful trades are worth entering. Always pay attention to which mirror you want to look at.

REMEMBER

Set yourself some subgoals as well. The resulting step-by-step approach, which is immensely motivating, creates regular experiences of success. Psychologists say that this is the breeding ground for mental strength and self-confidence. Studies show that achieving small, planned successes has a greater impact than the normal, positive experiences someone has in everyday trading life.

Avoiding Trading Stress Traps

Because you're risking your own capital when you trade, it's impossible to avoid psychological pressure. You're acting in an environment of risk and uncertainty and you will regularly suffer losses. This can cause an immense amount of stress — stress you'll somehow have to deal with. That task isn't always pleasant. Be honest with yourself: If you're looking for a stress-free environment, trading is the wrong place for you.

Working with positive stress

Stress isn't generally detrimental to your health — it's quite a natural response to perceived stressful situations (those times you feel under pressure, in other words.) Stress sharpens the senses and inspires performance. You can cope better with challenges. The output of the stress hormone adrenaline provides for increased attentiveness and muscle tension. Positive stress mobilizes the body and mind, without causing damage. From an evolutionary point of view, a minimum level of stress and excitement is necessary for survival.

REMEMBER

Winning is a rush. It triggers a shot of adrenaline in all traders and puts them in a joyfully excited state. Winning is sure to motivate you and increase tremendously your willingness to perform.

Stress and fear of loss of control

That adrenaline rush can definitely be positive, but it can also be dangerous if the feeling of stress continues and turns into a fear of losing control. Negative stress can easily throw you off track. If the psychological strain of trading becomes overpowering, you'll lose your emotional balance and make mistakes.

REMEMBER

In research, a distinction is made between two types of stress: positive stress (known as eustress) and negative stress (known as distress). Positive stress occurs when you're highly motivated; successful moments work to drive you. Negative stress occurs as a result of frequent overtaxing or threatening situations. Over a longer period, the physical and psychological consequences of negative stress are sometimes so serious that they can lead to burnout syndrome.

Stress is a social phenomenon. According to surveys, an overwhelming majority of the workforce suffers from stress symptoms.

You can probably imagine that trading contains numerous stress triggers. After all, you're risking your own money in an unpredictable market environment. If this isn't fertile ground for negative emotions and stress factors, or stressors, what is?

WARNING

The need to be in control in trading (the desperate need to get a grip on the markets, in other words) may emerge when you have lost control in other areas of life. The sense of powerlessness triggers negative stress. Subconsciously, you want to compensate for this loss of control. However, the markets are the worst place to do it.

Letting go of false beliefs

Sometimes, you may put pressure on yourself with false expectations or unrealistic ideas of trading. You have probably never consciously thought about it. Typical stress triggers are, for example, the following convictions I often hear in my practice:

>> Only a day with wins is a good trading day.

>> I must trade a lot to be successful.

>> I must earn money with trading every day/week.

These beliefs inevitably lead to negative stress. You're emotionally dependent on winning days. If you believe that you need to earn money on the stock exchange, the market will take your self-esteem for a ride. Any unexpected market volatility inevitably causes a roller coaster of emotions. It's well known that a loss of control leads to stress and anxiety. How will you be able to focus on the rule-compliant implementation of your trading strategy under those circumstances?

You can control neither the market nor your trading results. A good day is a day in which you successfully implement your strategy. Some days will bring wins, and some will bring losses. The number of trades doesn't determine your success, either. In fact, it's sometimes better to wait and observe the market until appropriate trading signals appear. You're unnecessarily putting pressure on yourself if you think you need to trade frequently. And you're bound to make mistakes. Don't let the market decide how you feel.

REMEMBER

Mental strength also means being patient. Patience is a virtue that isn't easy for traders to develop. Being patient means waiting and trusting that what you forecast will occur. It requires self-discipline and courage to endure the uncertainty, however the market develops. Patience requires a firm belief that your strategy is the right one and that the appropriate entry signals will come. When you develop mental strength, you'll be in a position to surpass yourself.

TIP

Be aware of your assumptions and expectations by writing down your beliefs. Consider carefully how realistic your goals are and be clear about what is actually important in trading in order to be successful. (Chapter 6 talks more about setting aside beliefs that are keeping you from achieving your goals.)

Reducing stress in a targeted manner

Here's the burning question: How can you relieve stress in trading? The usual stress management methods mostly aim at symptoms and their results. This isn't enough. A sustainable form of stress management goes deeper and explores the reasons and causes. The goal is prevention instead of having to come up with a cure.

The following recommendations are derived from the flood of psychological self-help books on the topic of holistic stress management strategies. Let's start with the short-term measures:

>> Take a break from trading and try to relax.

>> Release the mental tension by physically reacting to it (maybe by letting loose a primal scream or two, pounding the table, or running around the block).

>> Consciously distract yourself by concentrating on a completely different topic.

Now, for some long-term measures:

>> Identify your stressors.

>> Consciously avoid stressors by preventively correcting and adapting your trading.

>> Change your attitude to the stressors you cannot change.

The short-term stress management measures are easier to implement than the long-term ones. To set the long-term measures in motion, you need regular phases of regeneration when it comes to your trading.

REMEMBER

The truth is, you can't change most of the stress factors in trading — but you can preempt these and control your stress response more consciously by recognizing those triggers early on and assessing them more positively. This requires personal self-reflection. When you can consciously perceive your triggers, you can control your response. If you use this window of opportunity effectively, you can break old stimulus-response patterns. That's how you can avoid the stress trap.

TECHNICAL STUFF

The Austrian neurologist and psychiatrist Viktor Frankl (1905-1997) once stated: "There is a space between stimulus and response. This space gives us the freedom and power to choose our response. Our growth and our freedom lies in our response." In other words, it's up to us humans whether (and how) we respond. How you react is a mirror of your trading development. Stress responses start in your head. The thing you need to change is how you think. It's possible for you to learn how to stop automated reaction patterns before they start. It's up to you to decide which response is appropriate in a given situation. Use your response space consciously and actively. As a result, you can maintain control. With the right attitude, you can develop your personal trading development potential. (You can also gain mental strength and resilience.)

TIP

Traders often follow way too many markets on too many screens. That practice is strenuous and distracting. The resulting sensory overload can cause stress. Stay focused and concentrate on the essentials. That way, you can stay on top of everything. The flood of information usually provides no added value, anyway. Also make sure you have a stress-free trading environment. It's important that you can work undisturbed in a focused manner. Avoid unnecessary distractions.

REMEMBER

You can try out a variety of relaxation exercises to relieve stress — yoga, meditation, autogenic training, or progressive muscle relaxation, for example. Special breathing techniques can also calm the nerves. Regular exercise reduces stress hormones and pent-up energy and has been proven to make people more stress-resistant. You can find out more about the benefits of exercise and other relaxation techniques in Chapter 6.

Becoming More Resilient

Each trader responds differently to stress factors. Personality traits have an effect, obviously, as confirmed by resilience research. Though some initially respond to stress by acting powerless and helpless, others immediately respond to the challenges and overcome any crisis. The crucial difference is this: Traders with resilience respond and act faster. They have a healthy sense of self-confidence and don't perceive uncertainty or pressure as stress. And they don't take loss trades personally.

Psychology understands resilience as *mental* resilience — the ability to cope with stress, crises, or setbacks and to grow from them, in other words. Resilient people have a realistic picture of what's going on around them and their abilities to deal with events and occurrences that get thrown their way. They're happy to take their fate into their own hands. This positive assessment style, known as PAS for short, ensures that someone can still act appropriately and make decisions under difficult circumstances.

A person's own assessment of the stressful situation naturally plays a major role. It's a question of character strength whether someone can continue powering through rather than getting stuck at a low point.

TIP

If you tend to take losses personally, make sure your mental resilience remains in harmony with your emotional risk tolerance. When choosing the *position size* of your trades (the dollar amount you invest in one trade, in other words), always ask how you would feel if you got stopped out for a loss. Answering this question determines the amount of risk you're willing to take.

What makes for a resilient trader? A truly resilient trader can control themselves so that they maintain an overview and can implement suitable strategies for stress management. This isn't a static condition — it's a dynamic process. Markets are constantly changing, and mentally resilient traders can better cope with changes. They can, for example, survive a losing streak without feeling like a loser — a streak that might make others lose their emotional balance.

TECHNICAL STUFF

Brain researchers assume that the activation of stress and fear centers in the brains of resilient people can be inhibited to such an extent that such individuals can respond with a controlled reaction.

REMEMBER

Traders aren't naturally resilient by nature. It's a predisposition that presupposes certain personality traits and can be initiated and strengthened by way of targeted training.

Seeing what constitutes a resilient trader

Here are some important traits and competencies of mentally resilient traders:

>> Being solution- and goal-oriented (self-control)

>> Accepting what comes your way and remaining calm (self-awareness)

>> Fostering personal responsibility and control (sense of responsibility)

>> Being (realistically) optimistic and having a positive self-image (self-efficacy)

These properties, the resilience factors, serve to protect you when adversity strikes, and they mutually reinforce each other. They act preventively, which is how they protect you against stress traps when dealing with markets.

What does this mean in practice? It means that resilient traders

>> Practice non-attachment by not identifying with losing trades. (Think of the teachings of Gautama Buddha here.)

>> Dissociate the outcome of a single trade from your self-esteem as a trader.

>> Manage to cope better with difficult market conditions

>> Avoid perceiving markets as threatening

>> Act in a considered and controlled manner

>> Maintain emotional distance (think non-attachment again) when monitoring markets

>> Find appropriate coping strategies and trust that these strategies will be successful

WARNING

Self-confidence in trading can easily lead to overconfidence. When it comes to markets, believing that you and you alone have control over your destiny quickly becomes an illusion of control. The reality is, you have no influence whatsoever on market price action.

Personality traits and characteristics remain largely stable throughout life. Even if more recent research has come to the conclusion that the human personality is more changeable than previously assumed, this doesn't apply to the age group of 30- to 60-year-olds — which is where most traders will find themselves.

And none of this means that you can't train yourself in ways that increase your resilience. Resilience is a dynamic process and, with the right challenges, humans are definitely capable of becoming more resilient.

TIP

Take a look at Dr. Eva Selhub's *Resilience For Dummies* (Wiley) in order to learn more about psychological resilience and inner strength.

REMEMBER

Your trader personality influences how you perceive and assess what is happening on the market. You also need to factor in your personal experiences of the stock market. When you assess these two aspects together, it explains why traders with different personalities and different experiences have such varying experiences when it comes to markets.

Starting your training regimen

Scenario analyses are a useful method for training mental resilience. Each time you execute a trade, imagine how you might react if the completely unexpected occurs:

>> **Worst case scenario:** The market turns suddenly against you, and you're repeatedly stopped out in the shortest time with accumulating losses. Or a large price gap when the markets open forces the trade of a security you held overnight, leading to an unexpectedly heavy loss.

>> **Best case scenario:** Your timing is perfect, and you hit a winning streak. Or you unexpectedly profit from a large price gap when the markets open.

The psychological trick is to truly imagine your emotional state for both cases in advance. If you can imagine both cases in concrete detail, you can already think through what your next steps should be. Admittedly, this strategy requires a goodly amount of empathy to simulate strong emotions, such as anger and resentment on one hand and greed and euphoria on the other, but it's worth it.

The main benefit here is that it takes away the power of these emotions in the real-life situation. You have played through the emotions of the scenario; you're therefore prepared, meaning it's much harder to knock you off balance. And you have managed to write a script about how you will react before the event occurs, while still in a calm state. This is a good method for increasing your resilience in trading.

REMEMBER

Traders often say that setbacks have made them more resilient. Resilience research confirms this observation. People who experience many setbacks and recover from them will know that things always pick up again. In my experience, you cannot completely avoid errors and losses in trading. If you have gained the inner conviction that you'll be able to weather any setbacks that come your way, you have the required emotional resilience for trading.

WHICH REALITY DO WE HAVE TODAY?

In trading, you see now and then a wide gulf between reality and perception. "The map is not the territory" is one of the main assumptions of the neurolinguistic programming (NLP) model. ("The theory isn't what it describes" and "A model of reality is not reality itself" are different ways of saying the same thing.) This map/territory distinction defines the relationship between objective reality and your own subjective perceptions of the world. Each trader creates a mental representation of the markets. On the basis of each trader's own filtered sense impressions, the brain creates internal maps and determines what someone perceives. Typical filters are individual experiences, beliefs, attitudes, values, and assumptions. In other words, every trader constructs their own reality and their unique model of the markets. The selective filter we traders use to perceive the markets determines how we trade.

Only by changing your language — namely, describing your internal map — can you change your perception of the outside world. With positive beliefs and a self-aware attitude, you will adapt your map of the real world. You will undertake a reevaluation in your head and thus create new perspectives. The brain doesn't distinguish between the actual event and the visualized and desired event. The biochemical processes are identical. Body and soul are aligned with the desired destination. They create a new reality.

Successful trading requires mental strength and mental resilience. Resilience is a competency that you can learn and develop. Nowadays, you can find a multitude of training methods for increasing resilience. The exercises are primarily based on methods of behavioral psychology, positive psychology and neurolinguistic programming (NLP). I explore some of these methods in the next few sections.

The journey is the destination

The secret to good goal-setting is to boost your goals with positive emotional energy. That way, the goals become wishes you absolutely want to achieve. You won't become a better trader just because you think it might be nice to be one. You need this yearning feeling in your bones compelling you to chase all your goals in a highly motivated way, no matter the consequences. Goals should always be formulated positively and build on your strengths.

Think about what you did best over the course of your most recent trading days. Is there a pattern that shows specific abilities or strengths? Can you derive a specific goal from this? Allow your competencies to become visible so that you can use them to drive your progress. (For more on leveraging your competencies, see Chapter 5.)

REMEMBER

Realistic and achievable goals are the foundation of success. Goals you have achieved create self-confidence and motivation.

So, what is the determinative factor when it comes to your success? Decisive here is that your goals should aim to improve the trading process rather than focus on boosting your profits. Why? It's very simple: You can design and control process goals, but you can't control the achievement of profit targets. Too many incalculable factors beyond your sphere of influence determine your profits. Focus on what you can control. Those are your processes, the implementation of your trading plans, and your strategies.

EXAMPLE

Do you want to improve the timing of your trade entry points? Simply adjust your setups and select an entry with half of the planned position size, and then buy the other half after a predefined time. Depending on how the price moves, you'll have either lowered your average purchase price or doubled your position in profit.

Your focus should always be on the continuous improvement of your trading strategies. Each experience brings you one step further. The learning process is the path that leads you to your goal. A good strategy implemented according to the rules is automatically profitable over time.

STRATEGIES FOR BUILDING RESILIENCE

A few years ago, the website for the American Psychological Association posted a guide to strengthening resilience. The guide, entitled *The Road to Resilience,* presented these ten tips:

- Accept that change is a part of living.
- Avoid seeing crises as insurmountable problems.
- Nurture a positive view of yourself.
- Take decisive actions.
- Move toward your goals.
- Maintain a hopeful outlook.
- Take care of yourself.
- Keep things in perspective.
- Look for opportunities for self-discovery.
- Make social connections.

REMEMBER

Every trading day turns into a positive learning experience if you focus on your strengths and consistently implement your trading plans. It's not about making a profit every day. That is unrealistic. It's about optimizing processes and strengthening your confidence in your competencies.

Accepting emotions as a source of information

Emotions are the formative part of your personality and character; they determine how you perceive the world. Can you exert any influence on your perception of the markets and how you react emotionally? I'm here to tell you that you surely can. Admittedly, you can't change the core of your personality; your character traits will remain broadly stable for the rest of your life. But you can learn how (and in what form) your emotional personality comes to the fore.

Neuroscientific experiments with brain-damaged test subjects have proven that humans are unable to make decisions or act without emotions. As paradoxical as it sounds, if someone has lost access to their own memory of past emotional experiences, they no longer have a rational strategy for action. Traders get tangled up in weighing all the options, leading to an infinite loop. Brain researchers say that humans lack freedom of will at a conscious, rational level.

Who else remembers Mr. Spock, the emotionless Vulcan from the starship *Enterprise*, who always acted rationally? It's a pipe dream, as everyone knows today.

It's impossible to use the mind to get a grip on emotions, and it's most certainly impossible to suppress them. In fact, it works the other way around: When you become angry about losses or errors, lightning-fast biochemical processes occur in your brain that don't give reason a chance. The adrenaline boost, depending on someone's temperament, favors the kind of outbursts that have led to the destruction of quite a few keyboards and monitors.

As long as your emotional state is at equilibrium, you have full access to your logical and analytical mind. This state of equilibrium is the key to your cognitive performance.

How can you manage to maintain this condition while trading? The decisive step is not to try to suppress or block out emotions but rather to consciously observe and accept them as valuable information you can use to inform your trading. Are your emotions telling you that you need to adjust your trading strategy?

TIP

Accept your moods. Take away the hold that negative emotions have on you and you won't lose control so fast. By consciously perceiving your subliminal feelings, you can achieve a change of perspective and take a more constructive point of view.

TIP

Psychological studies confirm that it's helpful to speak about your own emotions or to write about your emotions in a journal. In this way, you can observe your behavior from an observer perspective and reevaluate it.

Use your own emotional reactions as important additional information. You can use in trading much of the implicit knowledge in your emotional world. The rational mind has no access to the emotional treasure that lies hidden in your subconscious mind. This treasure has immense significance. Brain researchers have concluded that the area in human memory devoted to preserving emotional experiences is many times larger than all other areas for memory storage combined.

Your intuition, or your gut feeling, sometimes produces valuable information — results that cannot be achieved by the rational mind alone. You can find out more about this sixth sense in Chapter 3.

SAY HELLO TO THE LIMBIC SYSTEM

Is it all in your head? It depends on which part of the head you're talking about. Reasoning certainly isn't the highest authority — even if it sits in the uppermost part of the brain. Behind all that reasoning power is a much older brain area that can override and turn off reasoning at any moment: It's the *limbic system* — your emotional control center, composed of a variety of networked structures. (As most people know, decisions are usually made in the back room, and the human brain is no exception.)

Emotional memories are stored in the areas of the limbic system, co-controlling both vegetative and psychological patterns. Information coming from outside is always assessed by (and filtered through) the limbic system first. This information is compared with previous life and learning experiences and only then is passed on to the higher-order brain functions. Only a small fraction of the masses of information you unconsciously perceive through your senses arrives in this upper chamber.

Brain researchers have demonstrated that the limbic system of the brain is also its emotional control center; it's also way ahead of the intellectual areas when it comes to decisive action. In fact, if the emotional centers are over-activated, access to the cognitive areas is severed — meaning that the much-touted prefrontal cortex, the seat of all complex cognitive behavior, is supplied with less oxygen and glucose. The person then acts impulsively and without reflection. Whether it's greed and euphoria or fear and panic hijacking your thinking and actions, both areas of the brain are involuntarily on autopilot and act aimlessly. The rational mind has been switched off.

EXAMPLE

An inexplicable internal quiver, a grumbling in the belly, a tense neck, and pressure in the chest are often cited as physical warning signs that have saved many a trader from making a bad decision.

Even experienced traders react emotionally from time to time, but they never let emotions take control. They stay disciplined and stick to the rules. You can learn about maintaining emotional equilibrium in Chapters 7 and 8.

REMEMBER

You can't lock away your emotions in a deep, dark dungeon when trading. The best strategy for dealing with your emotions is to consciously perceive, accept, understand and (where appropriate) take them into consideration.

2

Making a Successful Trade

IN THIS CHAPTER

» Setting up a demo account

» Developing and testing your trading strategies

» Finding your personal trading style and your market niche

» Improving your explicit and implicit pattern recognition skills

» Developing your personal strengths — and accepting your weaknesses

» Designing frictionless processes and continuously developing them

Chapter **3**

Developing Your Personal Trading System

oes anyone really and truly enjoy doing dry runs? Most human beings, if they're honest with themselves, would take a pass on completing all the prep work and just jump right in, get their hands dirty, and tackle a task head-on. And, to be honest, most humans would fail miserably if they adopted this as their primary strategy. In this chapter, you'll find out how important and useful it is to improve your trading skills, by setting up a demo account and working through some trading scenarios. No one should be forced to learn how to swim by being thrown straight into the deep end of the pool.

You can also improve your trading strategies by testing and improving them with *paper trading*, which allows an investor to practice buying and selling without risking real-life money. (Back in the day, paper trading involved real paper, on which you wrote down your [simulated] stock buys and sells; nowadays, most "paper trading" takes place on a computer, where one simulates trading on the real stock market.) No matter which simulation strategy you use, it's sure to save you some painfully expensive lessons. Over time, you'll find a trading style that matches your strengths and personality. You'll also find the markets and instruments that suit you best.

With a lot of practice, you'll learn the art of pattern identification. When it comes to markets, explicit patterns — chart constellations, for example — are quite common. Although these tend to be easy to spot, there's also an intuitive form of pattern recognition — one that requires much more experience to discern and is also much more difficult to explain from an intellectual viewpoint.

REMEMBER

Always ask yourself whether you're allowing your skills and talents to shine when you're trading. Continue to develop your strengths and accept your weaknesses and shortcomings. Nobody is perfect.

Markets are constantly changing — sometimes, quite dramatically. You have to be careful or you'll miss the signs and get taken down. Routines and habits constitute an important psychological support in trading. You must have a fixed set of rules, but the rules must not interfere with your adaptability and willingness to change. You must be able to adapt your trading strategies and setups to changing market conditions. Process orientation and flexibility must go hand in hand.

Working with Demo Accounts

Trading is quite a demanding and complex activity. Beginners sometimes underestimate the cognitive and emotional challenges they face. Theoretical knowledge alone is insufficient to survive on the stock exchange. Without practical experience, starting out as a trader can be an *expensive* proposition. This is because the markets work differently from the way most people expect them to work.

A demo account makes it easier for you to step into the world of trading while saving you a lot of money. Because you're trading in simulation mode and risking no money, you get a chance to try out your strategies and test everything in a sandbox environment. Regardless of the results of the individual trades or if you make an error, you lose nothing — you just gain valuable insights.

You'll find numerous suppliers on the market willing to provide you with a simulated trading environment, where you can practice your trading skills under real-life market conditions. Most brokers are happy to provide you with free trading software, but of course this act isn't completely selfless. You should get used to the platform with the aim of entering real-life trading with your own capital. Keep this info in mind when selecting a broker.

WARNING

The barriers to entry are low, which means you can open a trading account in no time — that means your access to the market is also quickly established. I strongly recommend, if you're an inexperienced trader, that you reign in your greed and resist the temptation to immediately get started using your own money to trade. Without practice and planning, you'll have beginner's luck at best; the worst case scenario involves your losing all your money in a short period. Do you remember my words of advice about not diving into the deep end of the pool if you don't know how to swim? Patiently develop your abilities in the shallow end of the pool. With your feet firmly on the ground, test and train various techniques and styles. By starting out with a demo account, you can avoid a whole slew of painful experiences.

Practicing without risk and side effects with paper trading

Paper trading is the technical term for trading without real-life capital on a demo account. The expression stems from a time when there was no Internet and when every step of the simulation was meticulously written down on a piece of paper. The term is still in use, even if the digital world now requires investors to make only a few mouse clicks rather than laboriously write out every transaction they complete.

Paper trading allows you to try out, to your heart's content, all possible strategies, markets, and trade instruments. This type of trading has a playful component as well. (Yes, trading can be fun. Trust me.) Be creative and play with the markets. Go on a journey of discovery. Become familiar with market dynamics. That way, you get a much better sense of your strengths and weaknesses.

You'll be surprised by how many experienced traders regularly take advantage of these opportunities. Professionals practice their trading skills in a real-time market environment to find out which strategies work best.

Each trade strategy undergoes a two-level test phase before it's used:

» **Back test:** How successful would the strategy have been in the past?

» **Real-time test:** Is the strategy in the simulation profitable under real-life market conditions?

Paper trading on a demo account offers a rich learning environment. You can

» Test different trading instruments, indicators, and markets in different periods

» Train the implementation of your various trading ideas and plans

» Gain practice in the market-driven timing of your entries and exits

» Test the different types of limit orders (variations of stop loss and take profit, depending on volatility)

You'll gain lots of knowledge, focused on these benefits:

» You get a feel for market dynamics and volatilities.

» You learn about your own strengths and weaknesses.

» You find out which trading style and market niche best suits you.

» You learn which specific time frame lets you feel comfortable and offers the greatest benefit.

The list goes on. You should practice under the most realistic conditions possible. That means you should make sure that your simulated trades are well prepared and actively managed as well as fully documented and evaluated. You should also act as you would in a real-life trade transaction. This strategy results in a continuous improvement process, which can easily take a few months to complete.

REMEMBER

You need discipline and perseverance, and I can assure you that the effort is worth the trouble. When you have found your style and niche and you know where your strengths are best employed, you will have the mental prerequisites for successful trading with your own money.

TIP

Just do it! You'll be surprised by how hard it is to implement (and maintain) a trading strategy on a demo account across several weeks. You'll get an idea of how important dry runs are. In real-life trading with your own money, the processes must function smoothly.

Paper trading: A paper tiger without emotions?

A common criticism of paper trading on a demo account is that it has little to do with real-life trading. Many traders lack the motivation or patience to trade in demo modes, for several reasons:

» **No true emotions are involved.** Investors have no skin in the game, so to speak. No one loses any real-life money in demo mode.

» **There are no deviations in the execution of orders in the simulation.** This doesn't reflect reality in volatile markets.

» **Trading errors have no consequences.** You can press the Reset button at any time.

» **In simulations, you're able to trade with unrealistically large sums.** These amounts give you too much leverage.

It's true that you'll be mostly emotionless in the simulation, and therefore it seems you're acting unrealistically. And that is a good thing because, in paper trading, your most important task is to get to know your trader personality. You can then use it as the basis for finding your trading style and market niche. Almost as important is the fact that you can implement your trades as long as it takes to perfectly master the processes. If you lack the discipline in paper trading, how will you act when it comes to real-life trading?

By repeating defined processes, you create routines and automatic behaviors that you can retrieve at any time — even under great emotional stress. Rehearsed, frictionless processes give you the self-confidence and security you need in emergency situations, where your emotions and your ego might come into play.

TIP

Do you feel that simulations fail to provide the motivation or the emotional kick necessary for you to take them seriously? Then take part in one of the many public stock market games. The competition puts you under pressure. Or you can make public whatever trades you make on your model portfolio via your broker. If that's too much of a spotlight, you might organize a trading competition with your trader colleagues. You might be surprised by how difficult it is to implement your own strategies according to your rules across several weeks.

Professional paper trading is purely a matter of attitude. Take the trade simulation as seriously as if it were real money. Then you will make the most of it.

TECHNICAL STUFF

Many neuroscientific studies have proven how important the repetition of recurrent processes is. Brain scans show how intensive training consolidates and strengthens neural circuits.

EXAMPLE

Pilots train for hundreds of hours in a flight simulator before being allowed to fly a real-life plane. Even experienced pilots spend a minimum number of mandatory hours in the simulator cockpit. They intensely train processes and procedures. It's necessary to be able to recall these automatically in emergencies where the pilot is under extreme time pressures. That is the prerequisite to be able to manage difficult situations — namely, to be capable of decisions and actions at any time.

The best place to focus on processes and structures is on a demo account — real-life trading might overwhelm your trader psyche. You'll avoid serious errors and painful, expensive experiences if you train your skills with paper trading. In the training phase, order execution deviations are initially irrelevant.

Of course, you have to trade with realistic position sizes on your demo account and consistently implement your strategy — after you've concluded the testing-and-experimentation phase and you want to train process flows, of course. It goes without saying that it makes no sense to juggle millions in the demo account when in reality you'll be trading with significantly smaller sums. To have the desired learning effect, paper trading should be as realistic as possible.

The learning phase significantly increases your chance of success in real-life trading. It means that you have successfully tested your strategies and can cope better with unexpected market fluctuations.

TIP

After you add some actual money to your trade account and you want to start with real-life trading, start with small positions in order to obtain a feeling of safety with the processes you've trained on. Then you can slowly move toward any planned larger positions.

REMEMBER

Develop and train your abilities in the simulation without the disruptive impact of emotions. Frictionless processes are a prerequisite for emotional sovereignty in real-life trading.

Pattern Recognition: Where Practice Makes Perfect

The king of all disciplines in trading is pattern recognition. Though you certainly have to master processes as steps of the trading craft without even having to think about them, the ability to recognize recurring patterns is trading's true art. Your goal is to gain a statistical advantage — the edge that traders often talk about — by taking into account the increased probability of those price developments that repeatedly occur in your strategy. Your ability to factor in these developments to your trading practice is precisely the reproducible advantage that determines your profitability over the long term.

Explicit pattern recognition: Technical analysis (and much more)

When talking about patterns, the trading world cordons off one set by labeling them explicit patterns — this subset includes repetitive chart patterns, fundamental interrelationships, and market price action as well as calendar effects or seasonal patterns, all of which are governed by statistically verifiable regularities.

EXAMPLE

Typical chart patterns that are said to indicate a trend reversal are double top (or double bottom) patterns, triangle patterns, and head-and-shoulder patterns. These patterns can form the basis of a profitable strategy.

Technical analysis is a popular and widely used method to evaluate historical price action and current trends using charts of individual securities or of entire markets. The assumption is that promising entry and exit levels can be derived on the basis of price support and resistance, momentum, volatility, and the direction of the current trend. Traders assume that obvious patterns will repeat themselves and that similar price movements will occur in the future. If the probability of this occurring was more than 50 percent in the past, you can derive a winning trade strategy from this context.

It shouldn't surprise you that the kind of pattern recognition I talk about here requires hard work and a lot of practice in simulation mode. Before you risk your money, you need to be sure that your trading ideas and strategies will work. In other words, you should carefully check whether the identified patterns can be translated into profitable strategies. If it hasn't worked in the past, it probably won't work in the future. (This process is commonly referred to as back testing.)

Jesse Livermore (1877–1940), often celebrated as the best trader of all time, didn't put much stock in using technical or fundamental analysis when it came to forecasting markets trends. He felt that positioning yourself at an early stage and anticipating movement is just a game of luck. The secret of his success was to prepare his reaction patterns and then to wait patiently for specific market signals.

Pattern recognition includes the ability to recognize one's own thinking, feeling, and behavior patterns. (For more on these topics, see Chapter 2.) When you systematically analyze the profitability of your trades, you soon gain valuable tips about your trading style — take a look at these questions, for example:

>> Are you more successful with small or large positions?

>> Are you more successful in volatile sideways markets or during stable trend periods?

>> Do you tend to prefer long or short setups?

>> Do you follow the trends (momentum trading) or go against trends (contrarian trading) and try to time the market movements or a trend reversal?

>> Is there a connection between certain emotional states and your profitability?

The list goes on. Learn to observe yourself and to write down any patterns that catch your eye. Based on subsequent analyses, you can further develop your setups and strategies. (To find out how to detect and interrupt problematic psychological patterns, check out Chapter 5.)

WARNING

Everyone is constantly on the lookout for promising patterns in the market — and if you happen to identify a repeatable trading edge, you can safely assume that you aren't the only one. The hit rate of your strategy won't always be over 50 percent. In addition, market conditions can change at any time, and your advantage can dissolve into thin air.

REMEMBER

Stay alert and flexible. Use the opportunities that present themselves and regularly adjust your strategies. The search for a surefire strategy is understandable, but there is no sure thing on the stock market.

Intuitive pattern recognition: The sixth sense

Explicit patterns are obvious and understandable for every trader — even if it might take several years of experience for you to identify patterns at an early stage and to act accordingly. Still, it's not rocket science.

Recognizing implicit patterns is a horse of a different color. First, you won't discover the secret of implicit patterns in a how-to book. They cannot be perceived with the naked eye, and they can't be grasped intellectually. The intuitive ability to recognize implicit patterns is based on implicit knowledge that is anchored deep in the subconscious and can be acquired only by experience and repetition.

Research shows that very experienced traders are naturally in a position to see complex patterns in certain market situations — without being able to explain how they recognized them. This has little to do with extrasensory perception. Experienced traders can often perceive the smallest deviations or subtle changes at a subconscious level — proof that the human brain is a perfect pattern recognition machine. It's continuously processing all sense impressions by checking for regularities and whether they comply with existing rules, intuitively comparing these with previous experiences. When a pattern is perceived, it's automatically compared with patterns stored in memory. If the pattern is known, the neural circuits are strengthened. If it's new, it's saved in our memory store of emotional experiences for later use in case this occurrence returns. Physical reactions, such as the much-cited gut feeling, serve as useful somatic markers, indicating when the brain detects a pattern.

REMEMBER

Generally speaking, it's easier for the brain to identify known patterns than for it to recognize and store new, unknown patterns. Simply put, it's much harder to recognize things we don't know. Perhaps this explains the difficulties that even experienced traders face when market conditions change fundamentally.

Professional traders report making decisions based on gut feelings, or *intuition*. This is a kind of subconscious intelligence, the result of repeating similar patterns hundreds of times. Intuition is outside the range of normal sensory perception. Intellect cannot explain this special instinct for market movements. Rather, this ability is the result of years of experience and strong powers of observation. If you're distracted or unable to concentrate, you lose this special gift. Good intuition requires your undivided attention. That's why an emotionally balanced state is vital.

AN IOWA GAMBLING EXPERIMENT: HOW EMOTIONS HELP IN EARLY PATTERN DETECTION

In an interesting card-playing experiment, neuroscientists were able to prove that humans make decisions on the basis of emotions and physical reactions without knowing what made them decide the way they did. Most trial participants in the experiment were in a position to subconsciously anticipate repetitions of recurrent card patterns. The experiment demonstrated that somatic markers — physical indications, like sweating or a grumbling stomach — precede a conscious decision. The group of trial participants with brain damage in certain emotional areas weren't in a position to recognize advantageous strategies in the card games at an early stage. Due to this lack of emotional reactions, the learning effect occurred only at a much later point.

Gut decisions are good mostly when you have implicit expert knowledge and a lot of experience. Then your gut feeling becomes a darn clever mind. Professional traders have developed fine antennae for stock price developments. They have learned to trust their sixth sense.

WARNING

If you have little experience in trading and insufficient expertise, do not rely on your intuition. Good intuition is based on many years of acquired abilities to spontaneously recognize implicit patterns and to be able to bring to the surface subconscious knowledge.

Recognizing and Developing Your Trading Strengths

A popular leadership development motto says something along these lines: "It is important to know not only what you want — you also need to know what you can *do*." Humans naturally spend more time and energy focusing on eliminating weaknesses. This effort generally doesn't pay off. Weaknesses rarely turn into strengths; you'll probably only manage to become average in that area. If you never were really into sports, for example, you'll never become an exceptional athlete, even if you train intensively.

Accepting weaknesses

If you ever want to truly advance your personal development, you need to face your weaknesses. Every change is a challenge because you need to learn to recognize and accept your personal deficits or defects without damage to your self-esteem. Admitting weakness is a challenge to someone's sense of self.

Your ego is supremely powerful when it comes to hiding unpleasantries or sweeping them under the carpet. But weaknesses don't just disappear if you block them out. Quite the contrary — they steal your chance to learn. That means stagnation.

Suppose that one weakness is that you lack the self-discipline to keep to loss limits. You experience major losses, but you subconsciously block out the incorrect behavior. You don't want to accept this as a sign of a lack of discipline, and this inability to face facts ruins your performance.

Are you being honest with yourself? Do you know your trading weaknesses and shortcomings? Can you honestly admit your deficits, or do you play the victim and always blame the markets when things go badly? I am sure your experiences with paper trading will force you to recognize some of your weak points.

If you recognize that a lack of discipline is your specific Achilles' heel, you can take steps to counteract that weakness. You can, for example, practice the rule-compliant implementation of your trading plans on a demo account until you have internalized the processes necessary to keep you focused and on track. Admittedly, this process requires a lot of patience, but it strengthens your self-discipline.

A weakness is a learning task with three steps:

1. Look for the mistake in yourself before looking for weak spots elsewhere.

2. Recognize and accept that weaknesses are a normal part of your personality. (Nobody is perfect.)

3. Take the necessary steps to keep your weaknesses at bay.

REMEMBER

You'll learn from your mistakes only if you're able to demonstrate a) the necessary willingness to accept mistakes as part of you and b) the humility to see that you aren't perfect. Ignoring or stamping out weaknesses doesn't work in trading — they are a part of you, just as your strengths are. The whole is your personality. This is simply clearcut evidence of life's imperfections — nothing more and nothing less.

Having bad experiences is part of the nature of trading. Even losing streaks statistically occur more frequently than is commonly believed. Accept that each trading loss is an opportunity to gain new insights and a better understanding of the market or your setup.

It helps to write down loss trades. Make a table with three columns. In Column 1, write down the loss trade. In Column 2, write down the reasons for the loss and what you have learned. In Column 3, spell out what you can actually do to improve your performance in your next trade. This exercise can help you develop yourself. (For more on keeping a trading journal, see Chapter 5.)

TIP

Be consistent when it comes to carrying out your trading plans and following your own rules. That way, you can keep your weakness from adversely affecting your trading performance.

Developing your strengths

Representative surveys show that most people believe it's more important to concentrate on their weaknesses than on their strengths in order to improve themselves. This is the result of our educational system. This focus on eliminating defects and correcting deficits starts in school. The system wastes your energy and traps you in mediocrity when it comes to trading.

Personal weaknesses are no excuse for wallowing in exaggerated self-doubt. It's much more effective to identify and develop strengths. This leads to outstanding achievements.

The success factor in trading lies in knowing your own, natural strengths. What skills and talents do you bring to the table? Here are some examples of natural strengths:

>> You're a quick learner.

>> You possess pronounced analytical skills.

>> You stay flexible and adaptable.

>> You maintain inner peace and a clear overview of your current circumstances.

>> You demonstrate mental and physical resilience.

>> You can count on gut feelings and your intuition.

REMEMBER

Are you using your talents when you trade? Consider carefully what you can *do* to take full advantage of your true strengths. Otherwise, you'll be like the 80 percent of people out there who fail to put their abilities to use in their profession.

TIP

You are your own biggest critic. Accepting yourself with all your strengths, weaknesses, and needs isn't always easy. Do it anyway.

The likelihood that you'll be a successful trader if you develop your strengths and talents is much greater than if you work only on your weaknesses. It's possible to get a grip on the latter with process-oriented and rule-based trading. Continuous further development creates success experiences that make it easier for you to accept your deficits. Success motivates and creates self-confidence.

REMEMBER

Find your trading strengths, and then strengthen them. Find the market and trading style that uses your strengths in the best possible way. At the same time, be sure to weaken your weaknesses by consciously accepting them as a part of who you are.

Developing your change competence skills

Financial markets are complex and change dynamically. They're also (unfortunately) unpredictable by nature. Rules and correlations that have worked for years can lose their validity in the blink of an eye.

EXAMPLE

Shocks from outside the system can trigger technological developments that earlier would have seemed inconceivable. Disruptive innovations can accelerate the complete restructuring of an economy. Who would have guessed, for example, that the global lockdown that occurred as a result of the coronavirus pandemic would have resulted in such a rapid digitalization of economic processes?

The truth is, the year 2020 turned on its head much of what experienced players in the financial markets had experienced in the past. Traditional valuation benchmarks and causal relationships seem to have been overridden. As a result, the valuation of the stock markets has completely been decoupled from the real economy. The billions intended for rescue programs from central banks and governments has triggered a glut of liquidity that has flooded the financial markets. The free play of market forces or the control function of prices seems to have been undermined for now.

What does that mean for you in trading terms? If, for example, you're acting as a position or swing trader, you can no longer rely on traditional analyses. In the long term, the (partially) excessive overevaluation in some sectors will correct itself, but this can, under certain circumstances, take years. If you have a shorter investment horizon, you should take other criteria into account when it comes to your trading strategy. For very short-term-oriented traders (scalpers and day traders, for example), fundamental analyses play a subordinate role.

What can you learn from these examples? Change is the only constant and markets are constantly changing — and you'll have to change, too, if you want to continue being successful at trading. If you stand still, you'll go backward, just like on a treadmill. In other words, you're forced to continually develop your strategies and trading plans. Admittedly, this requires a high degree of flexibility and adaptability on your part, but you have no other choice.

REMEMBER

It is your task to continually design your own change process despite any setbacks that might occur and to refuse to fall back into old patterns. For this task, you need solid processes and routines as a bulwark against emotional overreactions in difficult market phases, but you also need to remain flexible and continually adapt your trading to changing market conditions. That is the core of change competence.

Successful trading is a permanent process of development. Your willingness to change is a key competence in trading. And it's fundamentally a matter of attitude.

Psychological studies about successful changes indicate two prerequisites:

>> Process orientation

>> Intrinsic motivation

The next few sections look at both prerequisites in greater detail.

Processes are your shelter from the storm

Without planning and structures, you can't focus on your development process goals. Direct access to markets makes it quite tempting to jump right in and place a few orders in real-life trading. You may even succeed and profit from it initially. But what you're doing is speculation, not professional trading. And it won't get you far.

For you to have success in the long term, you need smoothly functioning processes. You also need to have clearly defined goals for what you want to achieve with your trading. And every single step you take, from strategy development to implementation of each trading plan, aims at that goal. This structured approach allows you to withstand the emotional waves that are sure to roll your way. You control the processes; the market determines the amount of trade profits you make. That is why process orientation is the key to success.

REMEMBER

Professional setups are the prerequisite for profitable trading. Establish firm rules about which setups you'll trade with and in which market phases. That way, you're sure to have the right setup, depending on market volatility.

Many traders are afraid of the effort required to include fixed structures and practice their processes. However, if you aren't fully convinced you know what you're doing, you'll lack the motivation and emotional strength to pursue your goals. You'll end up following the trading plans and rules you have established in a half-hearted way, and you won't learn from your mistakes. Your development process will stagnate.

What are the triggers for an individual's willingness to develop? In theory, it stems from the positive emotional experiences that you internalize. Success experiences are truly motivating, but they aren't sufficient when it comes to trading. Without strategies and a plan, you may confuse luck and ability. Short-term success can be deceptive. I continually experience this in my coaching practice. Occasionally raking in a big score tricks people into overestimating their own abilities.

Short-term profits make many traders cocky. The decisive aspect is a functioning strategy, not random gains. Such traders too easily overestimate themselves. Greed is not a strategy.

Humans change only when they're ready for it. A willingness to change usually comes with the realization that something has to change. According to psychologists, crises are an opportunity for change. Crises shatter your foundations and force you to act.

In my experience, traders understand what is required of them only after they've experienced large losses. (For more on this topic, see Chapter 4). Unfortunately, in the trading world, only those painful experiences motivate and move traders to undertake serious change.

REMEMBER

Define your goals in your trading processes and not in terms of the absolute results you hope for. Initially, it's all about trading well. Concentrate on what you can do every day to improve.

Motivating yourself for change

It's not enough to know that you need to change your trading; you must want to do it. Traders who still don't give up despite serious loss have an intrinsic motivation to establish professional processes. The internal drive provides the necessary self-discipline for further development. Change competence arises when you manage to develop yourself continuously. In particular, this means rule-based trading must become part of your routine. If your trading strategy is profitable, the profits will set in automatically. Then it's your skill driving your success, not mere luck or coincidence. And if your trading strategy is no longer making profits, you know that the market conditions may have changed. Then you adjust your strategy accordingly.

TECHNICAL STUFF

Psychologists often speak of *self-efficacy*, where someone has developed the internal conviction that they can successfully navigate difficult situations. Without this firm belief in your own competencies, you are incapable of acting efficiently under stress. Experiencing success strengthens your self-efficacy. In uncertain environments you can't control, it's important for your self-confidence to experience self-efficacy. (For more on this topic, see Chapter 6.)

WARNING

The belief in one's own abilities sometimes leads to an illusion of control. Don't let that happen to you. Your mantra should be, "I can't control the markets — I have no influence on what is happening there." Don't forget that, even when you're experiencing a winning streak. Stay adaptable and follow the market closely.

Gauging your aptitude: Personality traits and competencies

In trading, you're constantly making independent decisions in an environment of risk and uncertainty. For that, you need to be equipped with a special ability for self-organization. You won't get far with expert knowledge alone. You must be able to implement and adequately apply your knowledge. Activation makes or breaks the competence concept. It's all about your ability to act — the ability to find means and solutions and act in an accountable manner.

Acting in accordance with your own organizational principle requires that you're motivated to initiate the right steps. What drives you when you're trading? You know that trading is personality development and that it requires developing mental strength. How can you develop a success-oriented mindset?

The following performance formula clearly demonstrates how you behave when you're trading and your potential performance:

Performance = Desire × Ability × Environment

» **Desire** describes your intrinsic motivation — namely, your inner drive according to your own needs. In short, it's your commitment.

» **Ability** describes your actual performance — namely, your self-organized capacity to act. In short, it's the competent application of your knowledge.

» **Environment** describes the context of the performance frameworks — namely, the given market environment as well as your trading strategies and rules.

You need all three performance factors; it's the combination and interplay of desire, ability, and the environment that leads to performance. The performance formula will be close to zero if any of the factors are close to zero.

I discuss the desire and ability performance factors extensively in the next couple of sections. Just a quick note before jumping into that discussion: Desire can be captured by means of a motive profile, and ability can be illustrated using a competence profile.

Your personal competence profile

Competencies consist of much more than technical knowledge and qualifications. Only the application of your knowledge creates a competency. That's why competencies describe one's ability to set in motion independent action.

You can use competence models to test which of your competencies is stronger or weaker. In the competence model I use here, I differentiate between four basic competencies:

>> Personal competence

>> Activity and decision-making competence

>> Methodological and professional competence

>> Social-communicative competence

From these four basic competencies, you can derive 64 additional key competencies.

In general, basic competencies depend on context and are related to action; that means they come into effect in real-world situations. By contrast, personality traits are independent of a situation. One's character doesn't change; competencies, however, do, depending on internal and external conditions.

The KODE competence model (www.kodekonzept.com) was developed in the 1990s to record and strengthen one's performance and self-organizational skills. Based on a scientifically based competence model that has been continuously developed since 1996, the model has been verified and used widely on a national and international level.

This competence model, which is universally applicable, is based on a basic capacity to accurately reflect competencies under normal — as well as difficult — working and living conditions. This distinction is important in trading: You may respond completely differently under stress and emotional pressure than when you're in a relaxed state. Experience shows that some traders lose access to their competencies and make avoidable mistakes when psychological pressure is great. The reactions can vary considerably, depending on how pronounced your four fields of competence are. Ask yourself the following questions:

>> Are you capable of acting and making decisions under stress?

>> Do you react impulsively and tend to act merely for the sake of acting? (Can you say "overtrading"?)

>> Do you become rigid and stare at the markets, frozen like a deer in the headlights?

>> Do you hide behind charts, analyses, and models and thereby remove yourself from the responsibility to make decisions?

>> Do you discuss potential trading strategies endlessly with real or virtual trading colleagues because you're afraid of the consequences of your decisions and therefore don't act?

The KODE competence profile shows your competence under normal conditions as well as difficult ones.

You *must* not lose the access to your competencies under difficult conditions. This requires mental strength. Also keep in mind that, in contrast to personality traits, the capacity to act can be developed and expanded into old age. In other words, you can learn and develop key competencies for lasting, successful trading.

I have filtered out the relevant core competencies for trading from the 64 key competencies. There is a certain range for each individual competence. The result is a set of profile requirements for your success in trading. Your personal competence levels are automatically entered into the target profile when you complete the online test. The result is used to determine your current position and provide you with some orientation. Comparing your personal competence profile with the required range shows you possible strengths and weaknesses. You will be above the benchmark for some competencies and under it for others. Certain competencies are particularly important for trading. Your personal competence profile provides you with an initial overview of your talents; more specifically, whether you have the competencies required for trading. You also get advice that will help you find the trading style that suits you.

Figure 3-1 shows an example of a competence profile for traders. The spectrums show you where you should be in an ideal situation. (Again, your personal competence levels are automatically entered into the display when you've completed the online test.)

The competence atlas (see Figure 3-2) shows you how the 64 key competencies are spread across the four basic skills. The competencies labeled in the light-colored triangles are relevant to trading requirements and are an integral part of the requirement profile.

Your personal motive profile

What is your intrinsic motivation in trading? What influences your mindset? If you think these questions are easy to answer, you're wrong. It's never easy to find out what your innermost self truly wants.

You can find numerous personality tests online that are said to reveal your personality traits and characteristics, all in the service of getting to the bottom of your motivation. Generally, these are extensive online testing procedures where respondents answer or assess statements. Such tests are used for self-assessment as well as for external assessment.

Target profile competencies

Competency	Code
Planning ability	M
Analytical abilities	M/P
Judgement	M/P
Objectiveness	M/P
Systematic-methodical approach	M/A
Conceptual strength	M/A
Ability to act/execute	A
Consistence	A/M
Resilience	A/P
Result-oriented action	A/M
Personal responsibility	P
Discipline	P/M
Decision-making ability	A/P
Self-management	P/A
Ability to learn	P/M
Conscientiousness	S/M
Problem-solving capacity	S/A
Openness to change	P/A
Awareness of consequences	M/S

Scale: 1 2 3 4 5 6 7 8 9 10 11 12

Legend:

■ KODE®X Competence channel
Trader competencies

P Personal competence
A Activity and decision-making competence
M Methodological and professional competence
S Social-communicative competence

1	not very developed
2-3	partially developed
4-5	developed
6-7	significantly developed
8-9	strongly developed
10-11	very strongly developed
12	excessively developed

Source: Kode GmbH

FIGURE 3-1: A requirement profile for traders.

In my practical experience with professional as well as private traders, the motive structure analysis, or MSA, has proven itself to be the most reliable one available.

The MSA (https://msaprofil.com) is a resource-oriented procedure that represents your individual motivational structure. Based on a total of 18 basic motives, it captures your emotional core character as well as your intrinsic drive and self-motivational potential.

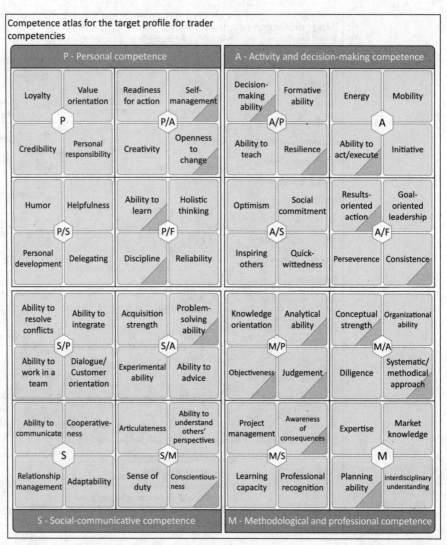

FIGURE 3-2: The competence atlas for traders.

Competence atlas for the target profile for trader competencies

P - Personal competence				A - Activity and decision-making competence			
Loyalty	Value orientation	Readiness for action	Self-management	Decision-making ability	Formative ability	Energy	Mobility
Credibility	Personal responsibility	Creativity	Openness to change	Ability to teach	Resilience	Ability to act/execute	Initiative
Humor	Helpfulness	Ability to learn	Holistic thinking	Optimism	Social commitment	Results-oriented action	Goal-oriented leadership
Personal development	Delegating	Discipline	Reliability	Inspiring others	Quick-wittedness	Perseverence	Consistence
Ability to resolve conflicts	Ability to integrate	Acquisition strength	Problem-solving ability	Knowledge orientation	Analytical ability	Conceptual strength	Organizational ability
Ability to work in a team	Dialogue/ Customer orientation	Experimental ability	Ability to advice	Objectiveness	Judgement	Diligence	Systematic/ methodical approach
Ability to communicate	Cooperative-ness	Articulateness	Ability to understand others' perspectives	Project management	Awareness of consequences	Expertise	Market knowledge
Relationship management	Adaptability	Sense of duty	Conscientious-ness	Learning capacity	Professional recognition	Planning ability	interdisciplinary understanding
S - Social-communicative competence				M - Methodological and professional competence			

Source: Kode GmbH

Your internal driving forces and motivations are completely individual and can be compared to a personal fingerprint. The motivational profile provides you with insight into your personality.

In trading, your character traits are more important than your qualifications. Which ones are helpful and which are not? It's all about recognizing at an early stage whether you have the mental strength or whether you can develop it. Ask yourself the following questions:

>> How suitable are you for the challenges you'll face as a trader?

>> How do you deal with stress, risks, and emotional pressures?

>> What is your strength and energy potential?

>> What truly moves you deep down and what drives you forward?

>> What motivates you to permanently be at your best?

The MSA analysis determines your individual motivational structure. When you have recognized and understood what drives you, you may have the key to developing your performance, stress resilience, emotional control, and self-discipline — characteristics that are critical in trading because this is where the psychological pressure is particularly burdensome. A better understanding of your personality will help you recognize personal hurdles. Self-knowledge helps to develop mental strength for trading.

From all that we can determine, there seem to be timeless stable character traits and intrinsic basic motives that form the emotional core of a personality. These basic emotional drives change little over the course of a lifetime. Your motivational profile holds up a mirror to you and explains why you behave the way you do when trading.

The expression of a fundamental motivation is naturally a special performance motivator. You do the things you like to do well, and they motivate you. Stress factors arise when characteristics required by a particular situation are ones you lack — or lack to a sufficient degree.

The following motives have proven themselves over time to be worthy of attention:

>> **Desire for knowledge:** Theoretical versus practical

>> **Adherence to principle:** Principle-oriented versus purpose-oriented

>> **Relationship to power:** Leading versus being led

>> **Status seeking:** Elitist versus down to earth

>> **Relationship to order:** Structured versus flexible

>> **Attitudes toward freedom:** Going it alone versus team-oriented

>> **Desire for close personal relationships:** Sociable versus distanced

>> **Desire for recognition:** Sensitive versus self-assured

>> **Competitive drive:** Combative versus harmonious

>> **Attitude toward risk:** Willing to take risks versus aware of the risks

The characteristics listed here indicate that each individual basic motive has two poles. They complement each other, which means that you'll always have both drives — though the expression of the drives can be quite different.

The MSA test evaluation (see Figure 3-3) shows the individual motivational expressions specified in percentage points and normally distributed. The sine-shaped curve shows your personal characteristics in relation to the population as a whole.

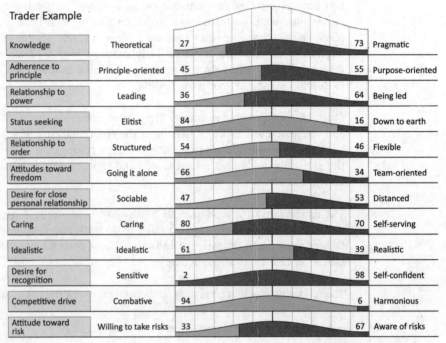

Trader Example

Knowledge	Theoretical	27	73	Pragmatic
Adherence to principle	Principle-oriented	45	55	Purpose-oriented
Relationship to power	Leading	36	64	Being led
Status seeking	Elitist	84	16	Down to earth
Relationship to order	Structured	54	46	Flexible
Attitudes toward freedom	Going it alone	66	34	Team-oriented
Desire for close personal relationship	Sociable	47	53	Distanced
Caring	Caring	80	70	Self-serving
Idealistic	Idealistic	61	39	Realistic
Desire for recognition	Sensitive	2	98	Self-confident
Competitive drive	Combative	94	6	Harmonious
Attitude toward risk	Willing to take risks	33	67	Aware of risks

Source: MSA Motivation Systems GmbH

FIGURE 3-3: A motivational profile as a graphical overview.

The two complementary drives are clearly visible in Figure 3-3. The lightly shaded bar shows the level of the drive on the left, whereas the darkly shaded bar shows the level of the drive on the right. For the competitive motivation, assume that you're 94 percent combative and only 6 percent harmonious. You still have both drives, but how they express themselves varies widely.

Interpreting profiles

In the interpretation of any motive profile, it's both interesting and fruitful to pay attention to the motivational combinations, because they're particularly relevant to the trading business. To show you what I mean, let me share with you two examples of how to interpret and analyze a motivational profile.

Trader A's profile shows that they are a risk-seeking, combative, and self-confident trader. You can assume that they have mental resilience and are possibly stress resistant. These are clearly useful properties when trading. The flip side of the coin is that — you guessed it — under certain circumstances, Trader A is predestined to make catastrophic miscalculations. Trader A also has a tendency toward overestimating their own powers (they assume that they're in control of a situation when they clearly aren't), negligence, or dogmatism.

WARNING

I consciously chose this example because I have met some traders with this motivational combination who have fought the markets as Don Quixote fought against the windmills. Here's how their stories usually ran their course: an aggressively averaging down, massively expanded loss position, and then negligently ignoring rules and risk management, recklessly bloated position size, and, finally, selling at the lowest point in a panic (or freezing in panic and closing out at a worthless position).

Because I don't want this topic to be all doom and gloom, let's take a look at a less drastic case. **Trader B** is a team-oriented person who enjoys meeting people. They are definitely friendly and possibly the life of any party. The opposite personality type would probably be more helpful for trading. The question is whether Trader B would truly be satisfied spending the day alone in front of a screen with no human interaction.

As you have seen based on both cases, knowing both of the drives within basic motivational structures are of fundamental importance. Multiple motives are activated simultaneously. The impact on trading can be significant.

It's interesting to note that, by nature, humans search for balance in other areas of life if they can't live out certain personality traits or basic motivations in a specific area. For example, a person who loves order and who works in a creative and flexible vocational field will probably live out their need for order at home.

This subconscious search for balance and compensation opportunities in other areas is something you can take advantage of in trading:

> » **A risk-seeking, combative trader may consciously balance these traits by looking for a competitive sport or an adventurous hobby.** This would address their motivational expressions and they would be in a better position in trading if they stuck to the rules there and were more prudent in their trades.

> » **A sociable, friendly trader could join a group of traders who are similarly inclined.** Or they would trade for only an hour at a time and spend the rest of the day surrounded by people.

Both examples are meant to illustrate that you can always look to other areas of your life to create the balance you need. Finding that balance always makes sense if not doing so means specific characteristics might have undesirable effects on your trading business. However, this strategy has its limits. In case of heavy inclinations toward one side or the other of the motivational scale, the compensation options may be limited. Self-discipline will suffer. The risk remains. For example, the gambler in you makes an appearance when your emotions are running high. A trader's true character mainly makes an appearance when things get hot.

Use your motive profile to create a stress balance sheet — a way to identify trading situations that act as strong stressors for you, in other words.

The motivational influences of your internal drives can work together in a positive manner (leading to synergies) or act negatively (causing tension). Trading is all about character. A certain combination of personality traits and basic motivations is necessary in order to be able to deal with the special requirements and conditions of trading. A motive profile may be able to provide you with the clarity you need in order to see whether trading is for you.

Caution, autopilot: Staying flexible

Rules, systems, and fixed structures in trading are important parts of your process orientation. They help you maintain your emotional balance and avoid errors.

The flip side of the coin is that routines can affect your change competence. You're walking along a tightrope here. If you're not careful, your brain switches to autopilot — which is convenient and saves cognitive energy. That's why habits are powerful, because they have proven their worth in our evolutionary development. This default energy-saving mode, however, involuntarily leads to the shutdown of other areas of the brain. Your thought processes are in a holding pattern, going round and round — and missing out when the need to adjust to a new situation arises. Many traders can tell you a thing or two about this situation. Always having to be prepared to change and adapt is cognitively quite exhausting.

You must be able to respond flexibly because the market environment is constantly changing. Otherwise, you lose your trading edge. Make sure that you always

>> Act differently in volatile markets or strong trends than you would in quiet, sideways phases.

>> Recognize that the correlations as well as the relationships of cause-and-effect evolve during various phases of the market. New trends emerge.

>> Change your strategy and setups depending on whether it's a bull or bear market.

For example, when markets are characterized by extreme volatility, the price development range may vary considerably. For example, if you set stops to secure your position too closely, you run the risk that you will regularly get stopped out.

How can you remain mentally flexible and simultaneously avoid habitual (self-destructive) behavior patterns? Brett Steenbarger, the psychologist and trader coach, recommends four steps that can help you to react to market requirements in a predictable and careful manner:

1. **Look for alternative opinions to your market assessment.**

Question your basic assumptions regularly, discuss contradictory scenarios with your trader colleagues, and search the Internet for other points of view. Stay adaptable and gain a different perspective.

2. **Change your observation period.**

If you mainly trade in short time frames, it may be worth your time and effort to take a look at medium- or long-term trends. A glance at the big picture may provide you with insights that can help you classify price developments in the short-term arena. In any event, you're sure to gain a different perspective.

3. **Consider the entire market.**

Don't just compare various views and perspectives. The trick is to look at the correlated markets as well. This expands your viewing angle and provides you with valuable information for the markets and instruments you use.

4. **Keep your distance.**

Regularly interrupt your trading and take breaks. That step protects you against tunnel vision and helps you maintain an emotional distance from the markets. That's because Steps 1–3 require lots of cognitive energy.

If you follow these four steps, you'll remain adaptable without questioning your process orientation when trading. You'll regularly put your market assessment to the test and identify outdated thinking and behavior patterns. From a bird's-eye view, you'll learn how to carefully monitor the markets. You'll be in a position to detect changes in the market at an early stage and implement the knowledge gained in your trading plans. This is practical change competence.

REMEMBER

You need fixed processes as well as adaptability to changing market conditions in order to succeed as a trader.

IN THIS CHAPTER

» **Formulating profit objectives**

» **Using risk-reward ratios**

» **Seeing that *greed* is another word for *fear***

» **Dealing with drawdowns**

» **Managing positions**

Chapter **4**

Implementing Your Trading Plans

'm sure you've often heard that, in trading, you limit your losses and let your profits run. One fundamental rule of trading sounds like this: If you focus on consistent loss limitation, the profits will come by themselves. This statement is correct, as empirical studies demonstrate. (In Germany, for example, 80 to 90 percent of the surveyed portfolios of private investors show a negative performance because their losses repeatedly get out of hand.) In other words, losses are realized too late, and the profits gained are insufficient to compensate for the losses incurred. Traders tend to take out profits too early.

REMEMBER

It isn't enough to chalk up a 60 to 70 percent average of winning trades if you don't run up profits and your losses are significantly higher than the profits.

Your average profits and losses depend on the selected position sizes and the market fluctuations. The management of your portfolio risks should consider the answers to these two questions:

» What daily fluctuations are you willing to tolerate?

» Have you adapted your position sizes to reflect market volatility?

Combining good money management skills with good risk management skills helps you keep a firm grip on your overall risk exposure and the total return of your portfolio.

TIP

For a solid overview of the important subjects of money and risk management, I highly recommend Lita Epstein and Grayson D Roze's *Trading For Dummies, 4th Edition* (Wiley).

Some traders confuse large market fluctuations with profit opportunities. They increase their positions with increasing market volatility, hoping for fat profits. That strategy can easily go wrong because portfolio fluctuations tend to increase drastically in such conditions, so you'll be under severe psychological pressure to act — and act quickly. Greed is a bad counselor and sometimes leads to overconfidence.

Risk management with foresight means that you adapt your position sizes to current market fluctuations in order to protect your portfolio. If your trades are too large in relation to your portfolio, the portfolio fluctuations can reach dangerous proportions. Follow a simple rule: If the volatility of the market increases, reduce your stakes. The aim is to control the impact of loss periods on the overall portfolio. What risks are you willing to take? Where is the pain threshold for your portfolio? Your risk tolerance determines your portfolio risk and thus the position sizes you trade with.

Managing Your Opportunities Intelligently

No one would argue that the focus in trading should not be on the consistent use of stop-loss orders for loss limitation. Yet that is merely a necessary — but by no means sufficient — condition for successful trading.

REMEMBER

If you want to be profitable in the long term, you need to make bigger winning trades.

As the trading psychologist Brett Steenbarger rightly points out, the problem many traders face comes from how they deal with existing opportunities, not from how they deal with the risk of loss. If you have no clear profit goals in mind, it's difficult to become profitable.

In Chapter 2, I talk about how process goals are more important than profit goals because designing your trading processes means you have everything under control — though you can never hope to have any real control when it comes to achieving your profit goals. The markets are the only factor that determines things like profits. Don't draw any wrong conclusions from what I say here, however — establishing frictionless processes certainly takes priority, but this includes establishing a consistent loss limit. At the end of the day, you still want to earn money from your trading. In other words, despite the fact that much is out of your control, you should think very specifically about the profits you want to achieve. Ask yourself the following questions:

>> What is your absolute take-profit target for each trade?

>> What is the time frame (hourly/daily/weekly) for achieving your profit target?

>> How do you define the risk/reward ratio for each of your trades?

>> What rate of return do you want to achieve with your trading account weekly, monthly, and/or annually?

Set your focus on achieving realistic profits, and plan these to the letter in advance. Part of your plan should include

>> Finding out how high the opportunities and risks are before opening a position

>> Playing through all possible scenarios in your mind beforehand

>> Knowing exactly what you'll do if you're racking up profits or if the market is against you

REMEMBER

Experience shows that most traders pay a lot of attention to finding the right entry point. Perfect timing rarely works in the real world, and it should not be your goal either. Pay attention to managing your trades from entry to exit rather than to finding the perfect sweet spot.

TIP

If you find it difficult to take the plunge and enter the market, start with a partial opening. Once you're in the market, you'll find it easier to actively manage the position and expand it, if necessary. Brain research states that even the smallest activities work to break up mental blockages.

The entry is only the first part of the practical implementation of a trading setup. Stop-loss limits, position size, holding periods, and establishing realistic profit goals are further components. The next section deals with the correct ratio of profit opportunities to loss risks.

Balancing Opportunities and Risks (Risk/Reward Ratio)

The risk/reward ratio (also known as the *R/R ratio*) is the central control instrument in trading. It's one of the fundamental principles when it comes to managing money as well as risk. The R/R ratio sets out the potential losses for each individual trade in proportion to the potential gains. In this way, you can measure an investment's potential performance. You get a feel for the risks you're taking in order to reach a specific profit goal.

Say you purchase a share at the current price of 10 dollars. You secure the position with a stop loss at 9 dollars. Your take-profit limit for closing the position is 12 dollars. Your loss risk is the difference between the purchase price and the stop loss. Your potential profit is the difference between the purchase price and the target price. Then you divide the potential profit by the potential loss. In this simplified case, the R/R ratio is 2:1 (12−10/10−9).

REMEMBER

The R/R ratio says nothing about the probability of your trade being successful. Instead, it shows you what profit you can expect when you risk a dollar — assuming that you achieve the profit goal.

Empirical analyses show that you should seek an average R/R ratio of 2:1 per trade in order to be successful in the long term. That sounds obvious because the larger the R/R ratio, the more loss trades you can cope with.

Therefore, an estimated success rate of 50 percent means profitability for you. As sobering as this statement sounds, few traders manage to continuously close more than half their trades with a profit. That's why controlling profitability with a sufficiently high R/R ratio is important.

However, some traders make it too easy for themselves. You must consider the relationship between your hit rate — the percentage of your positions that have actually reached the profit targets — and your R/R ratio. The higher the R/R ratio, the lower the hit rate. That means if you set an unrealistically high profit goal, the probability of achieving it is comparatively low. With a R/R ratio of 10:1, for example, the question naturally arises of whether it's possible to ever achieve this profit goal. In short: The larger the R/R ratio, the less likely it is that you'll achieve such ambitious goals.

REMEMBER

Never daydream! Price targets should be realistic and not influenced by your pipe dreams or euphoric moods.

Be aware that trading only deals with probabilities determined by the market. You should keep that statement in mind when you're calculating your profit opportunities. It seems that, for certain traders, the temptation to cheat themselves is just too strong. Errors in reasoning, as illustrated in the following list, sneak in involuntarily:

>> Such traders plan a trade and increase their profit target higher until they get a better R/R ratio — even though the probability of reaching that price target is quite low.

>> Such traders drag the stop-loss limit closer to the purchase price in order to make the R/R ratio appear more attractive. Here, the danger comes from being stopped out prematurely.

>> To compensate for a trading loss, they increase the price target for the next trade. In this case, you're fighting the market, indulging in what is known as revenge trading. You want to recoup lost money.

In all three cases, you're ignoring market mechanisms. You're no longer following the market — you've devoted yourself to the unnecessary manipulation of R/R ratios. Calculating the R/R ratio in a subjective manner is obviously a weakness and a counterproductive use of this particular control mechanism.

The dilemma is simple and poignant. Although a high R/R ratio has a positive impact on expected profitability, it nevertheless leads to a lower probability that your price targets will be achieved.

REMEMBER

Your trading style always influences your risk reward ratio. A scalper who trades on very short-term time frames with low position sizes may choose a significantly lower R/R ratio than a swing trader who may keep positions over several days or weeks.

If you have extensively tested and trialed your trading strategy, you will usually be good at predicting what R/R ratio is realistic for your trades. By paying attention to the price movements, you can calculate the required hit rate and a R/R ratio that's appropriate to the market. This is the way to compensate the advantages of a high R/R ratio with the disadvantages of lower probability.

REMEMBER

You need to plan a realistic R/R ratio for every trade you make according to the market environment and what suits your trading strategy. Successful traders are the ones who enter positions with low risk and relatively high profit opportunities.

LOOKING AT CALCULATION METHODS

If you're a mathematically gifted trader, you have two formulas for exactly calculating the required hit rate, or R/R ratio.

To determine the lowest possible hit ratio needed in order to achieve the desired profit threshold (the break-even point, in other words), use the following calculation:

- Hit Rate = 1 ÷ (1 + R/R Ratio)

The R/R ratio you need for a given hit rate is calculated this way:

- R/R Ratio = (1 ÷ Hit Rate) – 1

Say you have an R/R ratio of 2:1. In this case, a 33 percent hit ratio would reach the profit threshold. That means that at least every third trade would have to reach your take-profit target.

Resisting the Evolutionary Urge to Cash In

Our evolutionary heritage weighs heavy on us humans. Allowing your profits to run up requires enormous self-discipline because you have to act against your nature. Your trader psyche will always find *creative* excuses for why you need to quickly close a position that is making a profit. Maybe you tell yourself the following:

» Many pennies make a dollar.

» No one has ever died from taking out their profits.

» Greed is a bad advisor.

TECHNICAL STUFF

From an evolutionary point of view, we humans have a natural reflex to realize profits quickly. Without even thinking about it, your brain will automatically fall back to trusted behavioral mechanisms. This desire for immediate reward (instant gratification, in other words) is controlled by the release of the neural messenger substance dopamine, also colloquially known as the happiness hormone.

Recognizing That Fear Is a Bad Advisor

The list of excuses you can come up with for taking early profits goes on and on, but it shows one thing, above all: A person is mortally afraid of losing the profits they have made — a fear based on the pain they will suffer if they, after making a profit, manage to later lose the unrealized book profits.

The problem is a lack of confidence in your own trades. Your whole attention span is absorbed by the development of this one position. You're suffering from tunnel vision and can only focus on how much money you could win or lose with this single trade. You involuntarily interpret every price movement as a potential danger or threat. You're caught up in your emotions and have lost sight of what is happening in the market.

From a psychological point of view, you aren't really worried about a single trade; rather, it's your ego that identifies with these concerns. That throws your emotional balance off kilter.

TIP

If you feel emotionally off balance, leave the room. Take a deep breath and make sure to use physical movement to relieve the emotional tension. This strategy allows you to bring a planned trade to an end as planned and in accordance with your rules.

Gaining Emotional Distance

I'm asking you to keep in mind these three principles, which will probably help you act objectively and with emotional distance:

>> Define a profit goal for each trade beforehand.

>> React only to market changes, not to individual positions.

>> Concentrate on the profitability of the entire portfolio in any given period, not on individual trades.

As long as you maintain the perspective of a neutral observer, you're in a position to control your subjective concerns about the outcome of individual trades. Clear price targets will help you keep a cool head. Whenever you feel that you're starting to think about the profits or losses of an individual trade, distance yourself and take a break. Use the break to think about what triggered your loss of concentration or distracted you from what was happening on the market. Ask yourself these questions:

>> Was it the fear that you cannot endure individual losses?

>> Was it a sense of excitement at the prospect of making possible high profits?

>> Was it the fear of later losing your book profits?

The triggers vary depending on the situation and the general mood. In addition, every trader reacts differently, depending on their personality. You must learn to recognize such triggers at an early stage. After you recognize them, ask yourself these questions:

>> Are there recurring patterns I can observe?

>> How does my ego react to particular triggers?

If you can find the answers to these questions, you'll find it easier to stick with the three principles I mention at the beginning of this section. I admit that it isn't easy to keep calm when profits increase under significant fluctuations. Experienced traders know that only those who have the most trust in their own strategy can endure the uncertainty about the outcome of a trade. It often seems as though you need more self-confidence in order to stay with a trade that is making profit than with a trade that is running sideways or even at a loss. The reason is obvious: Sometimes, high book profits are at risk!

TIP

In Chapter 6, I talk about some mental self-coaching techniques that may help you to remain both calm and confident. I recommend checking out that discussion.

You can spare your nerves by trailing the stop loss to your purchase position or even into the profit region. This enables you to render the position risk-free although such an assurance may bring with it smaller book profits under certain circumstances. Be sure not to place the stop too narrowly and get picked off on the next counter-movement.

Alternatively, you can realize partial profits and let the remaining position continue to run according to plan. This gives you a feeling of freedom of action and reduces your fear of completely losing book profits. At the same time, you find out that it can be worthwhile to allow profit to run up to the target price. In effect, you hit three birds with one stone.

The practice of meditation is an excellent exercise for observing thoughts without judging or identifying with them. Thoughts come and go, but you remain relaxed in the observer role. You'll find that meditation makes it easier to tolerate uncertainty.

Keeping Greed in Check

An old German proverb states unequivocally that "Greed rots the brain!" It's meant to describe what happens when someone's intellect is overridden, and greed takes over. On the other hand, you have the (fictional) Gordon Gekko's famous dictum "Greed is good!" as expressed in the Hollywood film *Wall Street.* Which point of view is correct here?

Before answering that question, let's start with a simple definition. *Greed* describes the excessive desire to want more and more: more possessions, more money, more success, more fame.

So, is greed bad, as the German proverb insists? If you were to answer from a purely biological evolutionary point of view, you would have to say no. After all, without the strong drive to find more food and reproduce, humanity would not have survived. Here are some other benefits of greed:

>> Greed helps people overcome obstacles and fears.

>> Greed increases the willingness to take risks and provides unexpected powers.

>> Greed makes people curious and increases their thirst for knowledge as well as their willingness to learn.

However, times have changed. People are no longer living in the Stone Age. Money and the stock market are products of the modern era. The truth is that the human brain has its origins in a much different time. It wasn't made for rational investment — and certainly not for short-term trading.

You say money isn't everything? Well, neuroscientific studies show that any monetary gains someone obtains without having to work a 9-to-5 job for it brings with it significantly more happiness hormones than money they might earn from a paycheck. Maybe that's why traders are prone to emotional outbursts.

Besides fear, greed is one of the two most dangerous emotions in trading. In fact, you can think of greed as just another form of fear — the fear of not getting enough. When combined with an inflated ego, greed and fear can turn trading into a vicious circle. (See Figure 4-1.)

FIGURE 4-1:
Trading's
vicious circle.

You know how important it is to take advantage of existing profit opportunities. If you're unable to regularly realize greater profits, you'll never be a profitable trader, for the simple reason that you'll suffer frequent losses, no matter what you do. Even the best traders out there rarely have more than 60 percent winning trades.

REMEMBER

The natural and deep-seated reflex to quickly take out profits is difficult to control. That's why clearly defined profit targets for each trade and emotional distance are important.

So, how and when does greed come into play? How about "with overwhelming force" and "all the time"? (That's certainly more than you want when trading.) As for the consequences of greed, this list gives you some answers:

>> Greed drives you to continue what you're doing even if you have suffered a losing streak.

>> Greed drives you back to the market after a crash.

>> Greed can sometimes make you forget your rules and take disproportionately large risks (over-leveraging, in other words).

>> Greed makes you resort to gambling and risky speculation.

>> Greed leads to overconfidence and loss of control.

>> Greed leads to overtrading or revenge trading.

>> Greed keeps you from learning from your errors.

>> Greed is responsible for market excesses and speculative bubbles.

Neuroscientific studies confirm that greed rots your brain, by effectively switching it off. At the same time, some part of your brain must still be available to you in order for greed to function. This offender sits in the emotional centers of the brain, functioning as the core of the limbic reward system. It is the *nucleus accumbens*, which, when over-activated, ramps down access to your intellect. When the *nucleus accumbens* comes into play, you don't stand a chance.

TECHNICAL STUFF

The *nucleus accumbens* (NAc) plays a central role in the limbic reward system and is responsible for the development of addiction. Dopamine receptors in the NAc respond immediately when dopamine — the happiness messenger — is dumped into the system. The NAc looks to repeat that pleasurable release, reinforcing the already strong human desire for reward and pleasure. Sexual desire, gambling addiction, drug addiction, and mobile phone addiction are controlled by dopamine. The dopamine output sends a signal to the body and the mind, demanding that the desire be satisfied.

Greed triggers motivation to move *toward* something. The deep-seated desire for profit is superimposed on your fear of loss. The determining factor is the prospect of profits — the *expectation* of profitable trades, not the actual profit. It is this expectation of a reward that triggers neural fireworks in your brain and releases dopamine. This expectation anticipates the profits and reacts physically and mentally as though the profits have already occurred. That may tempt you into ignoring the risks and your own rules. You react according to the motto "Anticipation is half the fun" and enjoy the dopamine hit.

WARNING

Following the rules when trading is boring for your brain. Subliminally, you're looking for the risk and the adrenaline rush. Dopamine is addictive. The brain is hungry for reward. The human reacts to expected profits as it does to drugs or sex. The neural and biochemical processes in the brain are identical when it comes to any of these desires.

When the profit actually occurs, your dopamine output returns to normal and the rational parts of the brain are reactivated. Disillusionment returns. As soon as a trade enters the profit region, the fear of loss takes over. This fear encourages risk-averse traders to realize smaller profits rather than let them grow. It is a to-and-fro action between greed and fear.

Imagine that you have realized a few smaller winning trades. You think this must be your lucky day — it's happening. This may be when you get cocky. Your happiness about the profits you've made is buried under the prospect of further, higher profits. Your NAc is activated, and the release of dopamine leads to an increased willingness to take risks. You increase the size of your positions and leave out the stop-loss limits for now. After all, you expect a winning trade. The prospect of additional wins makes you forget all the rules. The stronger your expectation of a reward, the stronger the activity in the NAc. Your intellect is powerless against these forces. And afterward you have no idea how it happened. How could you have lost control? It's quite simple: Your thinking apparatus was in a waking coma.

When your neural mechanisms kick into gear, it's nearly impossible to stop them. You must react at an early stage because, frankly, you don't have much time. That's why prevention is important: It's critical to have trained processes and a fixed set of rules in place when trading. You need iron discipline and mental strength so that you don't fall victim to greed. Above all, keep the following guidelines in mind:

>> Keep your distance by adopting an observer role.

>> Never take the losses personally.

>> Never identify with your trades (non-attachment).

>> Take a break and move your body when you have the feeling of becoming cocky or euphoric.

For an overview of mental self-coaching techniques that might help you in managing your neural mechanisms, see Chapters 6 and 7.

REMEMBER

Greed that is difficult to control in trading leads to a lack of discipline and points to addictive behavior. Psychological studies indicate that there may be deficits in personality development. The German Central Bank and the European Securities and Markets Authority (ESMA) regularly warn against the consequences of excessive speculation with leveraged products. The large number of individuals who are essentially addicted to playing the stock market is a cause for concern.

Managing Losses: The Trader Psyche at Its Limit

I return time and time again in this book to the depressing topic of trading losses. After all, it's not easy to have an occupation where losses are a normal part of everyday life. In any other job, you receive a fixed salary for the work you've done, and you may even earn a performance bonus. Imagine a situation where, if your performance were poor, you would not only forfeit your paycheck but also have to hand over money to your boss. Unthinkable! But this is how it works on the stock exchange. It's not simply the case that you earn nothing if your strategies and setups don't work out. What's worse is that you have to come to terms with the fact that, despite all the hard work you may have done, you still have to pay out on top of that and lose money.

This unfortunate series of events occurs in half of all trades, according to statistics. That not only hurts a great deal but also runs contrary to our evolutionary development. Human nature was not created for trading. Impending loss inevitably triggers ancient programs in your brain. If you were to follow your natural instincts in trading, your portfolio would probably be ruined in the shortest possible time.

If you don't want to belong to the vast majority of private traders who, according to statistics, fail on the markets in either the long term or the short term, you need to learn to deal proactively with losses. More specifically, you need to build up your defenses against your own evolutionary heritage — an emotional bulwark, as it were. The building blocks for such a bulwark consist of frictionless trading processes and explicit rules — not particularly exciting, I admit, but it's the only way to get a grip on your emotions, your ego, and your deep-rooted response patterns.

Recognizing (and limiting) your portfolio risks

What is your trading nightmare? You will undoubtedly answer this way: the dreaded drawdown — a continued losing streak.

TECHNICAL STUFF

The concept of (maximum) drawdown is an important tool in risk management. A *drawdown* is a measure of risk — the maximum loss of a portfolio between the peak and the subsequent low in a period (the peak-to-trough metric).

Imagine that you have capitalized your broker account with $50,000. Your trading strategy has been profitable, and you reach a portfolio of $60,000 within a few months. Then a losing streak reduces the portfolio to $40,000. You recoup your losses to bring the portfolio back to $55,000 before the next losing streak sends it to the initial level of $50,000. The maximum drawdown of the account — the highest interim loss, in other words — is $20,000 ($60,000 – $40,000). The risk level amounts to −33 percent.

When you suffer several trading losses in a row, it has a grave effect on your portfolio and your psyche. Many traders lose their nerve, break the rules, intervene, and make unforced errors. Drawdowns are the main cause of emotional stress and anxiety — and they're also the main reason that traders give up.

REMEMBER

How you deal with losing streaks determines if you will become profitable at trading over the long term.

Let me assure you: A losing streak in trading is as certain as an amen in church. Living in denial or hoping you'll be spared aren't sensible strategies. The statistics are clear. Assume that you want to achieve an average hit rate of 50 percent with your trading. That means that five out of ten trades are winners and five are losers. Now calculate how likely it is that several loss trades will occur, one after the other. (Table 4-1 does the math for you.)

TABLE 4-1

Doing the Math

Number of Consecutive Losing Trades	Probability of Occurrence
2	25% (0.5×0.5)
3	12.5% $(0.5 \times 0.5 \times 0.5)$
4	6.25% $(0.5 \times 0.5 \times 0.5 \times 0.5)$
5	3.125% $(0.5 \times 0.5 \times 0.5 \times 0.5 \times 0.5)$

The statistics aren't meant to scare you, but merely to prepare you for the fact that, as an active trader, you'll have to reckon with losing streaks at regular intervals and you need to be prepared for it. If your positions are large in relation to the size of the portfolio, a series of losing streaks will ruin your annual performance.

TECHNICAL STUFF

A striking number of traders overestimate their hit rate. In practice, the vast majority of traders don't achieve more than 50 percent of winning trades. By all accounts, it's not the success quota that's critical. Far more important is to know when you're in the wrong position and when you're positioned correctly in order to limit your losses and expand your profits.

REMEMBER

A drawdown is not the same thing as a loss. The balance sheet value of the portfolio in the drawdown example earlier in this chapter did not change. You suffered no losses, so at the end of the day, you still have $50,000. The fluctuation range, however, is enormous. The risk level amounts to a worrying −33 percent. Most of the traders underestimate the fluctuation range because they see losses only in relation to the purchase price. In addition, they underestimate the emotional roller-coaster. (For more on the dangers of fixating on particular reference points, see Chapter 11.)

The concept of drawdowns is an important measure to determine your portfolio risk. As has become clear, I hope, it makes a lot of sense to pay attention to the financial mathematics. The impact of a losing streak can be illustrated using the numbers, providing much needed clarity about the opportunities and risks from a higher-level perspective. By focusing on the financial figures, you can

» Analyze the risk of your entire portfolio, not just your individual trades.

» Determine the loss tolerance for your trades.

» Limit the effects of individual losses on your portfolio.

» Have an overview of the profitability of your total portfolio.

We humans are, by our very nature, quite happy to suppress thoughts of potential losses. After all, who wants to stare into the abyss? As a consequence, most traders underestimate the risks they face. Rather than correctly assess such risks, most people prefer to dream of profit opportunities.

Time for some straight talk: The proportional portfolio losses you suffer as a result of a large trading loss requires a significantly higher percentage of profit with the following trade to compensate for that loss. This is simple financial mathematics.

Table 4-2 shows why it's extremely important to keep losses within narrow limits.

TABLE 4-2

The Impact of a Drawdown on Your Portfolio

Initial Loss	Required Gain to Break Even
10%	11%
20%	25%
30%	43%
40%	67%
50%	100%
60%	150%
70%	233%
80%	400%
90%	900%
100%	Portfolio is ruined. . . .

The effects of large losses are frightening. The required percentage profit in order to compensate for such high losses increases disproportionately. Let's be honest: How realistic is it to achieve 100 percent performance to make up for a 50 percent loss? At least without excessive additional risks? How often do I hear of traders who have destroyed their entire annual performance with a single losing streak? How many traders try to recover lost capital with aggressive leveraged strategies and high stakes — and then lose everything irrevocably? Andre Kostolany summarizes it best: "You can win, you can lose, but winning back? Impossible."

REMEMBER

Keeping your losses small is one of the most important rules in trading. It's easier to recoup small losses, as Table 4-2 shows. Never forget that capital preservation always has top priority.

WARNING

Your trader psyche is a major stress factor over the course of a drawdown. How long will it take to recover your losses? The psychological pressure can be enormous during this time.

Surviving losing streaks

The laws of financial mathematics are clear: You cannot avoid losing streaks. The more trades you make, the more the probability of a drawdown increases. The numbers should provide anyone with a warning glimpse into the abyss, but many traders have nevertheless plunged right into that abyss out of ignorance or negligence because the emotional trap snaps shut. Summoning the psychological wherewithal to survive a losing streak is a massive challenge. You will manage to maintain your emotional balance only if you have an airtight set of rules you can hold on to. Process orientation in trading is the key to success in stormy seas; otherwise, you'll lose your grip and control — and end up drowning. (For more on self-coaching mental strategies for coping with loss, see Chapter 6.)

TIP

You can control the extent of your losses by applying the well-known 1 percent rule: Risk only 1 percent of your capital per trade. By sticking to this rule, you can limit your losses during drawdown. Just keep in mind that, in practice, this rule is harder to implement for smaller portfolios.

Experience shows that the fluctuation range increases dramatically with decreasing portfolio size. The reason is obvious: Position sizes don't match the size of your portfolio. Beginners with little starting capital tend to enter into large positions. Their impatience and their greed for major profits can sometimes overwhelm them. It's obviously hard to trade in small positions with proportionate risk. The danger here is that you won't survive your learning curves. If you trade regularly, losing streaks are inevitable. (Refer to Table 4-1.)

REMEMBER

A drawdown can result in portfolio losses so significant that you won't even have a chance to recover from them. (Refer to Table 4-2.)

Financial fluctuations increase the emotional stress that may prove unbearable under certain circumstances. Your error rate increases. If, in addition, you lose your emotional balance, you take the huge risk that you will ruin your portfolio in a short period of time. Studies confirm this phenomenon. A remarkably large number of traders with small portfolios suffer a total loss within a few months.

TIP

Calculate the historical maximum drawdown of your trading strategy. Carry out back tests on your demo account. You can then decide how much risk you're prepared to take and what fluctuations you're willing to accept. This is the foundation for determining position sizes and stops, and it has the added benefit of preparing you mentally for real trading. If you have worked out potential scenarios in detail in your strategies, you will be more prepared psychologically.

After you have successfully tested your trading strategy in a simulated environment, take the following actions:

>> Determine the maximum portfolio risk you're willing to accept.

>> Determine the maximum position size that doesn't endanger your portfolio in case of drawdown or exceed the selected portfolio risk.

>> Start with a few low stakes, and only increase your positions successively and only if you're able to transact your trade in an emotionally stable, consistent manner.

If you trade regularly, you soon discover that drawdowns are more common than people think. Be aware of the massive risks to your portfolio and your psyche.

Setting effective stop-loss limits

Placing a stop-loss order should be done sensibly and should take into account the market environment as well as your portfolio. Among other things, many traders make the error of determining a fixed sum as their maximum loss. This is understandable, but not professional: Either the amount is too large for your portfolio (in case you end up in a losing phase) or your stop is set too narrowly (with the consequence that you're stopped out too fast in volatile markets). It's more sensible to take into account the framework conditions of each individual trade. That means completing both of these tasks:

>> Set the stop loss depending on expected market volatility.

>> Take your portfolio aspects into account when setting stop-loss limits so that your total portfolio is protected.

You can choose from a variety of techniques and variants when it comes to using stop-loss orders in order to secure your positions. Besides the classic price stops, you can use time-based stops, technical stops, volatility-based stops, or trailing stop-loss orders, where you trail them into the profit region, piece by piece.

Generally speaking, a loss stop should clearly signal to you that your trading strategy isn't right for the current market environment. Find out the reasons for this. Doing the research here can help you resist the temptation to try to reenter hastily, without thinking.

I freely admit that it requires much patience to wait for your opportunity, especially if you've been stopped out. Your ego will surely try to get involved, hoping to get your lost money back. Hold back and trust your strategies. You should be trading only the setups with the best probability of success. If you know your opportunities and risks in the current market environment, you'll be successful in your trading.

Managing your positions actively

In my coaching practice I stress time and time again that one should always trade according to the rules one has set for oneself and with clearly defined setups. This process orientation is the key to success because it's the only way you'll have your emotions under control. Of course, you can always just sit back after entry and wait until you've reached the profit target or stop-loss limit you set for yourself. When it comes to beginners, the passive implementation of setups is often the best strategy.

Experienced traders master the art of the active management of open positions. That doesn't mean that you break rules and intervene arbitrarily — quite the contrary. You observe the markets *closely* and actively search for price-relevant information. You have a sixth sense to perceive and anticipate changes at an early stage. You act in a controlled and well-thought-out way. (For more on the special abilities of experienced traders, check out Chapter 3.)

The market is in a constant state of evolution, with new data and information arriving and being processed by market participants. The probability of gains or losses of your positions changes constantly.

Active position management means that you continuously keep an eye on the impact of market developments on your positions and reevaluate your opportunities and risks — for example:

>> If the market movements support your trading strategy, you increase your position, trail the stop to ensure low risk, and maybe increase your profit goal. (For more on this particular pyramid strategy, see Chapter 11.)

>> If the market environment changes to your detriment, you may dissolve a part of your position before reaching the stop-loss limit. Or you can simply close the entire position early on.

The decisive criterion for your active intervention in an ongoing trade is the change in probability. It makes little sense to hold a position if the prospects for profit have deteriorated. Experienced traders quickly recognize whether a trade is moving in the wrong direction and respond immediately. And it can make a lot of sense to expand a position if your trading idea is on the right track. Of course, this assumes you have a firm grip on your portfolio risk.

You're in a position to truly act proactively when you're quite clear about when you're right and when you're wrong. This requires a lot of experience and excellent market knowledge. When it comes to your profitability, it's just as important to develop position management skills as it is to have the best trading strategies.

REMEMBER

You're walking a narrow tightrope with active position management. It requires a lot of experience and iron discipline. Be careful that you don't unconsciously fall into the habit of tossing aside your own set of rules.

3 Emotional Sovereignty

Chapter 5

Seeing Trading as Personality Development

Keeping a well-structured trading journal is a useful way to get the learning process rolling as you develop your trader personality. The journal can work to focus your market analysis (as well as your self-analysis) at the end of the trading day. The aim is to uncover your trading patterns and, if necessary, change them. By keeping a journal, you get to put your thought and behavior patterns to the test. You self-critically ask yourself why you think and act the way you do when trading.

In other words, keeping a journal structures the self-observation process.

In this chapter, you learn how to lay the foundation of your development. You see how to draw your attention away from problems and toward possible solutions. You then can perceive the importance of comparing your character and personality traits to the requirements of various markets and financial instruments. The aim is to find a suitable trading style for you personally. At the end of this chapter, I make it a point to remind you that trading doesn't need to be an occupation for lone wolves — in fact, you can learn a tremendous amount by working together as part of a team of like-minded people. Real and virtual networks accelerate your development process.

Keeping a Trading Journal

Moments after the market closes, you still have vivid memories of each trade as well as the thoughts and emotions that accompanied each one. After a few days, you'll probably have forgotten or suppressed many of the details. Your ego is a master of self-deception and sees itself as being good at blocking out or reinterpreting unpleasant events. That's why it's vital that you make a record of what happened in a timely manner in the form of a trading journal. You don't want to delude yourself, do you?

REMEMBER

Your ego has the habit of focusing on what it wants to see. A well-kept journal forces you to see what you need to see in order to be able to trade well.

I freely admit that it sometimes requires a lot of self-discipline to write down and evaluate your trades after each trading day. It's not easy having to document how you feel about each trade. But you're leaving valuable information and insights on the table if you don't do this. It would be a shame not to take advantage of this learning opportunity.

In Chapter 3, I talk a lot about the high art of pattern recognition. Analyzing your trades after the fact helps you recognize important aspects you may have overlooked in the heat of the moment. In retrospect, you can see your trades with other eyes because you will have gained some distance and you'll be able to retrace your own thinking and behavior patterns. Maybe you'll even recognize some rather conspicuous emotional patterns. Doing so will give you an opportunity to learn from your mistakes. I'll be the first to say that it's definitely unpleasant for your ego to have to deal with the mistakes you made, but it's the only way you will learn.

Looking into the basics of journaling

A trading journal should always consist of two parts:

>> The technical part

>> The psychological part

The technical part documents neatly what actions you took and how you traded over the course of the day. The psychological part explains why you acted the way you did — what motivated you to act or to refrain from doing so, in other words.

Figures 5-1 and 5-2 show you examples of what the first two pages of a trading journal might look like.

Date _____   Time _____

Demo/Real money _____   Instrument _____

Setup (Signals/Indicators/Entries/Exits/Position size/Holding period:

_____

_____

_____

Trade rating: Grade: A / B / C

Random trade/opened by coincidence or   If not planned, why
planned?   not?

_____

_____

_____

Stop loss limit set before opening trade and adhered to?   Yes/No

If not, why not?

_____

_____

Profit target set before opening trade and adhered to?   Yes/No

If not, why not?

_____

_____

Emotional state and behaviour during current trade:

Were you tense as you followed the trade? Did you intervene in the
running and open position? Reasons?

Were you feeling relaxed in the observer position as you let the trade
run its course? If so, why was that the case?

_____

_____

_____

FIGURE 5-1:
Page 1 of a typical
trading journal.

Based on LR Thomas, Trading Journal.

Evaluation: These are the lessons I learned from the trade (technical as well as mental):

_____

_____

_____

_____

_____

_____

Profit/loss in dollars: _____

Profit/loss as a percentage of account size: _____

Did you realize rule based profits/losses or did your profits/losses come from breaking your trading rules? Reasons?

_____

_____

_____

_____

What can I do to improve my performance with my next trade?

_____

_____

_____

_____

Which mental preparation exercises did I employ for this particular trading day?

- Affirmations
- Visualizations
- Relaxation techniques
- Breathing exercises
- Anchoring

FIGURE 5-2:
Page 2 of a typical trading journal.

Based on LR Thomas, Trading Journal.

Use the trading journal for the trades you make. Record the feelings you experienced as part of each trade. Every individual profit-and-loss trade you write down helps you when you complete your postmortems. Documenting your trading day helps you with these two tasks:

>> Recognizing technical and emotional patterns.

>> Identifying opportunities for improvement.

The analysis also shows you whether you have managed to achieve profits and losses in accordance with the rules you have set for yourself or by flouting those same rules. Even if it sounds illogical at first, it's generally better to conclude a planned trade according to your rules with a loss than to break those rules and randomly close with a profit. Or is it a case where you simply lack the self-discipline and confidence in your own strategy necessary for success?

Unplanned wins trigger feelings of joy and lull you into a false sense of security. Your ego triumphs and lets you think you have excellent instincts. Hubris will probably lead you to break the rules further and indulge in impulsive behavior. Don't overestimate your abilities. You may in fact achieve wins even though you broke the rules; just don't attribute your success when breaking the rules to some magical "gut feeling" you had. You're confusing coincidence with ability.

WARNING

Without rules, you're at the mercy of your emotions. At some point, a lack of rules is sure to turn out badly and you'll lose control — which can become expensive.

A random win isn't an indicator of profitable trading. If you have a proven and profitable strategy, the wins will occur on their own if you stick with the rules.

REMEMBER

Your goal is to learn from each trade. You'll use your experiences so that you can continually improve yourself. That creates self-confidence and mental strength. Keeping a trading journal lays the foundation for your development to become a successful trader.

THE GOLDEN CIRCLE

The British author and business consultant Simon Sinek uses the metaphor of the golden circle to explain how successful people act and what inspires them. According to his model, successful people always start with the core question of Why and then work outward from the inner circle toward the outer circle.

(continued)

(continued)

Start with Why: How Great Leaders Inspire Everyone to Take Action is the title of his international bestseller. The basic idea behind it can be easily applied to trading. Your inner drive and emotional patterns explain why you trade the way you do, and they also reveal *what* you're trading for — the conscious and subconscious goals you're pursuing, in other words:

- **Why?** Motivation, beliefs, emotional patterns

- **How?** Trading behavior and how you implement the Why

- **What?** Trading plans and strategies and their results — the result of the Why

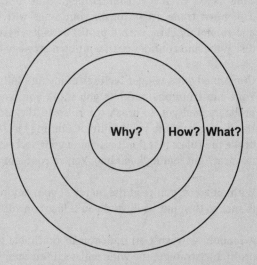

Most traders focus largely on market analyses and perfecting trading plans and strategies. This process works from the outside to the inside, a mechanical method that leaves you emotionally vulnerable. If you don't know your goals or what you're trading for, you'll lack the discipline and perseverance you need as soon as you're under pressure and stress. You'll lose your emotional balance, break your own rules, and make unnecessary mistakes. Your first losing streak will throw you for a loop; you'll give up because you have no inner drive to get back up and continue. You lack the mental resilience to prove yourself on volatile markets.

Successful traders know exactly what they're doing, how they're doing it, and why; they are inwardly convinced of the rightness of their actions. They have realistic expectations and a clear objective.

TIP

Search for the deeper meaning — your own vision, in other words — in your trading. In your journal, answer the decisive questions of why you're trading and what you're trading for.

Carrying out the technical analysis

In the technical part of a trading journal, you need to examine your market analysis and evaluate your trades. Among other things, you should be able to answer the following questions:

>> Were your technical and fundamental analyses correct?

>> What did you overlook or wrongly assess?

>> What did you get right?

>> Did your strategy and setup suit the market?

>> How was the timing of your trade entrances and exits?

>> Were the position sizes chosen and the number of trades made in proportion with market movements?

The daily analysis will help you to continuously improve your trading. It's a form of assessing your position daily. The day's experiences will teach you how mature your trading ideas are. Without being distracted or influenced by the ups and downs of the market, you'll be in a position to calmly develop your processes and strategies so that you can better prepare for the next trading days.

For many experienced traders, a trading journal is an important instrument for subsequent pattern recognition. With the perspective a little distance might bring, you may recognize chart patterns or formations that you may have overlooked during the hustle and bustle of daily events. You can compare these to historical situations. This process of daily repetition sharpens your awareness of implicit patterns. In short, you are training your intuition — and potentially developing new trading ideas. Finally, you can include these insights in your strategies.

Handling the psychological analysis

The psychological part of a trading journal is, above all, an instrument for recognizing your own patterns as a trader. It's a helpful process of self-observation that will improve your concentration and attention when trading. In general, patterns include

>> Recurring thinking and behavior patterns

>> Recurring emotional reactions in certain situations

EXAMPLE

Psychological problems affecting traders often go unnoticed and occur according to the same script: You have prepared thoroughly for the trading day and place trades strictly in accordance with your trading rulebook. At some point, a trade goes wrong and you start losing money. You get angry and subconsciously strive to get your money back. You start to flout the rules or ignore your planning for the day. You lose more money. Does this sound familiar to you? You want a successful close to the day, but you find yourself moving from frustration to frustration. You have long since lost your emotional balance and feel trapped. The market has become a threat and you're identifying with your trading losses.

What does that mean in concrete terms? In this example, the emotional pattern becomes clear: You posted a trade loss and feel like a loser. This triggers a chain reaction of poor decisions caused by your emotional state. You leave the straight-and-narrow and break your own rules.

Answering scaling questions

What is your emotional experience of trading? Do you notice psychological patterns in your subsequent analyses? Apply that same scale to answering the following questions:

>> Do certain market situations inspire fear, either making you freeze or triggering overtrading?

>> Do you have the tendency to force trades in order to earn money instead of waiting patiently for the right opportunity?

>> Are you revenge trading because you want to recoup lost money?

>> Are you (involuntarily) hesitating and missing good entry opportunities?

>> Do you feel worthless when, over the course of the trading day, no actionable trading signals occur?

>> Do you frequently change your trading strategy if it's not working?

>> Do you always behave according to the same scheme, regardless of how the markets move?

>> Do you tend to act against the market and fight to be right? Or do you prefer to follow the herd and run after every market movement, out of the fear of missing something?

>> Do particular market phases make you feel truly comfortable and confident?

Maybe you'll think of other emotional issues and challenges that apply to you. When your list is complete, I recommend this two-stage exercise:

1. **Evaluate your entries on a scale of 1 to 10, where 1 is the minimum impact on your trading success and a value of 10 is maximum impact.**

   The scaling results clearly show you how to assess your problems and how you weight them.

   This scaling technique is often applied in the field of systemic therapy. Because subjective perceptions and emotions aren't objectively measurable, allocating numbers allows comparability and weighting. This creates clarity and directs the focus to the solution of these problems.

2. **Rank your trading problems.**

   Start with the heavyweight problems. Make a table that consists of two columns: Write the weighted problems in the left column and write potential solutions in the right. Most of the time, you already know the solution, but your attention is still stuck on the problem.

The sense and purpose of this exercise is to make you aware of where your real problems lie and to draw your attention to the solution of these problems.

Creating clarity

As part of the journaling process, the psychological analysis provides you with valuable insights into your trader personality. I am sure you'll discover some typical reactions that you weren't aware of. If you carefully document your moods and feelings during the trading day, you'll learn how to identify the triggers for recurrent emotional patterns. The triggers are usually situational. When you're in a position to recognize these triggering situations, you can take precautions and adapt your trading accordingly.

REMEMBER

Be clear about the negative impacts of emotional patterns on your performance. Make sure this is readily apparent — that means notating in excruciating detail in your journal what losses occurred or what opportunities you missed and doing that day after day. When the costs of these damaging patterns become visible, you'll develop the motivation to interrupt these trading patterns.

TIP

Rethinking starts in your brain. Refuse to let problematic patterns control you by identifying with them. You're not the problem — the old patterns are. And you can change them.

Recognizing the issues behind certain behavioral patterns

Keeping a trading journal will become routine after some time and you'll discover more and more interesting peculiarities and regularities. You'll find out a great deal about yourself and develop a good feeling for your patterned trading behavior.

Experience shows that most traders don't usually have dozens of different patterns. Instead, there seem to be higher-level patterns that run like a common thread through all identifiable patterns. This may sound complicated at first glance, but it's important to understand.

For example, if your own personal issues stem from deep-seated fears, the effects of those fears will turn up in all problem patterns. If the following statements correctly characterize your trading actions, it's clear that the basic pattern that characterizes your trading behavior rests on fear:

>> You exit too early because you're afraid of losing book profits.

>> You move your stop-loss limits because you're afraid of realizing losses.

>> You choose position sizes that were too small out of fear of losses.

>> You miss out on good opportunities because you're afraid of entering the current market.

Superficially, these behaviors appear to be different problem patterns, but in reality, they're all linked to the single core problem you need to address: your fears. Chapter 15 deals extensively with this topic.

Replacing harmful patterns

The approach to moving from problem patterns to solution patterns occurs step-by-step:

1. **With the help of the self-observation documented in writing, you'll be able to recognize recurring problematic patterns.**

2. **Recognizing emotional patterns helps you interrupt them.**

   The entries in your journal will make you aware of the fact that certain situations trigger emotional behaviors that damage your trading success. You have calculated the costs of harmful patterns. Self-awareness interrupts automatic behaviors because you're now motivated and in a position to willingly undertake countermeasures.

TIP

Exchanging information with trader colleagues and comparing your approaches with theirs offer good opportunities to uncover thought and behavior patterns. When you look at your trades through the eyes of others and regularly solicit feedback from colleagues, you learn a lot about yourself. (You can read more about this topic at the end of this chapter.) The gap between your internal perception of the market and external reality may close.

EXAMPLE

If you find yourself falling into destructive behavioral patterns, one possible solution is to simply interrupt your trading. Take a break and create some emotional distance. (For some suitable techniques for regulating your emotions, see Chapter 6.)

3. **Replace a harmful emotional pattern with a useful behavioral pattern or new perspective.**

   Your focus will move away from problems and toward solutions. Admittedly, this requires a great deal of mental flexibility and adaptability, but you'll get there with lots of practice.

So, what would be a useful behavioral pattern or new perspective? Here are a few suggestions:

>> Avoid market phases that make you feel uncomfortable.

>> Trade only in time frames that suit your strengths.

>> Learn to accept trading losses as a normal part of any trading strategy.

>> Learn to immediately interrupt your trading when you find yourself reacting emotionally.

TECHNICAL STUFF

The trick to changing counterproductive behaviors lies in modifying the harmful pattern. To achieve effective change, you don't need to change the entire pattern; it's enough to change individual elements. The entire pattern is detected by the interactions between the contiguous elements.

You have had plenty of opportunity to test yourself and practice on the demo account. If, as a result, you have discovered that your trading style is one-sided — meaning you always follow the same schematics — you can extend your repertoire with the help of paper trading. In that way, you see how to react flexibly to various market conditions.

Finding solutions

See whether this situation sounds familiar: You are disciplined at keeping your journal and you have detected a series of harmful patterns, but you can't get rid of the damaging patterns in practice.

Systemic therapy formats often use the solution focus method. It's all about drawing attention to *solutions* — your abilities and strengths in trading, in other words. The thing is, there's more to your behavior than the effects of problem patterns; one can also point to patterns of success. The basic assumption here is that you either have, or can develop, the resources you need in order to be able to find the right solutions independently. When your perceptual focus is no longer associated with your problem patterns, your solution horizon expands automatically. Effective change means *differentiating* — introducing differences to the old patterns, in other words. Think of it as throwing a stone onto the still surface of a pond and seeing the ripples spread out to change the entire surface of the water.

Focusing on solutions: Consciously responding differently

Assume that your trading journal reveals that you keep making the same specific trading error (entering and exiting the market prematurely, for example). First of all, focus on the times when you did not commit the error:

>> What were the circumstances like when you ended up not making the mistake?

>> What did you do differently?

The answer to these questions will show you possible solution patterns so that you can consciously respond differently. Either that or you can set up rules to help you avoid such trading errors.

TIP

Problem patterns are always associated with specific emotional and physical conditions. Physical exercise, relaxation, and breathing techniques as well as conscious mental distraction are quite helpful when problems arise. When you change your underlying condition, you'll be able to see your problems with fresh eyes and reevaluate them.

Creating patterns of success

Problem recognized, problem gone, you might say. Being aware of a problem allows you to focus on possible exceptions and solutions. "If what you are doing doesn't work, do something else" is one of the basic premises of neurolinguistic programming (NLP). In trading, you should concentrate on what works well. In the past, you have demonstrated that you have the required skills to succeed; something has led you to be dissociated from your competencies, meaning you've temporarily checked out. To access your resources again, you need to place focusing on solutions at the core of your trading strategy. You need to find your pattern of success.

To do that, be sure to keep a trading journal, paying close attention to what worked well during the day. Ask yourself the following questions:

>> What went well today?

>> What did I do right?

>> What worked better than usual today, and why?

Concentrate on your strengths and opportunities for improvement.

Emotional patterns are the result of coping strategies from earlier phases of your life — strategies that subconsciously repeat themselves when trading. You see the world of markets through the internal conditioning you have experienced over the course of your life. The feelings and beliefs that result are your basic patterns. Obviously, there are similarities between your problems in trading and significant events or repressed conflicts in your earlier life. If you have experienced trauma and emotional wounds, I strongly recommend that you seek professional help. The market is the worst and most expensive place to work on psychological problems.

Setting up rules and establishing new habits

Identifying problematic patterns of thought and behavior and finding solutions for how to prevent these problems in the future is the key to your success as a trader. Initially, it may be hard to maintain these changes. You may fall back into old habits. What can you do to avoid relapses into old patterns? It's simple: You work through the solution patterns again and again until the new behaviors become habitual. Speaking from a neurobiological point of view, the neural circuits have consolidated to such an extent that you can automatically retrieve the desired behaviors without having to think about it. The key lies in repetition.

One important element is still missing: rules. To turn solution patterns into habit patterns, you need fixed trading rules you can follow.

A set of rules is your foundation, giving you support and stability in volatile markets. And it keeps your emotions under control.

Unfortunately, the behavior that's innate to humans isn't what leads to success in the stock market. That's why rules are an important corrective measure. Rule-based trading imposes discipline and forces you to do the right thing.

Try out this trading rule on a demo account first, for these two reasons:

>> You'll learn whether the rules make sense and show success.

>> Paper trading allows you to extensively train the implementation of new or modified rules. You learn to comply with tried-and-true rules. You acquire new, target-oriented habits.

A PROBLEM RECOGNIZED MEANS A PROBLEM AVERTED

Let's assume you have recognized that you set your stops too narrowly and are regularly being stopped out in volatile markets. Your aversion to loss is sometimes so strong that you keep closing positions before you reach the protective sell stop:

- **Problem recognized:** Your stops don't consider price fluctuations, you interfere in ongoing trades, and the fear of losses disrupts your emotional balance.

- **Problem averted:** You determine your maximum loss tolerance per trade in advance, and stops are set depending on volatility. The result is a solution-oriented rule: You're rarely stopped out, you have played through the potential loss per trade, and it's bearable. You remain emotionally stable and feel no urge to intervene.

Trading rules are more than mere specifications about what you should do or should not do. You have internalized the rules because you're convinced you're doing the right thing. You have understood that trading without an explicit set of rules is doomed to fail.

TIP

Evolutionary heritage and incalculable emotional outbursts leave you no other choice than to trade in a process-oriented, rule-based way.

REMEMBER

The advantages of keeping a trading journal are obvious: You train your inner observer, thus improving your ability to recognize patterns. You learn to interrupt emotional patterns and to replace these with solution-oriented behavior.

Getting to Know Your True Trader Personality

Keeping a trading journal is an important component of training your self-observation and self-reflection skills. By evaluating your entries, you're engaging in practical personality development. You learn a lot about your thought and behavior patterns as well as your strengths and weaknesses.

Part of practical personality development means you can make an unfiltered comparison between your self-perception and an objective view. Discrepancies often show up in your performance. Your trading results hold up a ruthless mirror to your true ability. You can't just run and hide, even if your self-esteem suffers. The profit-and-loss account at the end of each trading day prevents self-deception. The numbers are there in front of you in black-and-white.

WARNING

Again and again, I see traders who lack self-awareness. This includes the willingness to take a critical look at themselves. The result is that they overestimate themselves. In other words, they systematically misjudge their own competencies. That can be *expensive* in trading.

"Self-awareness is the first step to improvement" is a motto that is sometimes meant mockingly. The fact is, your trading is faulty and you can't help but notice it. In psychology, the ability to be self-aware is the decisive prerequisite when it comes to developing your personality further. You don't want to over- or under-estimate your abilities; you want to be able to judge them as objectively as possible.

Examining how personalities develop

Throughout this book, I stress the fact that your personality is one of the four factors for success in trading, alongside proven processes, sufficient practice, and awareness of one's own talents. So who are you, really? It requires courage to describe your own characteristics and shortcomings to see who you really are. You probably realize that being self-aware requires a healthy degree of confidence. It isn't so easy to accept who you are.

These are the three basic pillars of personality development:

>> **Self-awareness:** Awareness of one's major characteristics as well as one's strengths and weaknesses

>> **Self-acceptance:** The ability to accept yourself as you are

>> **Self-transformation:** The ability to develop further independently of others

Psychological studies have concluded that sustainable success in trading is a function of your personality and has less to do with intelligence or exceptional talents. That's why you should pay more attention to the further development of your trader personality.

TECHNICAL STUFF

Personality research agrees that the majority of the character traits and characteristics you possess are innate and largely remain stable throughout your lifetime. In this respect, personality development is rather a process where you mature your character. Some characteristics can be corrected or consciously and actively developed. In each and every one of us, potentials lie dormant that we can develop. That is the core of personality development.

Personality development also promotes resilience — a competence that comes in handy in a challenging trading environment. It strengthens our problem-solving ability, decision-making skills, and capacity to take action.

TIP

Would you like to strengthen your resilience? *Resilience For Dummies*, by Dr. Eva M. Selhub (Wiley), can show you how.

Finding the right market for your particular personality

"The personality of the market must fit the trader's personality," says the well-known trading psychologist Brett Steenbarger. In my experience, this is absolutely true. The markets, the financial instruments and time frames, the way you trade — all should be matched to your abilities and strengths.

Different trading systems provide different psychological challenges that fit different personality types.

What do I mean by that? You can't force your personality to match a different trading system. Your abilities and characteristics will show you your possibilities and your limits when it comes to trading. It's easier and more expedient to find the right market niche and a corresponding trading style than to bend your personality to fit another style. That won't be sustainable. It will take too much effort.

Use your demo account and try out the various markets and financial instruments using multiple time frames. You can play around in finding the right trading style for your personality, because it's all in demo mode anyway. Try to answer these questions:

>> What are your goals and expectations in trading?

>> What trading style matches your work and lifestyle?

>> How much time do you want to invest? How much time *can* you invest?

>> Are you a discretionary trader, or do you prefer system trading?

>> Do you take a fundamental or chart technical approach when it comes to analyses?

>> Do you prefer stocks or currency markets?

>> Do you prefer scalping, day trading, or position trading? In other words, which time frames do you feel most comfortable with?

>> How often do you trade (the number of trades per day or week)?

>> Are there times of the day or specific weekdays where you trade more successfully?

>> Do you follow trends, or do you like to swim against the current (looking for trend reversals, for example)?

>> Do you focus on a few big trades, or do you regularly run many smaller trades in different markets?

>> How flexible are you when it comes to implementing your rules? (Do you tend to make intuitive decisions, in other words?)

If you take the trouble to answer these questions honestly, you'll find clarity about which style and which niche might suit you. This is the foundation for developing trading strategies that fit your personality. You trade in your comfort zone, so to speak. In this way, you reap the benefits of your strengths. You trade by doing what you do best.

EXAMPLE

Are you the type who is glued to the screen and loves the hustle and bustle of trading and making fast decisions? Do you love taking numerous short-term positions that you hold for only a few minutes? Then scalping in liquid and volatile markets is probably for you. For the analyst with a fundamental approach whose strength lies in holding positions over several days or weeks, a completely different trading style is appropriate. And you, where do you see yourself?

WARNING

Don't mix time frames by turning a loss-making day trade into a longer-term position. That strategy usually goes wrong. You're leaving your niche.

Define the niche you want to trade in, clearly and unambiguously. A clear boundary imposes discipline and helps to ensure that you remain in your place of strength. The positive emotional experiences you make there will help to develop your personality.

REMEMBER

Many problems that traders report can be attributed to the fact that they're trading outside of their preferred niche. Even worse, traders often don't even know their niche and waste their abilities.

REMEMBER

It makes little sense to adjust to the markets or to force yourself to trade in a certain way. The best trading system is always the one that suits your personality, goals, and living environment. This system is the only one that will lead to success in a disciplined way.

Trading as a Team Sport: Avoiding Tunnel Vision

Most people describe *trading* as a lonely activity in small offices with countless screens. This preconception may also be a reason for the majority of beginners giving up out of frustration or failing after a short time.

REMEMBER

Humans are social beings who aren't naturally predisposed to sitting alone in front of screens all day. This is demotivating in the long term because you don't get feedback and can hardly develop. Silo thinking and a lack of adaptability are some of the consequences. Intellectual isolation is an obstacle to success.

Nothing says you have to sit by yourself in front of a screen. Look for like-minded traders, mentors, or sparring partners. Seeing trading as a team sport gives you another key to becoming a successful trader. Trading should be intellectual, personally challenging, and fun.

TIP

Build a network of like-minded traders, either virtually or real. Or join an existing network. Doing so brings with it multiple benefits:

>> You drive each other to think more intensively about the market and about trading ideas.

>> You get to share and discuss your observations, ideas, and analyses.

>> You challenge each other and are forced to see situations from another point of view.

>> You avoid tunnel vision and are thus able to broadly expand your horizons.

It's important to work together on a trust basis and have clear rules for cooperation. Virtual platforms or forums that mainly communicate via group chats in particular require regulated processes and a code of conduct. Otherwise, you won't have the confidence to openly discuss your trades and ideas.

Developing creative ideas

Albert Einstein is quoted as having said, "Creativity is intelligence having fun." Creative thinking can be fun and works best in teams. Creativity is a quality that has become increasingly important in trading as well.

Traditionally, it was sufficient to gain an advantage in the markets with a well-thought-out and successfully tested strategy. You could make good money with discipline and self-control. That is no longer sufficient. The times have changed, and with them, the rules of the game have changed as well. Market structures, actors, and interdependencies are changing even faster and more dynamically.

EXAMPLE

High-frequency trading, the use of algorithms and program trading, as well as the increasing importance of exchange traded funds (ETFs) are influencing liquidity conditions of markets irrevocably. The German Federal Bank has warned that, in periods of market stress, this can lead to distortions and sudden dips — the much-feared flash crashes.

Discipline and self-control are still important character traits in trading, but you also need new competencies, like adaptability and creativity, according to Brett Steenbarger. You need the ability and the instinct to recognize and adapt to market changes at an early stage. Creativity is the key to developing new approaches and ideas. Your trading processes should leave room for creativity.

TIP

Make use of one of the classics among creativity methods: brainstorming. Without passing any judgment, exchange with other members of your team any spontaneous trading ideas you come up with. Then assess and analyze the ideas. This promotes creative thinking and provides exciting results. You inspire each other. (Thinking against the grain is highly desirable.)

Putting your cards on the table

It never ceases to amaze me how many traders are reluctant to share their analyses and performance. This secrecy is an unmistakable sign of trading problems. Nobody is happy to admit their weaknesses, lack of preparation, or an inability to come up with a coherent set of rules. Or maybe you have found the holy grail and want to keep it to yourself? Disclosing your trading process is the first step to further development. You won't make progress if you isolate yourself and hide away. Successful trading is a creative development process that is at its most effective when you work on it with others. You exchange ideas and like to be challenged. You can learn a lot from other traders. Under certain circumstances, you may avoid the serious mistakes others have made.

WARNING

Merely copying other traders' strategies isn't a recipe for success. It won't get you far and is an indication that you have no confidence in your own abilities. You're afraid of making mistakes. You may be afraid of failure. You can find out more about trading fears in Chapter 15.

Ideally, you'll find trading colleagues on the Internet and in online communities with whom you can share regularly. It's important to be honest and disclose everything, to admit errors and be prepared to discuss controversial ideas and strategies. A frequent and honest feedback culture benefits all parties. It promotes a creative change in perspective and new ways of looking at circumstances.

TIP

If you can communicate openly and honestly about your trades, you have no place to hide. That imposes discipline and is incredibly liberating.

You will have good times and bad times with trading. Even when you have learned to accept this fact, it's good to share experiences with other traders. Frankly, it's comforting not to be alone on this emotional roller coaster. Everyone experiences these cycles and has various strategies to deal with them. You can learn a lot from that. Don't underestimate the value of professional and social interaction. An honest dialogue can energize you and give you renewed self-confidence.

THE ACCOUNTABILITY REPORT

Look for a mentor, trading coach, or a good colleague you can trust. Prepare a report at regular intervals (weekly/monthly/quarterly) in which you disclose everything — your profit-and-loss account with explanations, your entries in your trading journal, your development path. Account for everything. It should be a combination of a professional goals appraisal and a discussion of the psychological background to your trading behavior. I promise you that it will cause a quantum leap in your development as you make yourself into a successful trader.

Building networks

You can find lots of good newsletters, blogs, and online communities as well as trading platforms on the Internet that you can use to create a successful professional network.

TIP

Use independent reviews of brokers and online platforms in order to gain an overview.

Progress reports and comparative analyses are made by traders for traders. It may be worthwhile to initiate trial subscriptions for trading services from various professional traders to get trading recommendations and market assessments. Webinars, online seminars, and the exchange of information with other traders are also instructive.

I can recommend two trading services suppliers recognized by the market with a wide reach that are worth trying:

>> **Investing.com:** www.investing.com/

>> **Trading View:** www.tradingview.com

Both offer free and paid services. This includes up-to-date chart analyses of individual values and markets, fundamental analyses, real-time news and courses, expert forums, and webinars, for example.

TIP

Follow the best analysts and experts who regularly publish in online forums and communities and question their way of working. Get in touch with them. Try to understand their strategies and approaches. How did they arrive at these forecasts? Why are the charts drawn in that way? This strategy can be quite instructive.

REMEMBER

You can work as an independent trader without being isolated if you're part of a team of like-minded people and regularly share ideas and experiences, either virtually or in person.

Chapter 6

Practicing Mental Self-Coaching

One quite popular method you can use to develop your trader personality is self-coaching. You can use a variety of techniques and, because it's *self-coaching*, you get to decide which tools to use and when.

In Chapters 7 and 8, you get the chance to explore methodologies from the following fields:

» Systemic psychotherapy

» Hypnosystemic psychotherapy

» Positive psychology

» Neurolinguistic programming (NLP)

You also learn techniques that can help you to

» Process and dissolve harmful patterns of thought and behavior

» Transform negative beliefs into positive ones

» Take on new perspectives that enable you to deal with loss in a professional manner

>> Maintain a focused state of relaxation in order to maintain emotional balance

>> Increase motivation, self-awareness, and self-efficacy

>> Develop your potential as well as your mental strength

TIP

A simple but effective tool in self-coaching is the use of a success journal, which you can integrate with your personal trading journal. Recording your successes in writing can prove to be particularly motivating. (For more on trading journals, see Chapter 5.)

When it comes to self-coaching, one particular challenge is that you need to be able to ask yourself the right questions, including the uncomfortable ones. Problems you may have swept under the rug and left for years may inevitably come to light. You have to take on the role of your sharpest critic and overcome significant internal resistance. The subconscious strategies you've tended to use for tackling problems or difficult situations may work in everyday life, but they probably won't work when trading on the stock exchange.

REMEMBER

Self-coaching helps you to get to know yourself even better, with all your personal strengths, weaknesses, and inherent potential.

Looking at the development of your trading personality, what have you achieved so far? First and foremost, you have developed the ability to detect and correct specific trading problems, a correction that occurs by way of processes and routines that prevent these problems ever arising again. You also have learned that you'll be successful in trading if your core competencies as well as your trading style suit your personality. And, after you get used to keeping a trading journal, you'll set out on a journey of discovery. You'll write down your thoughts and feelings and discover your own personality. You'll assume full responsibility for your development.

The practical goal of self-coaching is that you come to a place where you can accept that at least half of all your trades, on average, will end with a loss. Beginners always want to avoid losing trades and be in the right. Experienced traders always expect losses, yet consistently work to limit such losses when they occur. They know when they have backed the wrong horse, yet they don't let such failures unsettle them. They have their emotions in check and know what they can and cannot manage and control. They are mentally prepared for trading and have achieved an emotional balance.

The market is what dictates the pace. Your task is to observe and to analyze and then to follow movements in the market when you determine that the probability of success is high. You trade based on what you see, not on what you believe or hope for. You cut out a slice of the recognized price pattern. No more, no less.

The path to becoming a successful trader is long and arduous. You will need to remove some boulders out of your way. In that sense, these are three largest psychological obstacles to success:

>> Letting emotions determine how you cope with loss

>> Becoming overwhelmed by stress and fear

>> Letting negativity dominate your internal dialogue

Using self-coaching methods, you'll discover ways to dissolve any psychological obstacles to your success while at the same time developing your mental strength.

Benefitting from Self Hypnosis: Seeing Your Subconscious Mind as a Trading Ally

Public perception of hypnosis varies widely, but the best way to describe hypnosis is to say that it's simply a natural state of total relaxation.

More specifically, *hypnosis* refers to the process of putting someone into a deep, relaxing meditative or trance-like waking state. It's a temporary altered state of consciousness that provides direct access to the subconscious. Conscious thought processes are restricted. This trance condition can also be induced by self-hypnosis.

When someone is in a trance state, it's possible to make suggestions that work directly on the subconscious. It would seem to be the case that recurring, problematic trading patterns can be resolved by the targeted influencing of an individual's subconscious and involuntary processes. In other words, one can use targeted suggestions to activate a variety of particularly desirable processes in an individual that's in a trance state.

TECHNICAL STUFF

Brain research has demonstrated the effectiveness of hypnosis. Using imaging techniques, researchers have been able to discern changes in activity levels in certain brain areas. Hypnotic suggestions evoke measurable changes to information processing in the brain.

Investigating the various forms of self-hypnosis

In principle, anyone can put themselves in a trance-like state. However, it requires some practice to achieve a stable and deep relaxed state. You've probably heard of *autogenic* training, a well-known self-hypnosis method: Mental relaxation techniques train your subconscious to believe in a desired goal. These auto-suggestions can be strengthened by mental visualizations because it turns out that the images in your mind have a greater impact than words do. The key lies in repetition so that subconscious thought processes assume the desired goal.

REMEMBER

The wide variety of meditation techniques available today all tend to serve one purpose: to achieve a state of consciousness where deep relaxation can be attained.

In addition to autogenic training, other methods of self-hypnosis can be considered as relaxation techniques or a form of meditation. For example:

>> **Targeted breathing exercises:** These can trigger a trance-like state.

>> **Progressive muscle relaxation techniques:** These can be used to achieve a deeply relaxed state. By alternatively tensing and relaxing specific muscle groups, you can reach a deep relaxation state encompassing the entire body. And, when the body is relaxed, the mind is relaxed as well.

>> **The eye fixation method:** In this method, which can be quite effective and fast-acting, you stare at an object of your choice without moving your eyelids. After a while, the eye muscles grow tired and your eyes close with a deep exhalation on your part and you automatically relax. When that occurs, you simply keep your eyes closed and take deep, conscious breaths.

WARNING

When attempting any form of self-hypnosis, make sure you're in a calm and quiet area where you will be undisturbed and, most importantly, where you can remain safe.

REMEMBER

Don't worry about how you'll remove yourself from a hypnotic trance. Just count backward slowly from 5 to 1. That reactivates your thinking apparatus. Or just imagine that you're returning to the surface of the water after a long dive and take a deep breath with your eyes open.

TIP

The Internet has lots of how-to's for self-hypnosis and trance induction, so you're sure to find plenty of literature on this topic. Progressive muscle relaxation and eye fixation seem to be particularly simple and effective techniques. Find out which method suits you best.

Initiating change processes in trance states

It's good news that you have many hypnosis and trance induction methods available to you, but the important aspect is that you actually use them to trigger changes in your problematic thought and behavior patterns. The whole idea is that you change your perceptions and also your emotional reactions.

Hypnosis isn't just for improving your trading personality. In psychotherapy, hypnosis techniques are used to treat stress and anxiety as well as to increase self-esteem. Try it if you're interested. Look for a hypnotherapist. It's worth it.

Internal dialogues: Talking to yourself when trading

Talking to yourself is a natural phenomenon. You probably don't even realize that this inner dialogue is always taking place. It's part of an important psychological process that is designed to work through impressions and experiences. Such incidences of talking to yourself are particularly intensive when strong emotions are triggered, and you can't confide in anyone. This is a typical situation in trading — a business dominated by lone wolves. Or do you have people in your circle with whom you regularly share your trading experiences? Does someone stand by you as you lay down your psychological burdens and express compassion for the joys and suffering of the trading business? If so, you're a lucky exception. Unfortunately, experience shows that you're more likely to experience a lack of understanding and a healthy dose of prejudicial judgments.

Be on the lookout for like-minded people who understand the ups and downs of trading. Build up your in-person network as well as your virtual ones. For more on how to do this, see Chapter 5.

These endless conversations you have with yourself determine your thinking, your behavior, the way you perceive the markets and, finally, your trading results. These internal dialogues control your emotional state and physiology in ways that mirror how your affirmations or core beliefs do. This inner voice of yours has a significant impact on your motivation.

Your self-worth and self-confidence depend on whether you come to terms with this inner voice in a friendly or hostile manner. In the end, how do you actually treat yourself? Are you appreciative and understanding of what your voice is saying, or are you derogatory and reproachful?

Your intellect believes the stories you are constantly telling it. It takes everything in, not bothering to distinguish between what might be positive and what might be negative.

It probably won't surprise you that the negative things you say to yourself are a big problem in trading. Many traders destroy their self-esteem and self-worth when they tear themselves down with their own self-directed derogatory thoughts. The result? A sense of inferiority, of not being good enough, of worthlessness.

That is partly due to the nature of the business. The psychological pressure is immense and enhances your natural tendencies and conditioning like a magnifying glass. In a worst case scenario, it leads to the following vicious circle of self-sabotage:

>> You make mistakes and suffer losses.

>> The anger and frustration lead you to blame yourself. (You even cuss yourself out to relieve the pressure.)

>> Your self-esteem suffers. (You doubt your abilities and may feel like a loser under certain circumstances.)

>> Your susceptibility to error increases and you're emotionally vulnerable.

Negative self-talk functions like a pressure valve: You impulsively allow your anger to run free, so you (momentarily) feel relieved. Yet such relief comes at a high cost: It causes lasting damage to your self-confidence and self-worth, and you end up doubting your skills. Negativity is self-destructive and has caused some traders to give up on themselves.

But it doesn't need to go that far. In this chapter, you learn a variety of techniques and methods that can get you back on the road to success.

Psychological studies show that anxiety and negativity are closely correlated. The bigger your fears and worries, the worse your inner dialogue. They tend to reinforce each other. Studies in high-performance sport demonstrate the impact of negativity on performance during competition. An athlete plagued by self-doubt cannot reach their full potential.

Developing positive conversations with yourself

How can you be successful if you constantly criticize and blame yourself and take all mistakes personally? Wouldn't it be more effective if you were to talk up your own courage, strength, and self-confidence? With that in mind, I ask you to be sure that you pay close attention to your inner thoughts and words.

REMEMBER

Negative thought patterns are learned habits and routines. It might be the case that you no longer have a choice. Perhaps you have no control over your internal conversations because you're unaware of them. The challenge of self-coaching lies in being able to recognize negative patterns, unlearn them, and then replace them with positive thoughts. Learning to take control of your inner dialogues can be your first step in radically changing your life.

WARNING

Identifying with negative thought patterns hinders your success in trading, not the negative thought patterns alone. It's a clear sign that you have lost control.

Here's a task for you to carry out: Pick up your trading journal and write down everything that spontaneously comes to mind when you think about your own inner self-talk. Pay particular attention to what's going on in your mind when you're trading. Make two columns: Enter positive statements that you say about yourself in one column and the negative statements in the other. Observe your thought processes in the coming days and weeks and add to the list. (*Note:* This exercise works best if you do this while trading.) Mark down whether you address yourself using the first person ("I") or you dissociate yourself from what you're doing by using the second person ("you").

The objective of this exercise is to a) identify your negative self-talk and b) create an awareness of your own thoughts. Then you can replace the negative attitudes you're holding on to with positive beliefs and affirmations. Adopting an observer role as you record what's going on helps you create clarity and emotional distance. It also allows you to document your development process objectively. As a bonus, you get to take an active role in designing your own thoughts.

You can implement this task by following these steps:

1. **Become aware of your inner voice when you're trading, and then write down all negative thoughts.**

   Here are several typical examples of self-doubt, self-denigration, and self-accusation:

   - You're just too stupid to find the correct entry point.

   - The fact that you didn't let your profits run shows how dumb you are.

   - I'm a loser, so it's no surprise that you're constantly losing money.

   - You never learn to implement your setups according to the rules.

   - It's all my fault!

- You just can't do it. You're a complete idiot, You'll never be a good trader.

- This is pointless. I should just stop this charade.

- You just don't deserve to earn any money from trading!

- You tend to take your losses personally, whining that you want your money back.

- You can't stop thinking about your losses and your missed opportunities.

- You're ashamed of your unprofessional and undisciplined trading.

- I do everything wrong.

- You're convinced that the markets are always against you, and you feel quite threatened.

- My strategies and setups are just *bad*.

The statements in this list might alarm you, but the fact is that what you see here is just a small selection of what traders think about themselves — and I'm not even including those words of a 4-letter variety that often crop up when traders criticize themselves. The truth is, you won't believe how hard some traders judge themselves. Their self-criticisms are filled with gross exaggerations, yet it all feels true to them. This is a self-destructive course.

TIP

Always ask yourself whether you're reacting so strongly to the actual market situation or to what you're telling yourself. Does your reaction have more to do with you?

2. **Categorize your notes.**

Do your inner conversations tend to focus more on self-worth, or are they more about managing trading losses?

3. **Spend some time thinking about how your inner dialogues outside of trading situations run their course.**

Ask yourself which parallels you see? Which differences?

TIP

If a single specific, negative limiting belief keeps turning up in your inner conversations, so much so that it's like a red thread running through all areas of your life, it can be a serious underlying problem for you. It might make sense to seek psychological help.

4. **Use the mental methods you learn about in this chapter to replace your negative thoughts with positive convictions.**

Affirmations and positive beliefs seem the most suitable methods here. Also, under some circumstances, dissociation and reframing techniques may also work well in trying to rewrite and reinterpret negative thought patterns in a more positive direction.

Suppose, initially, that your inner voice says, "I am such an idiot — I didn't let my profits run!" A dissociated reframing would state, "That was stupid not to let this profit run." The result? You no longer personally identify with the error, meaning you're able to protect your self-esteem.

The most decisive thing you can do is take control of your inner self-talk and no longer identify with negative thoughts. Let your own inner observer create psychological distance. The inner observer watches and takes action when necessary by reinterpreting, reframing, or replacing negative thoughts.

A consciously positive and appreciative inner dialogue, accompanied by thinking out loud, strengthens you mentally. You become more self-reliant and resilient. Positive beliefs and affirmations will help you reprogram your subconscious mind, dramatically changing your self-perception. At the end of that process, you'll have developed the mindset for successful trading.

One practical way to interrupt negative inner conversations is to personally intervene in a forceful way. That means every time your inner voice says something negative, shout out loud: *"Stop!"* or *"Nonsense!"* Such a distraction can work to abruptly interrupt the negative thought patterns.

Scientific studies have proven the effectiveness of positive inner conversations. In experiments with students, the trial participants who spoke to themselves frequently (also out loud) and asked themselves lots of questions were able to solve complex tasks better than those who remained largely silent.

Treat yourself as your own best friend. Be appreciative and benevolent. Think it through: Would you really swear at (and address derogatory comments to) a good trader colleague if they made a mistake, as you do to yourself?

Negative inner conversations indicate a lack of self-confidence and weak self-esteem. Mental self-coaching can work to help you strengthen your self-confidence and self-esteem in sustainable ways. Trust your inner voice — it will help you.

Promoting self-confidence and self-esteem

Trading is a volatile business and thus not necessarily suitable if your goal is to promote your self-confidence and self-esteem. Markets are unpredictable. Unexpected movements continually challenge your abilities and put you on an emotional roller-coaster ride, among other things. Regular losses and missed profits are a burden for the trader psyche and eat away at your self-image. Your need to be recognized by others for your particular talents will rarely be satisfied by the stock market.

REMEMBER

Know the difference between self-confidence and self-esteem. *Self-confidence* is confidence in your own abilities and depends on the situation. *Self-esteem* comes from inside and determines your perception.

EXAMPLE

You have mastered the tools in trading — the analysis methods, trading systems, and all that comes with it. This gives you self-confidence but doesn't necessarily give you self-esteem. This fact makes you emotionally vulnerable. Why do so many celebrities in the film or music industry suffer from depression? It's because, despite their outstanding performances, they lack self-worth and have low self-esteem. Conversely, you can have high self-esteem, yet have absolutely no trust in your athletic abilities. Such a lack doesn't dampen your self-perception, because you have a clear picture of your values and principles and you believe in your self-worth.

TECHNICAL STUFF

According to psychological studies, three-quarters of all people suffer from low self-esteem. The psychological and physical problems are sometimes severe. High self-esteem is the basis of any true measure of self-worth and self-confidence.

You've probably heard someone say at some point that trading is 80 percent psychology and 20 percent methodology. Professional traders have internalized this fact and continuously work on their personal development. Less experienced traders focus on methodology. Their factual knowledge of markets and instruments as well as technical and fundamental indicators can be impressive. However, with less experienced traders, it's often accompanied by a fragile self-confidence. Technical know-how doesn't help you for long in the trading world if deep down you don't believe in yourself. Doubting that you deserve success undermines your self-esteem. Subliminal fears are usually the result. You start sabotaging yourself if you think you don't deserve any reward. Your subconscious mind will prevent any success in trading. You'll not find the emotional balance you need for trading and, lacking confidence in your abilities, you'll also end up lacking motivation.

WARNING

Traders who make their self-worth dependent on their success in the stock market will constantly be afraid that the basis of their self-worth will be withdrawn. Losses might throw them off track.

What are the reasons for low self-worth when it comes to trading?

>> **Childhood experiences that continue to have an effect:** These are a lack of acceptance and appreciation and feelings of inadequacy, or of being worthless or rejected. Reproaches from others sound like this: "You can't do that," "You won't be able to manage that," and "You'll never get it."

>> **A series of traumatic losses:** These are feelings of inability and failure.

>> **Experiences of failure accompanying a total loss of some kind:** These are feelings of shame, guilt, or worthlessness.

>> **Negative inner self-talk:** These are feelings of inferiority and weakness.

>> **External negative influences:** These are contempt and misunderstanding on the part of others, "trading isn't a serious occupation," "it's just a dubious form of gambling."

Experience shows that most people hide or suppress the reasons why their self-worth is low. The fear of having to seriously deal with traumatic experiences and sabotaging beliefs naturally looms large. If you want to be a successful trader, however, running away from the truth isn't an option. You have to stop running when you end up at the stock exchange or else you'll run up against a brick wall (not a good outcome for your nose).

So, how can you build self-confidence and self-esteem in trading? What can you do to strengthen your self-image? It isn't an easy task; it takes time. This chapter focuses on a host of self-coaching techniques you can use, but for now I want to recommend a little exercise for self-reflection developed by the psychologist Catherine Stott. (I'm sure you have a good idea of how weak or how strong your self-confidence and self-esteem are, or do you?)

Here's what I want you to do: Choose five people from your immediate circle. Write down what you think these people think of you. What is it you feel you can offer these individuals? (Reliability? Humor? Trust?) What do you feel secure or confident about? (Trading? Your athletic ability? The ease with which you can get to know new people?) With that done, go ahead and write down all the characteristics you don't feel comfortable about. What would make you more self-assured?

This exercise should give you a good idea of what your self-image looks like. You have identified subconscious beliefs, and maybe you have an idea of what you need to work on to build your self-confidence and self-esteem.

TIP

If you have trouble imagining what positive statements other people might be making about you, this reflective mirroring exercise by Catherine Stott can help:

1. **Close your eyes and enter a deep relaxed state.**

2. **Imagine that your best friend is standing in front of you.**

   You see exactly what they're wearing and how they smile at you.

3. **Imagine that you've stepped outside of yourself, switched over to the other side, and now see yourself through that person's eyes.**

   It will look as though you're standing across from yourself. See for yourself the characteristics others love and appreciate about you. Feel all the joy that others feel when they meet you.

4. **Collect all your good thoughts and feelings and take them back with you to your side.**

5. **Spend some time enjoying these feelings of esteem and affection.**

   You know that it's real.

6. **Take a few deep breaths and open your eyes again.**

This exercise is simple and effective. Working through the steps works to help improve your self-image. You're sure to feel better and your self-esteem will surely benefit.

REMEMBER

Self-perception is often distorted. If you tend to underestimate yourself, learn to see yourself as others see you.

Here's another simple visualization exercise for recharging your confidence — it's called the *chair swap:*

1. **Pick two chairs — the desk chair you sit on when you're trading and another chair.**

2. **Place the chairs opposite each other.**

3. **Sit on the other, nontrading chair and close your eyes with a deep breath.**

4. **Imagine that your future self is sitting on the desk or trading chair.**

   This version of your self has significant trust in you and a strong sense of self-confidence.

5. **Use all your senses to put yourself into your future "I."**

   How does it feel? How does your body react? Your posture? Your facial expression? What are you wearing?

6. **Swap chairs so that you're now sitting on the desk chair of the self-confident self.**

   You have internalized the good feelings.

7. **"Drop into" yourself physically.**

8. **Breathe deeply and enjoy the newly gained self-confidence.**

In a figurative sense, you have charged the desk with good feelings of self-confidence and self-esteem. If you regularly repeat this exercise, you'll soon notice the positive effects.

TIP

The two exercises in the section on visualizations in this chapter are helpful as well. When you use them in conjunction with NLP's anchoring technique, you have the ability to strengthen your self-confidence for the long term. (For more on the anchoring technique, see Chapter 8.)

REMEMBER

Stop looking outside yourself for help and support. Stable self-esteem can come only from the inside. Building on your inner strengths means you won't doubt yourself and your abilities. Trading losses will no longer throw you off track, because you no longer have to impress anyone and you don't need confirmation from the market. You are confident and you know your limits. You have a positive self-image, regardless of any weaknesses you might have or mistakes you might make in trading.

REMEMBER

Over 50 years ago, the Austrian-American filmmaker Joseph von Sternberg (he of *The Blue Angel* fame) said that we humans spend the majority of our lives trying to earn the respect of others but spend hardly any time gaining our own self-respect.

Chapter 7

The Psychology of Coping with Losses

I n this chapter, you'll read about how trading losses can have a severe impact on your psyche. That definitely sounds like a hard pill to swallow, but don't worry: You'll also learn some mental strategies that can help you to better cope with your losing trades.

Most traders have great difficulty letting go of losses and not reacting emotionally. It's hard to accept losses as a normal part of the trading business. After all, you want to make money with trading. Instead, you're supposed to accept regularly losing money. What's up with that? Even if your intellect has learned to grudgingly accept losing money, it's still quite the irritant for the psyche. Let's face it: Our psyches find dealing with losses hard to bear.

In Chapter 4, I talk about everything concerning the professional management of losses and drawdowns, including practical recommendations (reframing losses, for example) that you can use to regain your emotional balance. I make it clear there that you should never trade without protective stops, that trade losses are a learning opportunity, and that you do not want to focus on individual trades. You must concentrate instead on the profitability of your entire portfolio. If individual losses hit you too hard, take a break so that you can regain your emotional distance.

It isn't sufficient to understand the rules for successful trading. You must also internalize them and be deeply convinced of them. Only then are you in the right state of mind to deal professionally with losses. For that to happen, it makes sense to look at the psychological causes of painful losses as well as the typical emotional reactions to such losses.

Registering the Psychological Impact of Losses

Maintaining a balance between cognition and emotion is a challenge when markets are volatile. (And when are they not volatile?). It's particularly difficult to avoid surges of emotion if one or more positions unexpectedly end up in the red. You must *not* become a victim of your emotions — otherwise, you're likely to lose control.

KEEPING A JOURNAL

Take advantage of any of the breaks you take when trading and immediately write down what happens to you when you make a loss:

- What feelings arise?

- What physical reactions do you experience?

- How do you respond?

Start making notes while you're experiencing a trading loss. The benefit: Your ego will have less scope for interpretation. You end up writing down your actual reactions in real time rather than thinking about how you reacted after the event.

Now write down the reasons you ended up taking a loss:

- Did you act impulsively, without due consideration, or chaotically — and, if yes, why?

- Did you implement your setup in accordance with the rules you had set for yourself?

Writing it all down forces you into the observer role and trains your self-reflective capability. It helps you gain the emotional distance you require in order to rethink your trading approach.

People suffer losses in trading for a number of reasons. Now, if the causes are merely of a technical nature, you simply have to adjust your trading strategy and setups accordingly. That's the easy part, because you can sort out this problem using your intellect. If the reasons behind your losses are psychological, however, your intellect can't help much — it simply switches off. What you need are other methods capable of affecting your subconscious.

Before I introduce you to some of those methods, take a look at some of the typical psychological reasons for losses (many of which you probably recognize right off the bat):

>> Emotions such as anxiety and fear lead to uncontrolled reactions that subsequently lead you to break your own rules and commit avoidable errors.

>> Your gut feelings that lead to impulsive trading aren't based on any plan or are not designed to meet a particular goal.

>> Either because you're convinced that you must trade often or because you lack the patience and grossly overestimate yourself, you end up overtrading.

>> Because you want to recoup money you've lost, you resort to revenge trading.

>> You trade out of feelings of guilt and regret because you ended up losing the unrealized gains of trades you had made earlier.

>> You play the victim or are unwilling to accept responsibility for your actions: "It's the market's fault" or "It's somebody else's fault."

>> You sabotage yourself by holding fast to beliefs that only limit you. You lack self-confidence and self-esteem. You might think you don't deserve success, so you subconsciously sabotage your chances of winning.

And now, take a look at typical emotional reactions to losses — some of which you might recognize:

>> **Shocked disbelief or even horror:** "How could this happen? But I was well prepared! What did I overlook?"

>> **Anxiety and stress in the face of the impact your losses will have on the day's performance, your overall portfolio, and your self-esteem:** You ask yourself, "Am I a bad trader? Am I a loser?"

>> **Helplessness and frustration:** These are faced by your lack of control over how your individual trades develop.

>> **Anger and rage at the market, brokers, experts, and especially yourself:** You may taunt yourself with the question, "Why can't I do anything right?"

WARNING

Your emotional responses may lead to a downward spiral. In a worst case scenario, you may end up trading out of desperation, impulsively trying (at great risk) to recoup your losses. That tactic never ends well and can potentially lead to financial ruin.

These emotional thought and behavior patterns seem to be a daily occurrence in trading. That's because they are quite normal human reactions — ones rooted deep in our human psyche. From an evolutionary standpoint, you react to impending loss as our forebears did to external risks and threats — namely, with fight, flight, or playing dead. Your subconscious is doing its best to help you avoid painful losses, but its best isn't good enough.

REMEMBER

The human brain doesn't distinguish between financial and physical pain. The threat of losing money activates the insula region of the limbic system — the region also tasked with processing physical pain. The impulses emitted from the limbic system all focus on avoiding pain at any price.

Natural reflexes are the wrong reactions on the stock exchange. You lose control over your trades because your emotions take over.

THE GRIEF CYCLE

Every trader who suffers a loss endures a grief cycle. You might think this description is a tad exaggerated, but it reflects the experience of many traders. This cycle applies to impending book losses that have spun out of control as well as to actual, realized losses.

The Swiss American psychiatrist Elisabeth Kübler-Ross worked extensively with grief and trauma. She described the five stages that characterize our responses to a loss of any kind. Every human develops subconscious coping strategies in order to be able to handle difficult situations. The stages last for varying lengths of time and they have no fixed sequence. Repetition may occur, and the intensity may vary.

The five-phases model in a trading context looks like this:

- **Denial, or wishing it weren't true.**

  This is a subconscious defense mechanism: You look away and try to ignore the loss. You deny the effect it has on your portfolio. Fear overwhelms you and may also cause you to freeze up.

- **Anger and rage**

  "Why me?" You feel jealous of others and alone in your grief. Pent-up anger is discharged and is directed against other people or objects. You want your money back.

- **Bargaining**

  Your need for control leads to hypothetical questions, such as these:

  "If only I'd not removed the stop, then . . ."

  "If only I had not doubled the losing position, then . . ."

  You then try to negotiate a deal with yourself:

  "If I regain this loss, I will promise to stick to my trading rulebook."

  "I will never again widen or take out the stops or double the size of the losing position."

- **Depression and grief**

  After freezing up and then indulging in outbursts of rage and helpless action, you begin to despair. You hide yourself away and decline to talk to anybody about your suffering.

- **Acceptance**

  The struggle and pain are events of the past You feel relieved. Now you're in a position to truly accept the losses and to learn from them. You have regained your emotional balance and can plan the next trade.

WARNING

A spark of hope exists in all phases of the grief cycle. Don't be fooled: Hope isn't a trading strategy.

You can't separate trading from whatever else is going on in your life. Tension, stress, loss, and grief in your family or circle of friends will influence your emotional balance and, with it, your trading. Sometimes it's better to take a break so that you can take care of the other important elements of your life before returning to trading.

REMEMBER

It's insufficient to understand that losing trades are part of the business. You must accept losses as a learning opportunity on an emotional level, in your deepest self.

Developing Mental Strategies for Coping with Losing Trades

The bad news: Under certain circumstances, the grief cycle can be a difficult, painful process. Some traders are unprepared for the emotional burden of loss and give up out of frustration.

The good news: A series of psychological techniques can help you better cope with loss. These techniques are designed to protect your trader psyche and develop your mental strength.

These techniques and methods shift the focus from the rational processes found "upstairs" in the brain's frontal lobes to the depths of subconscious emotional processes in the deep, dark "dungeon rooms" in our brains. Quite possibly, this is where you've stored some serious emotional baggage throughout your life. Beliefs that limit you, subconscious self-sabotaging traps you've set for yourself, traumatic experiences — they all pile up here. Making the effort to clean up these dark spaces, muck them out, and create order will probably solve many of the problems that may emerge in your trading practice — and maybe not only in your trading life. Your life as a whole may change. You may become a different person.

In the following sections, I present you with some mental strategies that aim at maintaining or regaining your emotional balance in trading. You'll see how to develop positive beliefs, how to remain calm using the right breathing techniques, and how to build up your emotional defenses to be used when required.

Letting your trading losses go up in smoke

Don't you wish you could simply leave your mistakes and losses behind you and get on with your life without all the emotional scarring? You could then just analyze the causes, draw the correct conclusions, adjust your setups, and take care of the next trade. Life would be so easy, right? Unfortunately, reality is different. Your intellect will keep going, but your emotions will pull you down. That's how nature has programmed you. Losses hurt, and it's difficult for the ego to deal with them. You end up doubting your abilities and desperately need to avoid further losses. Psychological stress and pressure seem inevitable. You have lost your balance.

You know and understand that trading losses are simply a part of the business. As long as you aren't sabotaging yourself and you aren't hampered by limiting beliefs that are subconsciously driving you into a loss spiral, a simple exercise may help — I'll admit that this particular exercise may appear unusual at first glance:

>> Sit comfortably and relax with a few deep breaths.

>> Take out a piece of paper and write down the particulars of your trading loss, with all its associated emotions.

>> Crumple up the paper and burn it.

Each negative experience in trading is associated with corresponding emotions. You may not be able to reverse a loss, but you can dissolve the associated negative emotions. The moment you start to write, you become truly aware of your emotions because you have to experience the pain of the loss again. You have brought these negative emotions to the light and figuratively bound them by the piece of paper. You may feel how the negative energy flows through your pen into the words you have written down.

TECHNICAL STUFF

Neuroscientific comparative studies show that it makes a difference when you write out your thoughts by hand. Doing so demonstrably strengthens creativity and your powers of memory. Writing down your thoughts by hand activates multiple different areas of the brain simultaneously because handwriting is deeply anchored in your person and has personal significance. You fill your handwriting with feelings and energy.

Does burning the paper destroy the emotion? No, but the fire transforms the emotions into literal smoke and ash. Depending on how intense the emotions were, you can repeat this exercise several times. You would be surprised about the relief you might experience when the negative energy of the emotions dissolve.

The psychologist Catherine Stott proposes a similar technique, however, that requires a lot more imagination. Briefly put, you first move into a deep relaxed state and then imagine yourself writing down all your negative experiences. You collect all these (imaginary) pages in an imaginary box that you then close. You attach balloons to the box and watch as it lifts off and disappears over the horizon, never to be seen again. It seems as though the burden is falling away. You feel liberated.

Reframing your losses

Trading losses are a matter of perspective. Emotional reactions are quite different, depending on the context you construct for them. That's where reframing comes in. A technique used in systemic therapy as well as in neurolinguistic programming (NLP), *reframing* deliberately reinterprets an event to create a new perspective that lets you see the situation in a different light. If you change the context or the framework of an event, you also change its meaning. New choices and interpretations emerge.

EXAMPLE

It has been raining all day, and you have planned a garden party for this evening. This is bad news for you and you're upset. This is good news for farmers because it hasn't rained for weeks and the fields have dried up. The meaning could hardly be more different. The frame/context determines the meaning and, with it, the emotional response.

Many traders focus only on earning as much money as possible with trading. Greed is a bad advisor. After all, this framing will make it hard for you to deal with losses. If you focus on keeping your losses small instead, you'll find it much easier to accept trading losses as just part of doing business.

What can you learn from that? The meaning of losses for you personally depends on how you frame the losses. If you change the frame, it changes the meaning, and as a result your emotional reaction to the loss will change. Reframing creates a new perspective — a more meaningful way of perceiving trading activity.

REMEMBER

To reframe something in accordance with your goals, you must distinguish between intention and behavior. You would think that good intentions are the basis of all behavior, but a gap may in fact exist between what you do and what you want to achieve with your behavior. You may not necessarily reach the goals you want to achieve with your perspective in trading.

Assume that you want to change your perspective on losses so that you can stay more balanced. You know that you can't stop undesired emotional reactions by willpower alone — quite the contrary. The negative emotions solidify because you pay too much attention to them.

Your intention is clearly formulated. Your plan is to change your behavior by reframing it. Start an inner dialogue and use your trading journal to put your thoughts in writing:

>> Name the emotional reactions to losses that you want to change. Are you experiencing fear? Rage? Frustration? Anger?

>> Ask yourself what good intentions could possibly be intertwined with these negative emotions. Does your subconscious mind want to protect you against the pain of loss? What else can you think of?

>> Accept these good intentions with appreciation and gratitude, but then be sure to separate the positive intent from the negative behavior.

>> Name the desired behavior and suggest a change of perspective that aims to harmonize the good intentions with the desired behavior.

For the implementation in the last bullet, use affirmations (positive beliefs, in other words) to make the transition. (See the next section to find out more about affirmations.).

Here are some examples of the kinds of affirmations you can use for dealing with losses:

>> I will quietly and serenely deal with individual losses because I will never risk more than 2 percent of my total portfolio.

>> I will quietly and serenely deal with individual losing trades because I am focusing on the profitability of all trades in a day/week.

>> I am a good and successful trader; losses are a normal part of the trading business.

>> Losses are always an opportunity to learn and improve.

>> I will stay quiet, calm, and confident because I am on the right path.

By regularly repeating these positive beliefs to yourself, you maintain your emotional balance when you suffer inevitable losses.

REMEMBER

You alone decide what your trading losses mean to you. You alone provide the framework. With reframing, you can assign new meaning to your losses and achieve a change of perspective. The key is to always learn from losses and not repeat them often.

Benefitting from the power of positive thinking

Behavior patterns and your belief systems are deeply rooted in your subconscious mind, far beyond the reach of your intellect. You don't achieve anything with good intentions and declarations of intent. Willpower has no chance against involuntary processes. You need to start on a deeper level. Positive affirmations support behavioral changes because you feed your subconscious with repeated and targeted messages. And the best way to achieve this is in a relaxed, trance-like state.

REMEMBER

Affirmations are clear and positive principles, formulated to directly influence your subconscious mind. Affirmations are simply formulated goals you can and want to achieve. The trick lies in repetition: You tell yourself the selected new belief again and again in order to reprogram your thoughts.

Thoughts, feelings, and actions are linked. When you change thought patterns, you change your mood and your physical state.

TECHNICAL STUFF

Neuroscientific studies show that every thought triggers a cascade of biochemical processes in the brain and has a direct impact on your body.

After a while, your convictions, mindset, and behavior will change. Does that sound surprisingly simple and logical? It is, if you consistently apply this tried-and-true therapeutic method.

EXAMPLE

"Yes, we can!" the famous slogan of Barack Obama's 2008 US presidential campaign, is an effective affirmation. Affirmations are particularly effective in advertising and mass communication because they produce enthusiastic responses that prove infectious. They are meant to interest and motivate target groups to buy a particular product.

There are a few prerequisites you need to fulfill to ensure that positive affirmations are effective. Always ask yourself these two questions:

>> Does the selected key phrase suit your problem?

>> Are you really willing to solve the existing problem and to change your behavior — perhaps radically?

For the successful use of affirmations, the key phrases you choose *must* make sense to you and be consistent. If you feel uncomfortable with an affirmation or you can't cope with it, it makes no sense to apply it.

WARNING

Affirmations do not work if they are unrealistic. For example, if you say that your portfolio will double every month, your inner doubter immediately pipes up. The truth is, you don't even believe it yourself. You may even damage your self-esteem if you fail to achieve unattainable goals.

Affirmation is a simple and effective self-coaching method that requires no additional resources. By using affirmations, you learn how to control your own behavior more reliably and accurately. Psychological studies prove that it's possible for you to develop a positive mindset and mental strength. When you transfer these assets to the trading environment, you experience the following positive impacts on your emotional balance over time:

>> You find it easier to trade in a more focused, concentrated, and disciplined manner.

>> You gain self-confidence and increase the stability of your self-esteem.

>> You can work quietly and calmly at achieving success.

By regularly repeating your new positive affirmations to yourself, you reprogram yourself to be more self-confident. You replace doubts and negative thoughts with positive ones. From a hypnosystemic therapy perspective, you move from problem trance to solution trance. Your goal is to develop the best trading mindset that you can.

Developing effective affirmations

You're probably wondering how you can develop meaningful and effective affirmations for yourself. I recommend starting out with some concrete rules:

» **Make affirmations reasonable and realistic and have them address a specific problem or concern.**

Otherwise, your inner critic stokes doubt and takes the wind out of the sails of your affirmations. Pipe dreams don't make effective affirmations.

» **Formulate the affirmation in a positive and encouraging way.**

The human brain can't deal with negatives. Avoid negative formulations: "I want to trade less impulsively," for example. Your subconscious only reacts to the word *impulsive*. It's better to say, "I react calmly and serenely in all market phases.

» **Use the present tense.**

By suggesting to your subconscious that your wish has already become a reality, it becomes a done deal. It's much more powerful when you say, "I am a successful trader" than to say, "I want to be a successful trader." The secret of success lies in your ability to convince your subconscious that you're already in the desired state with all your senses.

» **Use powerful images along with your affirmations.**

The human brain responds much more strongly to images than to words. (As everyone knows, "A picture is worth a thousand words.") Affirmations you can visualize have a stronger effect. (You can find out more about visualization techniques at the end of this chapter.)

Here are some additional techniques designed to support the effect of affirmations:

» Ensure that you're in a calm and relaxed state. Say the affirmations loudly and clearly. That increases the effect.

» Write down your affirmations on a piece of paper that you attach to places you regularly look at (your computer screen, for example, or your refrigerator). The effectiveness of an affirmation increases if you're continually reminded of it.

» If you're an auditory learner and you find it easier to remember content you can listen to, it may be useful to record your affirmations and listen to them regularly.

TIP

You can further enhance the effectiveness of your affirmations if you write them down by hand at least 20 to 30 times a day. This practice is time-consuming, but it fires up those gray brain cells.

The goal is to make the daily repetition of affirmations a habit, no matter in what form. Affirmations can be fully effective only when you have internalized the key phrases and programmed them into your brain. As a rule, you notice changes and results only after a few days. However, it takes one or two months of intensive training to anchor these new beliefs deeply in your subconscious mind. Does this process sound tedious? Well, it takes only a few minutes a day. Ultimately, the question is how seriously you take your trader career.

Looking at the practical applications of affirmations in trading

How can you practically use affirmations as part of your trading day?

Here's a tip: You may have noticed, while formulating key phrases for an affirmation, that the principle of focusing on solutions comes into play. You focus on what you want, not only what you no longer want. For example, if you have trading fears, the temptation to move away from such fears is immense but not effective. The internal drive to escape and flee from what you have confronted before obscures the actual solution. You want to get rid of your fears, but you don't know what to replace them with. In this case, an affirmation is a well-formulated motivation-to-something rather than a motivation-away-from-something. What could replace your fears? The goal might be courage, self-confidence, and serenity.

REMEMBER

Positive affirmations can help you to solve recurring problems in trading. These affirmations remove obstacles, limitations, and harmful patterns and replace them with positive, goal-oriented beliefs and behaviors. This strategy works best in a deep, relaxed state. To do this, you can use self-hypnosis techniques.

Identifying and resolving inner resistance

Your inner resistance competes with your desire for change. This power struggle continues until you've been able to install your newly desired ways of thinking and behaving. Don't give up, even if the training feels strange for the first few days.

WARNING

Sometimes, your initial affirmation training can make you feel less confident than before. Your internal resistance — the doubter, the critic, your limiting belief system — will initially fight back. It may be difficult at the start to apply your chosen affirmations in your daily life.

FORMULATING AFFIRMATIONS

Now it's your turn. Pick up your trading journal and write down as many affirmations as you can spontaneously come up with. Then check whether you have followed the rules I lay out in this chapter. You'll notice that it takes practice to formulate appropriate and consistent affirmations. It's important that you address your trading problems.

To make this task easier, I give you some examples of affirmations that some traders have successfully implemented:

- I patiently watch the markets, waiting for proper entry signals.

- I easily adapt to changing market conditions.

- I deserve to have success in trading.

- I earn money on the stock market because I'm worth it.

- I'm able to control my emotions and stay relaxed, maintaining a state of equilibrium.

- I am self-confident, and I make good decisions.

- I learn fast and constantly develop myself.

- I let my profits run.

- I limit losses according to my set of rules.

- I see individual losses in the context of the entire portfolio.

- Rather than look at individual trades, I look at the sum of trades in a day or a week.

I hope that these examples provide you with suggestions for your personal affirmations. It's important that you use only those formulations you feel comfortable with. Try it and see what comes up.

The trick is to learn how to deal with these resistances. Start out by taking a look at the causes, because there's always a positive intent behind even the most harmful behavior. Ask yourself the following questions:

>> What is this behavior protecting you against?

>> When and why were these patterns useful to you?

>> What is your behavior trying to keep you from doing?

ASKING THE RIGHT QUESTIONS

When forming affirmations, the idea is to always make positive statements of belief. You shouldn't follow that path when it comes to positive beliefs. Rather than just stating a belief, ask yourself questions that encourage you to go the next step. In other words, ask yourself open and positive Why questions:

- Rather than say, "I deserve to have success in trading," ask yourself why you deserve to be successful at trading.

- Rather than say, "I am able to control my emotions and stay relaxed, maintaining a state of equilibrium," ask yourself why you're able to maintain your emotional balance while trading.

Pay attention to the insightful answers that come to light. With this approach, focus your attention on possible solutions.

The psychological trick here is to ask yourself the questions that are sure to steer you in the desired direction. Subconsciously, you behave as though you have already reached that goal. Your subconscious automatically searches for answers and evidence instead of doubting your statement when it's posed as a question. It makes it easy for you to make clear decisions.

This approach helps if affirmations alone don't help you to get ahead. In this manner, you can skillfully bypass your internal resistances and doubts. In such situations. clever questions can be more effective than positive affirmations for your brain.

It's often the case that there are deeper reasons for your behavior that may be grounded in events that occurred some time ago and have not yet been processed. There may have been a time when these patterns served you well. In this respect, you need to use your inner persuasive skills to make it clear to your internal resistance that you require other behaviors for you to succeed as a trader.

Building emotional defenses

Sometimes, it can be useful to shield your emotions in trading. You want to remain calm and collected in turbulent market phases. In particular, you want to make sure that emotional outbursts don't ruin your trading day.

So, how can emotional outbursts ruin your trading day? Let's say you make an unforced error and need to close a position at an early stage. Or your stop was too tight and you were stopped out prematurely. In both cases, you're extremely angry. And, when you're upset or angry, you involuntarily carry these negative emotions on to your next trades. Typical reactions are revenge trading or excessive trading in order to recoup losses.

The British psychologist and hypnotherapist Catherine Stott has developed an effective technique designed to prevent the transfer and spread of negative emotions. The aim is to build an emotional barrier so that you remain calm and focused.

You can build this protective shield or barrier in six steps:

1. **Think of a protective shield and try to visualize it.** (You can find out more about visualization techniques in the next section.)

   Maybe you can picture a plate of imaginary, bulletproof glass that you erect between you and your computer screen or a suit of armor just waiting for you to don. There are no limits to your imagination.

TIP

   Do you feel you lack imagination? Are you more of a haptic learner, where you want items you can touch and feel? Then it might be helpful to search out a suitable Plexiglas miniature windshield you can place in front of your computer screen. Another example is wearing a specific piece of clothing when you trade. I know traders who always trade in a shirt and tie. A serious presentation emphasizes the seriousness of the business and promotes self-discipline.

2. **Imagine a situation where you're following the markets and your positions on your screen. Suddenly, a promising trade turns into loss, and your emerging anger bounces against the protective barrier.**

3. **Imagine that the shield serves as a filter that prevents any unwanted emotions and only allows the information you need for objective decision-making to pass through it.**

4. **When you have played through this technique a few times, apply it to your trading.**

   You behave as you always do and prepare your setups.

5. **Before you start your trading day, close your eyes, take a deep breath, and relax. Now imagine that you're building the chosen protective shield. Try to visualize the shield as realistically as possible. It's meant to keep your emotions in check.**

6. **Confident that the protective barrier is now in place, you start trading as usual.**

   During the day, if something happens that calls up an emotional response, you allow the emotions to bounce off the barrier.

As usual, practice makes perfect with these mental techniques. The more often you use them, the easier it will be for you to control your emotions. With time, it will become a subconscious automatic behavior.

With this technique, as with many mindfulness techniques, you must train while in a calm and relaxed state.

Mastering breathing techniques

Breathing is a subconscious process that tends to be beyond our direct control. Breathing also tends to change, depending on our mood. That's because breathing is part of the automatic nervous system and is thus intimately connected with all essential biological functions, such as heartbeat, metabolism, and digestion. Breathing has an immediate effect on the whole body and on the brain.

In a relaxed state, you breathe deeply and slowly. Under stress and emotional pressure, your breath becomes shallow and irregular. Permanent psychological stress in trading results in your nervous system and brain no longer receiving enough oxygen. This enhances the physical and psychological perception of stress — a vicious cycle if ever there was one.

You can break out of this vicious cycle by exerting just a little effort. Breathing is the only function of the nervous system that you can directly influence.

There are a large number of breathing techniques. The first step is to be aware of your breathing. The next few sections look at a number of various breathing techniques you can easily incorporate into your trading practice.

Abdominal breathing during emotional stress

Apply this breathing technique in case of emotional stress:

1. Sit upright, make yourself comfortable, close your eyes, and put a hand on your belly.

2. Breathe deeply and consciously, observing how the air flows through your nose to the whole body and then escapes through your mouth.

3. After approximately five breaths, insert a short pause after exhaling before breathing in again. Continue this for a while.

This technique is known as abdominal breathing. It's important that the spine remains straight. You can also count up to 4 when breathing in and out and pause the breath for a moment after each inhalation and exhalation.

Ten to twenty repetitions are recommended. After a few minutes, your breathing calms down and you feel how your body and mind relax during exhalation.

TECHNICAL STUFF

The Navy SEALs, an elite unit of the US military, use abdominal breathing to remain focused and efficient in situations of extreme stress. Neuroscientific studies have demonstrated the effectiveness of this breathing technique. It demonstrably strengthens stress-resilience and self-control.

TIP

You can enhance your abdominal breathing by completing visualizations. Remember a moment of joy and deep relaxation. Imagine this moment with all your senses to make it appear as real as possible before performing the breathing exercise.

You can also combine abdominal breathing with progressive muscle relaxation. When you breathe in, tense up all the muscles in the body, hold the tension for a brief moment, and then relax the muscles when you exhale. This exercise works well with stress-induced physical tension.

Breathing techniques for anxiety

The following technique may help you with anxiety:

1. Lie down flat on the floor or on a bed.

2. Observe where you can feel your breath in your body.

3. Breathe slowly and then deepen the breath with every exhalation until you can feel it in every part of your body.

After a few minutes, your physical tension and fears will dissolve.

BREATHING TECHNIQUES FOR ANXIETY PAIRED WITH STRESS

In case of both anxiety and stress, you can try these steps:

1. Sit down, relax, and breathe deeply a few times.

2. Imagine an empty chalkboard placed in front of you.

3. In the next step, take five deep breaths where you consciously breathe out slowly. Every time you inhale, imagine a number on the board. When you exhale, the number slowly disappears.

   Start with number five and count backward:

   5: When you inhale, visualize the number 5 on the board. When you exhale, the number slowly disappears.

4: When you inhale, visualize the number 4 on the board. When you exhale, the number slowly disappears.

3: When you inhale, visualize the number 3 on the board. When you exhale, the number slowly disappears.

2: When you inhale, visualize the number 2 on the board. When you exhale, the number slowly disappears.

4. When you arrive at number 1, say to yourself over and over again, "I am relaxed, calm, and confident."

The appeal of this breathing technique is that it reactivates your intellect because the counting requires concentration and doesn't occur automatically. This has been confirmed by experiments using a brain scanner. Counting distracts you from the fear and stress. The brain works sequentially, so it can't process two events at a time.

ALTERNATE BREATHING FOR RESTLESSNESS AND NERVOUSNESS

Are you restless and nervous? Then try this breathing exercise:

1. Sit up straight and upright.

2. Lay your index finger and middle finger of the right hand between your eyebrows.

3. Close your eyes and breathe in and out deeply through your nose.

4. Close the right nostril with your thumb and breathe slowly through the left nostril.

5. Close the left nostril with the ring finger and open the right nostril and breathe out slowly.

6. Breathe in through the right nostril, close it again with your thumb, and then open the left nostril and breathe out again.

You breathe alternately through each nostril. After a few minutes, you'll feel the beneficial effects. This technique, which comes from yoga, is known as alternate nostril breathing.

REMEMBER

These breathing techniques are the basis of most of the self-coaching methods I talk about in this chapter. They also happen to be the perfect mental preparation for every trading day.

Chapter **8**

Adopting Techniques for Coping with Stress and Anxiety

This chapter talks about various techniques for dealing more efficiently with stress and anxiety — techniques that, thankfully, are both effective and easy to learn. Whether you want to anchor new behaviors or work with mental images, the most important factor for ensuring your success is regular practice. Taking on the observer role — a crucial part of these techniques — may also feel awkward at first, but practice there as well will make it easier over time.

Fears are strong emotions that can suddenly throw you off balance. In Chapter 15, I talk more about the forms and causes of anxiety in trading and how to escape the fear trap. In this chapter, however, I want to focus more on neurolinguistic programming (NLP) and other mental techniques to cope better with stress and anxiety.

One objective of the various methods is to gain control over your emotional state. When trading, you can't allow yourself to fall victim to your involuntary emotional outbursts. You must learn to be conscious of your various states and to influence them at an early stage.

WARNING

The biochemical processes in the brain are generally faster than those of the rational mind. That means your emotions will switch off your intellect faster than you can think. Reacting isn't an option. Prevention is everything.

Harmonizing the Body with the Mind

Body and mind are closely linked. They influence each other. Your thoughts have a direct impact on your emotional and physical being. It's remarkable that we humans are usually pretty good at perceiving our moods but seem incapable of consciously registering the physical changes we experience, such as tension or shortness of breath — despite the fact that every emotion is clearly the result of observable physiological and thought processes. When you change your emotional state, your body and mind change as well — and vice versa.

Here's a simple exercise that clearly illustrates the neural link between body and mind:

1. Sit comfortably and relax by taking in a few deep breaths.

   If you like, you can close your eyes.

2. Try to remember a particularly beautiful experience from the past.

   Deliberately experience the beautiful images, the good feelings, and the sounds and smells associated with that event.

3. Return to the present.

   Can you perceive how your facial features, your posture, and your breathing have relaxed?

This exercise is designed to help you see the influence you have over your general state of being. The good feelings are as real as they were back in the past. In the words of neuroscientists, the biochemical processes are identical. Your brain doesn't distinguish between reality and fiction.

As always, every coin has two sides. Good and bad experiences can be arbitrarily and involuntarily recalled, with the corresponding consequences for your physical and emotional well-being.

EXAMPLE

Suppose that you experienced a severe losing streak in the past. This experience gets stored both emotionally and physically. It requires only a trigger and then the memories come flooding back. Your breathing may falter as you break out in a cold sweat and your body tenses up. The emotional stress is immense. Trading in this state of fear would be grossly negligent.

FOLLOWING PATTERNS OF SUCCESS

The positive side effect of working mental exercises is that you may come in closer contact with skills you already possess. In the past, you have obviously shown an ability to solve your trading problems. This provides a pattern of success with which you can associate yourself. The idea here is to draw your attention to the desired experience pattern and in that way reactivate this pattern. Focusing on solutions is key here. (For more information about focusing on solutions, see Chapter 5.)

As the exercise at the beginning of this section shows, you have a simple way to restore your emotional balance in trading: Just call up a time when you were in precisely that state of equilibrium. Unfortunately, getting this part right isn't so easy in practice.

TIP

The relaxation methods I talk about in earlier chapters (especially Chapters 6 and 7) can also be quite helpful in situations of anxiety and stress. The breathing techniques I discuss in Chapter 7, for example, can be particularly effective.

Adopting a bird's-eye view

In the heat of battle, you may not see the forest for the trees. When the markets get hectic, gaining some distance can make a lot of sense. That prevents tunnel vision and helps you keep an overview — which also helps protect your emotional balance.

I often talk about the benefits of taking on the position of a mental observer watching events from a safe remove. You know how important it is to maintain your emotional distance from the markets and the positions you've taken. The protected observer position — also known by those who indulge in highfalutin' jargon as a metaposition — allows you to gain a kind of bird's-eye view. At a safe distance, you can observe your behavior and emotional state from a different perspective, which (potentially) can create new insights and help protect you from errors.

TIP

Follow the exercises I discuss in this chapter to gain this new perspective.

It makes a huge difference whether you observe the world of trading from the outside in or from the inside out — this is especially true when it comes to your emotional state.

To illustrate this point, I propose a two-part exercise. Start by closing your eyes:

1. Imagine that your body is floating up to the ceiling of your office. You're looking down on your workplace. Now glide back down to your chair. You're in your body, observing your environment from an inside perspective. You are associated, having adopted the I-position.

2. Now imagine that part of you has left your body behind in its chair and is now floating up to the ceiling. You observe yourself from various angles as the body you left behind sits down there at your desk. Your body has not left the desk chair, but you don't care — you have dissociated yourself and have adopted the metaposition.

The crucial difference between the two positions is in how you perceive your emotions:

>> In the associated state, you identify with your perception, your behavior, and your feelings.

>> In the dissociated state, you observe your reactions from a safe distance. Your feelings refer to what you perceive from the outside. These are not the same feelings you immediately experience in the associated state.

TIP

Test whether you recall positive and negative trading experiences in an associative or dissociative state. What images appear, and how do you experience the situation today? Are you squat in the center of the situation, or are you standing on the edge? How present or how distanced are you emotionally?

Unfortunately, traders frequently forget or dissociate from their experiences of success, but losing streaks are often vivid and quite associated.

TIP

Turn the tables on your emotion. Use dissociations to distance yourself emotionally from bad experiences. Think of positive experiences in an associated way. Good feelings strengthen your self-worth and show you what you can do.

Anchoring: Finding a point of tranquility

From our own human experience, we know that emotional stress has a direct impact on trading. When you're under stress, your thoughts and actions are often beyond your control and the errors pile up. How wonderful it would be if you could jump from one role to the next — just like an actor jumping from one emotional state to the next — simply by flicking a switch. Actors need to be able to consciously control their inner emotional states. But don't think you need acting lessons in order to trade in an emotionally balanced state or to prevent anxiety; you can manage that role-switching quite well on your own.

The key to controlling your emotional states more effectively lies in your ability to consciously anchor the emotional state you want as your emotional foundation. Anchoring, as a technique, is something you can use in a variety of situations.

What exactly are you anchoring? In the neurolinguistic programming (NLP) model, an impulse or stimulus that always triggers the same response is known as an *anchor*. This chain of stimulus-and-response can, of course, be unintentional, but the beauty of the NLP model is that it can also be intentional.

Learning to anchor

Though human reflexes are innate and are the result of our evolutionary development, your anchors are learned over the course of your life by way of neurological connections. Just think it through: Over the course of your life, you have experienced various anchors — specific sounds, images, situations, or smells that evoke memories and automatic responses. The human brain naturally links experiences from the past and associates these with the present.

Anchors vary widely and are an important part of our lives. There are more anchors than you can imagine, because all the senses can act as triggers. Everything you see, hear, smell, touch, or taste involuntarily triggers reactions. These are natural conditioning mechanisms.

How, in practical terms, do anchors come about? Here are two ways:

» **Repetition:** Conditioning or habit, in other words. An example is the fact that you automatically stop your vehicle at a red light. Even better for your financial health: You generally set a protective stop-loss order for every trade.

» **Painful** experiences: Such experiences work to trigger you when similar situations occur in the present. An example is when earlier losing streaks regularly cause painful memories.

Anchors based on habits can automatically trigger certain reactions. This is a form of subconscious competence that preserves cognitive resources. Anchors are, so to speak, a stimulus-response coupling, a learned linking of certain stimuli with certain reactions.

TIP

To master your emotions, you need to find your anchors. Think about which habitual anchors you have set in trading. Are there certain trading hours or particular instruments or markets you subconsciously prefer? Long or short setups? Are there price patterns, market movements, financial news, or market correlations that automatically trigger a reaction in you?

PAVLOV'S DOG

You have probably heard of Pavlov's dog. The infamous experiment shows the effect of stimulus-response patterns. The laboratory dogs were always fed when a bell rang. After a few repetitions, the dogs salivated automatically whenever they heard a bell, even if they weren't being given food. Later, neurological experiments were carried out with humans. By combining images and scents and the measurement of brain activities, it was possible to confirm the principle of classical conditioning.

Anchoring in practice

Anchors can change your emotional state. They can positively overwrite and/or replace negative states. When you have experienced anxiety and stress from enduring bad experiences, the anchor method can help. You'll be able to reevaluate the situation from today's point of view by creating a positive association and thus the desired (positive) emotional reaction.

You anchor in several stages:

1. Choose the desired emotional state you want to be able to retrieve in specific trading situations.

   Be concrete and choose a specific state of being — serenity, for example.

2. Connect the desired state of being to an anchor that's always available to you.

   The trigger can be an object (figurine, lucky charm), an image, a key word, a specific movement, an affirmation, or even a sound (snapping your fingers, for example). A popular one is touching the thumb with the middle and index fingers, which comes from meditation, or you can use a combination of elements that address a variety of sensory channels.

   REMEMBER

   In football or other sports, you often see athletes who complete specific rituals before stepping on the field or before the game starts. Whether they cross themselves, kiss their talismans, touch the grass, or step onto the field with a specific foot, these are all anchor techniques that are intended to bring luck and success.

3. Choose a situation from the past when you felt serene and calm when you were trading.

   Stand up or change positions and try to embody the emotional state and relaxed physical sensation as intensely as possible. Associate yourself with all the sensory channels.

4. Just before you reach the peak of these sensory perceptions, return to the position where you felt dissociated.

Now you know how you can create the desired state.

5. Switch to the position in which you experienced the desired state and repeat the exercise.

Just before reaching the peak of the sensory perceptions, trigger the selected anchor. Link the anchor to the state of serenity, in other words.

6. Repeat the exercise until the connection between the anchors and the desired state is stable.

7. Imagine a concrete situation in the future when you will be in need of the desired state of serenity.

Think of those physical signs that should remind you that it's time to apply the anchor technique you have learned. This might be questions you have about yourself and your actions, a cramped posture, sweaty hands, nervousness, or emerging anger. Take whatever spontaneously comes to mind.

WARNING

Select an anchor that is unique and won't be triggered by chance. Shaking hands or being patted on the back are certainly not good ideas.

The anchor technique requires a lot of practice and diligent application. Otherwise, anchoring won't work. Make sure that

>> The desired state is clear and unambiguous so that you can reexperience it.

>> The anchor is only embedded just before reaching the peak of the emotional state — this timing is important.

>> The anchor is set in an exact and precise manner so that you can repeat it.

Now you can use this anchor or another one to intentionally create the emotional state you require for successful trading. With lots of practice, you'll be able to cope with situations of stress and anxiety. It's impossible to erase negative trading experiences from your memory, but you can reevaluate the experiences from today's point of view and suppress their negative effect on the future.

In the future, you cannot prevent making negative experiences and sometimes losing your emotional equilibrium. By adopting a protected observer role, you learn how to perceive and understand your emotional states. You also learn how to deal with them and consciously choose your response. You know that every state has a physical equivalent and a biochemical one. It's all part of the same system. Thought patterns, emotions, and physiology interact. When you change one component, it changes your entire overall internal condition.

REMEMBER

The anchor technique allows you to trigger a desired emotional state and dissolve undesired ones. You anchor the emotional balance you need for trading. You put yourself into the emotional state you want to be in. You have the choice. This is emotional freedom.

Working with the Images in Your Mind

Is imagination a recipe for trading success? The technique of visualization is a strong motivational technique, and it's a proven technology you can use to program success. You direct your attention to the goals you want to achieve by imagining them as specifically as possible and forming a clear mental image of each one.

REMEMBER

In psychology, visualization refers to the activation of ideas and images in your mind's eye.

Your imagination is immensely important. Visualizations are included, in one way or another, in every mental training method. Without the right images in mind, your trading problems will prove difficult to solve.

TECHNICAL STUFF

Humans have a visually centered sensory brain. Both positive and negative emotions are stored in the brain as images. Images are significantly more effective than language. It's the images in your mind that rule, not words, numbers, or facts.

EXAMPLE

Visualization techniques are used in high-performance sports to focus and to strengthen motivation. This method is applied in psychotherapy in order to practice new ways of thinking and behaving or to alleviate stress and anxiety. In both cases, visualizations are combined with relaxation techniques.

You naturally visualize constantly, whether you like it or not. Every formative experience in trading is stored in your memory as a short film. A losing streak you experienced in the past may be linked to a horror film in which a similar situation is played over and over again. You involuntarily end up in what hypnotherapists refer to as a *problem trance,* where you only see everything that can go wrong. The one-sided focus on risks and potential losses programs your subconscious to fail. That's why it's vital to refocus on solutions and success in trading. Concentrate on what you want to achieve.

To use visualizations in trading, you need positive and suitable inner images that you can align with your goals.

REMEMBER

It doesn't make a massive difference for your brain whether you only imagine something or have actually experienced it. The biochemical processes — the emotional and physical reactions, in other words — are identical. That's why visualizations are so effective.

Managing mental images for trading

Consciously or subconsciously, traders are constantly using images when they are trading. They always have images of charts and price patterns in their minds. They also have quite vivid ideas about how the trades will develop. Their assumptions and forecasts are based on likely developments that they can imagine.

Let's assume that, when trading starts in the morning, you're always a bit nervous and afraid of early losses. That makes you hesitate and you end up missing good entry opportunities. You lack the right mindset for a successful start.

With the correct visualization technique, you can learn to change your focus and mentally concentrate on winning trades.

In this exercise, make sure you're working from an "I" perspective:

1. Relax with a few deep breaths and close your eyes (trance induction).

2. Using all your senses, imagine an outstanding winning trade.

   Your analysis, setup, timing, and everything else are perfectly in tune. Which good feelings arise? What images do you see — the chart? The profit? How does your body feel? What do you say to yourself? As much as possible, try to put yourself mentally into that situation.

3. Enjoy this state of happiness for a while and select a particularly beautiful image that will serve as an anchor.

   The anchor technique ensures that you can recall this image at any time.

4. Accept this positive feeling as real and complete the exercise with a few deep breaths.

After this exercise, it's quite possible that you feel both relaxed and confident. You're motivated and focused on successful trading. You have strengthened your self-confidence. Trading losses, which inevitably occur, don't make you nervous or hesitant. You have an eye firmly on the prize. To support this feeling of confidence, you can reframe any trading losses that occur (reframing technique) or deploy an emotional barrier.

TIP

You can apply this exercise during ongoing trades and visually imagine how you complete the trade with a win. Visualization works just as well outside trading times as during them.

Seeing the future

If you like the visualizations and are having fun, why not go one step further? Are you brave? Do you want to create a coherent vision of the future? Or the vision of a successful trader who has achieved prosperity and wealth? It's no longer a question of an individual winning trade or winning streak, but rather it's about whether you can actually imagine having a successful career as a trader.

The psychologist Catherine Stott has developed an exciting and imaginative exercise to help you picture such a future:

1. Relax with a few deep breaths and close your eyes (trance induction).

2. Imagine sitting in front of a mirror that shows you in the future.

   Be sure to describe the mirror in precise detail.

3. Look in the mirror.

   You realize that *you* are the person you see there. It's your future You, the successful trader who has become wealthy with their trading. What images do you see? Which films play out in your mind's eye? Do you see a villa, a yacht, the luxurious life? Or is this You a major investor, top consultant, or sought-after speaker?

4. When you have found the appropriate images for your vision, imagine the perfect life with all your senses and let it play like a film, with all the voices, sounds, and images associated with it. (Movies don't usually engage your sense of smell, but go ahead and add smells as well.)

5. Imagine what you look like and what you feel.

   Are you happy? Relaxed? Motivated? Proud? Thirsty for action? How would you like to feel in an ideal world? Enjoy the good feelings as intensively as possible.

6. Look for a particularly beautiful image that you can use as an anchor.

   Now you can recall this wonderful state at any time.

7. When you're ready, end the trance with some deep breaths.

This exercise prepares you for a successful trading career. You have programmed your subconscious mind for success.

Or maybe not. If you have difficulty imagining this vision of the future, it might be because it isn't truly your path. Does the vision feel coherent, or does it not suit you at all? Or maybe you lack self-confidence and self-esteem. Perhaps limiting beliefs or other psychological obstacles stand in your way?

I am sorry if I may have spoiled all the good feelings you experience from the exercise. But if you lack the imagination to visualize a future vision as a successful trader, you will likely need to deal first with some mental obstacles to success. Just return to the beginning of this chapter or Chapter 7.

TIP

Break down this rather expansive vision of the future into partial goals or more manageable chunks of time. Visualize your monthly or annual targets and gradually increase from there.

4

Making Decisions Safely

Chapter **9**

Untangling Decision-Making's Hidden Path

Perception is a tricky thing. In Chapters 2 and 5, I talk a bit about how we humans construct our own reality and how subjective and biased our individual point of view actually is. This chapter is more about our perceptual skills. Here you'll discover that your personal perception of financial markets is often quite biased and easily influenced — involuntarily and unintentionally, to be sure. This does help to prove my contention, however, that human decision-making processes are inherently susceptible to failure. For you to be able to make good, reliable trading decisions, you *must* understand the implications of letting cognitive biases, emotionally-laden stories, and information overload affect your trading behavior.

Recognizing Systematic Perceptual Disorders

Do you know how human decision-making processes occur? I imagine it as follows: You collect information from a variety of sources. In this digital era, you have immediate access to a variety of information sources, which are often only a mouse click away. Using that access, you want to quickly gain an objective over-view. You think hard and long, looking through your memories to see whether any relevant experiences and knowledge might help the decision-making process. You then compare what you find with your current decision situation. Depending on how simple or complex the situation is, the process is made up of information processing and decision-making. Sounds logical and reasonable, right?

Unfortunately, reality is different. In principle, every person has their own way of making decisions. It starts with a variable ability to absorb information. Our human perceptual ability is limited and varies considerably, depending on our emotional state.

That's why you should know about three particular aspects of the decision-making process. As a trader, you will benefit greatly if you're aware that

>> Our perception is always selective and biased.

>> Our perception is always a gross oversimplification of reality.

>> Our emotions always work to thwart what we hope will always be purely rational decisions.

Tracing Selective Perceptions

Did you know that different people perceive and process even simple information in completely different ways? And that this is still completely subconscious? Studies show that 90 percent of what you do and think happens automatically — without voluntary control, in other words. In doing so, you subconsciously perceive things in a selective manner:

>> You don't perceive all the information presented to you.

>> You find it difficult to differentiate between relevant and non-relevant information.

>> You see patterns where none exist.

>> You subconsciously suppress things that don't make immediate sense to you.

>> You generalize, summarize, and compartmentalize your thinking.

Being perceptually selective serves to reduce the complexity of a situation so that you can remain capable of action and decision-making. The price you pay for such action is a distorted and selective perception of reality.

REMEMBER

Every trader inhabits their own reality of the markets. As a trader, you don't see the world of financial markets objectively; you see it as your brain constructs it subjectively. Your personal life experiences shape your view of the world. After all, this kind of behavior has so far proved successful over the course of human evolutionary history, so why change it now?

Dealing with Gross Oversimplifications

Psychological studies show that the phenomenon of distorted and selective perception is widespread:

>> Your expectations subconsciously influence your perception.

>> Information that supports your market assessment is overvalued.

>> Information that doesn't support your preconceived opinion tends to be weighted less or ignored completely.

>> You replace information gaps and missing details with your own experiences or with assumptions that fit.

You end up constructing your highly individual and remarkably harmonious overall picture, but in doing so, you show yourself to be shockingly biased. Such *confirmation biases* occur especially when making difficult and complex decisions.

Psychologists and behavioral economists have extensively researched decision-making processes and have concluded that humans inherently rely on *heuristics* — proven rules of thumb and simplifications that someone unconsciously apply to a situation — in order to arrive at a decision. This simple decision-making strategy is often quite error-prone.

This heuristic approach simplifies and accelerates the processing of information. It spares cognitive resources and is sufficient in most life situations. Humans are generally lazy thinkers. ("Googling instead of thinking," is the motto of many.) When it comes to complex financial markets, this behavior leads to hasty and systematically distorted decisions.

REMEMBER

In trading, a heuristic approach can result in your recognition of changes in the market situation only when it's too late. It can also mean that you regularly miss the right entry or exit point for a position.

THE BRAIN'S ENERGY-SAVING MODE

The reason for the weaknesses of our human perception skills can be found in our evolutionary history. Human brain processing capacity is quite limited. The areas of the brain responsible for intellect and logical thinking aren't as robust as you might think. The reason for it is the high energy consumption required for conscious analysis. Active thinking is exhausting and causes fatigue. Subconscious thought processes consume significantly less energy. That's why, over the course of evolutionary history, the human brain developed in such a way that we could rely largely on energy-saving automatic behaviors. This may have ensured our survival in the Stone Age, but in trading you need to be able to rely on your intellect. The stock market does not forgive mistakes.

It isn't surprising that traders rely on rules of thumb (*heuristics*) under stress and time pressure in order to reduce the cognitive load and act more quickly. However, this behavior is not useful for high-risk investment decisions. In trading, you need a clear head and full access to your intellect. That's the only way to avoid our evolutionary pitfalls. Self-discipline and analytical thinking determine your success in trading. Subconscious automatisms certainly don't.

Channeling Dangerous Emotions

It's time to talk about your emotions — feelings that can certainly become dangerous when you're trading. That's because you tend to see the world with different eyes, depending on your mood. Whether you're feeling euphoric or anxious, your mood significantly affects your perception of the markets.

>> **If you're afraid,** you'll place too much weight on negative information and you'll avoid risks.

>> **If you're feeling positive,** you'll block out negative information and automatically predict that positive events advantageous to you are more likely to occur. Your willingness to take risks increases significantly, as a number of studies have shown.

In both cases, you're no longer being objective. In fact, you're letting your emotions significantly influence your decision-making — and therefore your trading success.

Whether it's greed, anger, or frustration, whenever your emotions take over the helm, you'll experience a shipwreck on the stock exchange sooner or later. There's always a danger that, when you get stressed, you'll lose control and make mistakes. You can only concentrate, be disciplined, and be able to focus fully on what is happening on the market when you're calm and relaxed. Otherwise, you're sure to make mistakes.

However, it's impossible to completely empty yourself of all emotions. Neuroscientists have shown that a person without emotions is incapable of making decisions, as has been demonstrated in experiments with patients suffering from damage to the areas of the brain that process emotions. Without emotions, you're simply incapable of triggering decisions, because rational considerations on their own don't result in action. The balance between intellect and emotions is crucial. That's the only way you can have full access to your rational logical mind on the one hand and your gut feeling and intuition on the other. When your emotions boil over, however, you end up making bad decisions. Your rational mind is switched off — a dangerous state of affairs when trading.

TIP

Cognitive biases are a daily occurrence in trading, and they are difficult to prevent. However, you can ensure that you're in an emotionally balanced state when you trade — quiet, focused, and relaxed, in other words. That's the only way you have full access to your intellect. That way, you're in a position to act (and trade!) rationally.

Maintaining an Overview in the Face of Information Overload

You're surely familiar with the image of traders sitting in front of multiple screens, trying to get an overview of everything. This, of course, looks cool and gives you the feeling of being a pro. You have your eyes on the world, and you never miss a thing. Charts, rows of numbers, data, and a continuous news flow from every corner of the world give you self-confidence and a feeling of control.

Many traders believe that they need to know more than all other market participants combined. This is based on the conviction that having more knowledge and more information automatically results in better performance. But this is a fallacy, as the following list makes clear:

>> **Too much information leads to stress:** With the wealth of information available to us today 24/7 in real time, it isn't surprising that it quickly overwhelms our brains. The cognitive load required to process all this information is simply too immense and leads to stress. And when you're stressed, you're sure to make mistakes and lose your self-discipline.

>> **Too much information gets filtered automatically:** This is compounded by the fact that you automatically adapt the flood of news to suit your preconceived convictions, meaning you'll either winnow out the information that doesn't fit or reinterpret it to make it fit your preconceived notions.

>> **Too much information overloads our brains:** Neuroscientific studies show that the processing capacity of the human brain is quite limited. After all, our memory is not a supercomputer that can evaluate and weigh vast amounts of information in fractions of a second. The quality of the decision-making that computers are doing is constantly improving alongside the quantity of information they deal with, which means their forecasts are improving.

However, your decisions in trading aren't improving. After all, more information is not better information. It's a mistake to believe that information is knowledge. The human brain lacks the ability to process more information, let alone assess it or weigh it according to its importance.

>> Too much information will worsen your ability to forecast: The pointless hunt for an information advantage can have undesirable side effects. Psychological experiments suggest that your self-confidence increases with increasing information; however, your ability to make predictions doesn't. This is strange and frightening at the same time. Even if the information is completely irrelevant, your self-confidence will significantly increase; the quality of your decisions, however, does not. You're lulling yourself into a false sense of security by overestimating your forecasting abilities. Obviously, too much information is distracting and obstructs your view of what is essential.

TIP

Always focus on just a few price-relevant parameters. For example, look at previous price patterns. What were the triggers for larger movements? What drives the price? Is there a clear overall trend? Finding the answers to these questions saves time and energy, creates emotional distance, and prevents unwanted distortions in perception.

TIP

Reconsider how you reach decisions for trading. For example, imagine that you're thinking about investing in a specific technology share you've been watching for a while. You diligently gather all the information you can find about the company and the sector. In addition to a thoroughgoing fundamental analysis, you carry out detailed and extensive technical chart analyses. You want to identify resistances and supports and look for entry signals. You are satisfied with your thorough research and are now confident that you have made the right investment decision. From now on, you're essentially biased, even if you aren't aware that you are. You have developed an emotional relationship with the tech stock, which makes an objective point of view impossible. Your self-confidence is so great that you filter out any additional information that may run contrary to your conclusions and perceive only what suits your preconceived opinion. Studies show that you're hardly willing or able to change your mind, even if new factors challenge your assessment of the stock. Subconsciously, you only accept confirmations of your preconceived convictions. The trap snaps shut.

EUGENE FAMA'S MARKET EFFICIENCY HYPOTHESIS

"More information means better information and leads to better results." This belief probably dates from the era of traditional financial market theory. At that time, the dominant idea was that all markets are efficient and rational and therefore share prices reflect all available information, meaning it's impossible to outperform the market. This so-called *market efficiency hypothesis* was developed in 1970 by the American economist Eugene Fama and dominated thinking in the financial markets for many years. In 2013, Fama was awarded the Nobel prize in economics for his research.

Today, we know that financial markets aren't efficient and that market participants trade in a manner that's anything but rational. There are regular market anomalies from calendar effects, market exaggerations (up to and including speculative bubbles), and long periods of over- and underreactions on the part of markets. Despite this, most professional and private market participants believe that they can beat the market only if they know more than the others. The truth is, however, that more information doesn't automatically mean better performance. Markets are in no way efficient — certainly not in the short-term time frame where traders usually ply their trade. Market price action is much more random than you think.

SOMETIMES, LESS IS MORE

As part of a behavioral economics experiment, a group of MBA students were tasked with predicting the earnings per share for several companies in the next quarter. To reach a decision, they received more or less useful information about profit and sales during the last three quarters. The results of the study are noteworthy: The more information the students received, the more confident they were, independent of whether the information was relevant to the question. However, the increased self-confidence led to significantly worse earnings estimates, because the ability to identify what information was relevant decreased. Simultaneously, the irrelevant information distorted the students' ability to make forecasts. In other words, too much information was misleading or even harmful to the decision-making process. The less information, the better the students' earnings estimates. The noise is a distraction from what is relevant.

WARNING

I can only recommend in the strongest terms possible that you become aware of the automatic processes that accompany your trading decisions. It is nearly impossible to achieve an unfiltered information edge and it certainly isn't helpful in inefficient markets. It only creates too much self-confidence, which leads to your overestimating your own abilities. Attempting to cope with the flood of information from the markets isn't a good strategy for making successful trading decisions.

Acknowledging the Perils of Storytelling

We humans love stories. Stories convey emotions and values. We all think in terms of stories because doing so provides us with a foundation and can make sense of what is happening in the world. Sociologists speak of *narrative* — those significant or meaningful stories that explain information or specific events and are meant to place these into a wider context. This is how we orient ourselves, gain a sense of belonging, and achieve a feeling of security. As such, narratives help us make sense of everything. What counts is faith. Humans are constructed in such a way that they need to believe in something in order to be able to understand it.

REMEMBER

The noun *narrative* comes from the Latin word *narrare*, which means "to tell." Since the 1990s, this word has paradoxically become a buzzword because tried-and-true narratives of the past no longer explain or justify the political and social upheavals in this post-modern, digital era. Nowadays, political narrative strategies frequently serve to manipulate or to legitimize the interests of those in charge. Narratives differ depending on the culture and change with the times. New narratives tend to prevail in times of crisis rather than in stable and quiet periods.

Stories evoke strong emotions. They work not only to make sense of what we see around us and impose meaning in complex decision-making situations but also sharpen our senses in an environment where the flood of information widely exceeds our brain capacity. This sharpening creates feelings of self-confidence in relation to further actions. In this respect, emotional stories are an important part of effective decision-making.

EXAMPLE

A good example of such a narrative is the American dream (and myth) that every citizen can make it from rags to riches. This narrative brings forces together in order to create a common, radiant image. This has less to do with the truth and has more to do with providing people with orientation and confidence. The belief in the great American dream is now lost. Today, less than half of Americans in the United States still believe that hard work will make them rich.

Neuroscientific research over the past few years demonstrates to what extent stories and emotions determine our decision-making processes. Throughout evolution, the human brain has specialized in packaging a highly complex and uncertain world in simple stories. In that way, we assign meaning and purpose to every event and are convinced all along that we are doing the right thing. This gives us an orientation and helps us to concentrate on the essentials. Throughout the history of human evolution, it was essential to human survival that we be capable of making decisions and taking action at all times.

Telling Trading Stories

In a rational world, the sober assessment and weighting of figures, data, and facts would determine the strategies and trading plans of market participants. So much for the theory. In reality, the plans of market participants are far from rational.

Seeing that traders are suckers for stories

Traders let stories instead of facts determine their decisions. The information collected from trading serves to construct a story that is as plausible as possible. They put their story together in order to be able to classify and explain all price-relevant information. If it doesn't fit the story, it is unconsciously cast aside. Then, full of conviction, they make supposedly well-thought-out trading decisions. An advertisement from a large German investment company has aptly explained what criteria investors use to make financial decisions: "Stories, news, facts"— in precisely that order.

Puffing up price fantasies with the help of company stories

People tend to overlook companies that don't have much to say on the stock market. This is reflected in the valuation. A strong narrative attracts attention, spreads rapidly in the market, and creates price fantasies. A well-known American equity analyst once said that the stock market is not a pure fiction but, in the end, is always about storytelling. New buyers are attracted when they are enthralled by a company's story.

The stock market trades in future expectations, not numbers and data from the past. Expectations are always linked with emotions. This, of course, invites exaggerations. When reality catches up with the growth fantasies of market participants, the market corrects the overvaluation. In the long term, the fundamentals always determine price development.

Stories can put a spell on us. In experiments, psychologists have demonstrated how much we are subconsciously influenced by rumors on the market. We buy shares on the basis of rumors if the story behind it can explain current price action. In these experiments, the majority of trial participants bought shares offered even though they knew that these were only market rumors. The participants treated rumors as though they were real news. But all of them denied that their purchasing decision was influenced by the rumors! The control groups in the experiments who didn't know anything about the rumors didn't buy anything.

Be skeptical if the market wants to tell you exciting new growth stories. Narratives such as "This time, everything will be different" and the much-cited "paradigm shift" or "technological upheavals" have cost many an investor a lot of money.

The bursting of the Internet bubble in 2000 is a prime example of what can happen when hopes and dreams disappear into thin air. The story of a new market is a story of big promises and gigantic expectations. The prospect of big profits was simply too tempting. The story of the dawning of a new economic era caught and spread like wildfire; everyone wanted to be part of it. The mood was euphoric. A speculative bubble of gigantic proportions emerged.

When shares become a matter of faith, people no longer look at the fundamental data. A factual analysis of the future prospects of these Internet companies did not take place. The crash began as the first Internet companies had to file for bankruptcy and doubts about the fairy-tale growth story began to circulate. Greed and euphoria turned into fear and then panic. The speculative bubble burst.

Markets like to package groundbreaking innovations and megatrends in exciting and convincing stories. They magically attract us. Here are some current examples:

>> The rise of cryptocurrencies

>> The future vision of electric mobility

>> The digital transformation of the economy

>> The growth story of artificial intelligence

>> Demographic change in society

Evaluating the role of the financial press

The reporting by the financial press has a significant influence during periods of irrational exuberance. That's because they deliver the arguments and the story for price increases, thus reassuring people. Investors' trust in a continuing bull market grows. Belief in the boom solidifies with the rising markets, leading to a spiral of self-fulfilling expectations. Increasing prices underpin the story, which leads to a further increase in prices. This is how speculative bubbles occur.

TIP

The list goes on. The media loves trend topics and visions of the future. My advice: Don't let yourself be seduced, and don't make your investment decisions based on this kind of hope for the future.

Studies suggest that investors regularly pay a high price for growth fantasies. That's why it's important to keep the following advice in mind:

>> Avoid making the performance of your portfolio solely dependent on major stories you read about in the press.

>> Pay attention to the truth, and never forget the importance of a sober analysis of the figures, data, and facts before investing money.

In real life, stories make a lot of sense, but other laws rule the financial markets. Stories are irrelevant for your trading decisions for the short term. As for the long term, winners frequently show up during times of massive upheavals in the economy and society. You'll find shares that have multiplied over the years, especially in the technology sector. Peter Lynch, former investment manager in the US for the investment company Fidelity, came up with the term *tenbagger*, an investment that has the potential to appreciate in value ten times its initial purchase price over the long term. Lynch systematically searched for these kinds of investments. However, he knew that he would have to accept volatility and drawdowns in his long-term investments. Today, Peter Lynch is still considered one of the most successful investment managers in the world.

Chapter 10

Using Evolutionary Rules of Thumb

I n this chapter, you're going to find out what strategies your brain has developed over the course of the evolutionary process that have allowed you to conserve vital energy while leaving you still able to act. The other side of this particular evolutionary coin is that such strategies inevitably lead to cognitive biases, which in turn leads to behavior that isn't particularly useful when dealing with complex financial markets. I'll show you what you need to pay attention to when trading so that you don't fall into an evolutionary trap.

The perception and processing of information doesn't take place in a rational or objective manner, simply because your brain capacity is very limited. Whether you're filling your brain with objectively relevant or irrelevant financial news is of little importance; as a trader, you have your very own filter for what you perceive and how you process it all. And, despite all your attempts to be objective and rational yourself, your emotional state is what's critical when it comes to how you evaluate this information.

Leveraging Mental Shortcuts When Under Pressure

When under stress or faced with time pressures, we humans intuitively rely on mental shortcuts and rules of thumb in order to reduce our cognitive load and to speed up the decision-making process. This behavior was beneficial in evolutionary terms, even if it meant that it led us to (systematically) make wrong decisions. In trading, this behavior can cost you a whole lot of money. However, you will no longer be capable of decision-making and acting on dynamic markets if you try to carefully weigh and assess all the information in order to eliminate any and all perceptual distortions. Moreover, you can't just turn off your emotions when you're under pressure.

You *must* have a clearly defined strategy and a trading plan you can stick to. This fact alone supplies you with sufficient grounds for taking advantage of mental shortcuts. Consider the following:

» There is not enough time to obtain and assess all the available information.

» The flood of information can a) lead to emotionally charged stress reactions and b) impair the ability to act.

» The amount of effort required in order to analyze all scenarios and alternatives is out of proportion to the potential yield.

» Comparable market conditions have occurred in the past that you can use as a blueprint for your current situation.

» You may miss numerous trading opportunities.

As you can see, it's not that easy to make your way through the pros and cons:

» On one hand, you're trading on complex and dynamic financial markets.

» On the other hand, you have a brain that tends toward systematic biases when it comes to its information-gathering and decision-making processes.

TIP

Stick to the previously defined trading rules in order to avoid missteps — process orientation is the key to success in trading.

Fashioning the World You Want, Not the World That Is

You've done it. After careful analysis of all relevant information, you've finally made an investment decision. Your indicators tell you that the automotive sector needs to catch up. When the markets open, you buy a specific car stock, which should have, from a technical point of view, the biggest upside potential. You feel certain that you've made the right move, and you believe that you have everything under control. Your trading plan is set up. You lean back. You're relaxed. You follow along with a sense of satisfaction as the automotive sector starts to outperform the market. "I've done everything right," you say to yourself — until you notice that the particular stock you bought is not increasing in value. Worse, your stock falls in value compared to trends in that sector. The price of all the other automotive stocks you considered are moving up. Unbelievable. You start to get angry. And then you realize that you might have made the wrong decision. You are now in the midst of the tension of an inner conflict — cognitive dissonance, to be precise. The market is not developing as expected.

You now have two options to choose from:

>> **Rational:** You admit you've made a mistake, and you sell the shares immediately. (That's a rational decision.)

>> **Emotional:** You desperately search for reasons to hold on to the company. You tell yourself to be patient and that the share price will surely catch up. In the meantime, you shut out all the facts that speak against this decision. That is (as you yourself already know quite well, although you don't want to admit it) *selective* perception.

When caught up in your emotions, you are no longer in a position to objectively assess the situation. You have subconsciously fashioned a world where, by some miracle, that unpleasant state of tension inside you that is caused by external events melts away. Psychologists point to every human's need for consistency and absence of contradiction.

Take a look at another example. In response to the market movements just described, you are considering reentering the automotive sector with a bigger position. This time, however, you hesitate and miss your entry. Over the course of the first trading hours, the entire automotive sector has already risen by several percentage points. Basically, the valuation gap to the entire market has already closed. Worse, the stock you wanted to buy has had the best performance of the day.

DEFINING COGNITIVE DISSONANCE

In 1957, the American psychologist Leon Festinger presented his research in book form as A Theory of Cognitive Dissonance. His descriptions there mirror the kind of inner turmoil that market participants experience when, after having to decide between several options, the rejected alternatives turn out in hindsight to have been more advantageous. This results in what Festinger refers to as a "distressing mental state." According to the theory of cognitive dissonance, market participants attempt to overcome this contradiction between reality and their own conviction by rationalizing any errors in their investment decisions and overvaluing any positive factors. In that way, they regain their emotional balance.

You react angrily — quite angrily, in fact. Your ego is incapable of processing missed profits, because you just don't want it to be true.

To dissolve this area of tension, you make up stories to tell yourself, as in "I don't like the automotive sector anyway" or "It's just too volatile" or "Don't worry — the market is sure to correct itself tomorrow." Your tension fades away. Your picture of the world is once again free of all contradictions and is in harmony with the reality you've created for yourself.

To summarize:

>> As a trader, you'll always tend to reduce cognitive dissonance and you'll always want to make contradictions disappear as quickly as possible.

>> Your need for control is immense.

>> You want to avoid at any cost any feelings of regret that may arise from making a wrong decision.

>> Fear of failing at trading does not agree with your self-esteem. Your ego always wants to be right.

The consequences of these psychic hurdles are cognitive biases and misperceptions.

TECHNICAL STUFF

One particularly interesting neuroscientific experiment looked at human behavior when making hard decisions — decisions between two alternatives of equal value, in other words. It showed that, in hindsight, humans will always see the decision they made as correct and view the alternative they rejected in a negative light. Rational considerations don't come into play here. Our preferences subconsciously change after the fact. This adjustment process ensures that inner conflicts — the kinds of conflicts that can only waste your precious time — never occur. This protects our capacity to act.

Practicing Humility Instead of Indulging in "I Told You So"

Dogmatism prevents self-reflection. Successful trading is a continuous learning process and requires emotional intelligence. If you allow only your own point of view to be the right one and you stubbornly hold on to your own perspective, you'll never learn from your mistakes.

WARNING

A know-it-all can cause immense damage to a company. These folks, who are supremely aware of their own power, fight off any counterarguments or other opinions because they see them as threats. Only their own truth counts. Being right is self-confirmation. It is a power play that comforts the ego and can thus often be traced back to low self-esteem or even to an inferiority complex. Know-it-alls have the need to continually assert themselves and to exercise power. The addiction to recognition and approval is limitless. Making errors or having weaknesses cannot be reconciled with the ego's perception of itself.

It is difficult and exhausting for colleagues and other employees in companies to deal with know-it-alls. In contrast, the stock exchange quickly makes short shrift of them. If you believe that you need to fight for your rights on the markets, you've lost already. The famous economist John Maynard Keynes supposedly said, over 100 years ago, "The market can remain irrational longer than you can remain solvent." The stock exchange is basically always right. Regardless of how irrational market price action may be, setting yourself against the market is pointless and will ruin you.

If you want to stay successful in trading, you're going to need emotional intelligence — in other words, the ability to follow the markets, be open to other people's views, and constantly be prepared to learn. The markets require flexibility on your part and the ability to adapt on a regular basis to changing conditions. The stock market does not forgive mistakes.

REMEMBER

Humility is the polar opposite of dogmatism. Take that statement to heart. Successful traders learn more every day by embracing humility as well as their inner growth.

Escaping the Dissonance Trap

Almost everyone knows that regular losses are a part of everyday trading. You can't predict price developments. Finding the optimum entry or exit point is impossible. You'll never manage to perfect your market timing, but that's not essential for earning money in the markets, anyway. Be clear that this is about being profitable, not about being right.

You can't avoid cognitive dissonance when you make wrong decisions, but you can reduce its impact by not allowing feelings of anger and regret to gain the upper hand. You have the following (quite exemplary) options:

>> **Change your perspective.** Look at other perspectives before you trade. What technical and fundamental reasons speak in favor of a short position instead of a long position? What reasons speak in favor of the stock you didn't buy? What reasons speak in favor of the stock you *did* buy? You can flexibly adapt to changing market conditions and switch to the winning side. You'll be able to maintain your emotional distance and act more rationally.

>> **Keep looking ahead.** Tell yourself that your trading strategy is generally successful and that not every individual trade counts. You stick to your set of rules. Trading losses are normal and are handled according to your rules. Keep looking ahead for new opportunities. The only thing that counts is the balance at the end of a trading week or month.

Both of these strategies require lots of self-discipline and a structured approach. You orient yourself according to the processes you're following, not to the individual trades. You can practice that. When you practice and act in accordance with your processes, you'll get a handle on the effects of cognitive dissonance.

Chapter **11**

Finding the Right Basis for Decision-Making in Trading

I n this chapter, you get a chance to learn about what are considered to be the typical, well-researched behavioral patterns of investors trading on the stock exchange. You'll see that the very same coping strategies that work well in daily life can be damaging when relied on for trading. The trick is to realize that you'll be successful only when you can control your emotions and act according to the ways the markets work. Throughout this chapter, I give you some practical tips on how to get to that point.

Over the course of your life, you have developed strategies that have served to guide you, for better or for worse. You may not be aware of many of your behavioral patterns and conditioning, but they have worked to allow you to create, as far as possible, a living environment best suited for you.

By choosing to trade on financial markets, you have selected a field of activity that generally runs counter to human nature. You will fail in trading if you try to use the same tried-and-true coping strategies you use for daily life. You may have to learn other ways of thinking and acting.

Seeing Why Investors Hold On to Losing Shares and Sell Winning Shares Too Early

In difficult situations, you make decisions on the basis of selective perception — rules of thumb, in other words. Any cognitive dissonance you may be experiencing quickly dissolves away when you suppress or play down the negative factors and highlight and overvalue the positive factors. Your overall objective judgment is limited. This automatic behavior pattern is reflected in trading by the disposition effect, a term I'll introduce as follows:

> Imagine you've built up a position in a stock. The average purchase price is ten dollars. This is now your reference point. Profits and losses can only be made around this unconsciously anchored mark.

> Your decisions depend on whether your position is winning or losing. This is always in relation to the average purchase price.

Here comes the definition: In behavioral finance research, the disposition effect refers to the tendency of investors to quickly sell securities that increase in value and to hold on too long to securities that have fallen in value. Empirical studies confirm this effect: Investors realize their profits too early and let their losses run. In case of losers, investors reveal risk-seeking behavior by keeping the losing position. In case of winners, the same investors become risk-averse by selling prematurely to lock in the money. Apparently, investors dislike losing money significantly more than they enjoy making money. Rational behavior would suggest to hold on to winning trades and sell losing trades.

This phenomenon is called asymmetric risk behavior. It determines how you react, depending on how the security or stock develops in relation to the entry price:

> » **Scenario 1:** The share price increases to 11 dollars. You're happy that you made the right investment decision, but at the same time you're afraid of losing whatever book profit you may have gained. So, what do you do? You sell and take your profit, that's what you do. Your risk behavior has changed. You become risk averse when you're ahead and tend to realize the profits too early instead of letting them run. Under some circumstances, you may be missing out on some great profit opportunities.

TIP

> Use a trailing stop-loss order when winning. For example, in the case I just mentioned, you can set your stop-loss limit order to ten dollars — the purchase price — and continue to adjust upward if the price continues to increase.

> When you have moved your stop to the initial purchase price, you know that your position no longer entails any risk. The worst thing that can happen is that

you'll get stopped out without a loss. And you get to participate in further price increases without risk. Alternatively, you can take some partial profits, by closing half the position at 11 dollars and letting the other half run. In both cases, you're avoiding the (subconscious) impulse to close the position too soon.

>> **Scenario 2:** The price of your stock unexpectedly falls to nine dollars. You're upset and you don't want to accept that you were wrong. Losses create cognitive dissonance. You desperately search for indications of a speedy recovery. You ignore all the factors that go against your beliefs. You're plagued by perceptual distortions. So, what do you end up doing? Unfortunately, you keep the position and refuse to realize a small loss. You've removed or widened the stop to give the stock price more room to eventually bounce back. Your risk behavior has obviously changed. You've become quite willing to take risks when you're behind and thus let the losses run. In a worst case scenario, you average down your purchase by buying more at the "cheap" price and further expand your risk position.

Unfortunately, most investors and traders are trained by the financial press to anchor to a fixed point in the market. Markets are always up or down relative to this year's peak or bottom. Or for the calendar year. These reference points only lead to emotional decisions driven by fear or greed. The price at which you bought the security is not relevant for making subsequent rational decisions about your position.

WARNING

Never lose control and buy more when experiencing a loss. That means never, ever build up a position in case of falling prices if you don't have a plan. The risk of excessive losses is simply too great — and you no longer have your emotions under control. If things are going wrong, you obviously made a wrong decision. You need to extricate yourself from a risky situation, not get even more entangled in it.

Dealing with the momentum effect

Studies of price developments consistently show the same pattern: Shares that went well for the past six months will also have an above average performance over the course of the next six months. This pattern also applies in the case of those stocks that suffered losses over the past six months. These shares will also have a below average performance in the following months. Therefore, it would be rational to keep winning stocks in your portfolio and to sell losing shares quickly. The disposition effect shows that the majority of investors do the exact opposite.

Winners remain winners. Losers remain losers. Trends continue for longer than you think. Technical analysts speak of the statistically proven momentum effect. It should come as no surprise, then, that *momentum strategies* are popular with many traders — long and short strategies that place their bets on the continuation of relative strengths or relative weaknesses.

TIP

When you're trading, enter the market and ride the waves the market offers, and be sure to listen to the signals indicating that a trend is coming to an end.

Deploying the averaging down strategy

One can certainly argue quite persuasively that purchasing more shares at a losing position often works in practice. You will in fact manage to reduce your average purchase price so far that even a small movement is sufficient to return to profitability. (After all, it's impossible to find the right counter-move.) You can afford to be wrong for a while. You've mastered your craft and you're able to buy a lot more shares at the falling price. Most of the time, you manage to close the overall position after a certain period without taking a loss. This gives you the self-confidence to continue. This strategy of averaging down is quite popular with traders.

I agree that perfect timing in trading is a pipe dream and that regular losses belong to everyday trading. That's why consistent risk management is extremely important. Protecting your portfolio is your top priority. If you have lost 50 percent with a position, you'll need 100 percent performance in order to compensate for the losses.

A particularly aggressive method of buying further shares when you're at a loss is known as the *Martingale System*, a strategy where, in case of a loss, you keep doubling the position to increase the odds of returning to break-even in the first counter-movement or reversal of the share price. If, on the other hand, you're winning, you halve the position going forward.

This sounds temptingly simple: After expanding your position, you reduce the average purchase price (cost averaging) and stay close to the supposed profit threshold. This is why this strategy is so popular with many traders who enjoy risk.

From a psychological point of view, it's all about these characteristics:

>> Wanting to be right

>> Wanting to control the markets

>> Finding it hard to accept small losses

However, by buying into the Martingale System, you're breaking all the rules of good money and risk management. This is gambling with losing positions, not serious trading. You risk being squeezed out of the market because, if you happen to be unlucky and have set yourself against a stable trend, you end up seriously endangering your portfolio:

>> Your position size is out of proportion to your portfolio size (concentration risk).

>> You can't buy any more shares and you're unable to act (loss of control).

>> A heavy drawdown can ruin your portfolio for years.

The Martingale System is a risk-seeking trading strategy. It works only if the stock price reverses or bounces back. You're therefore living off hope and you're dependent on the next market movement. This results in a loss of control. Your brain automatically switches to alarm mode and you will lose your emotional balance. The market has taken control of your portfolio. You are utterly at the mercy of the market.

REMEMBER

Perhaps John Maynard Keynes never really said it, but it is nevertheless true: Markets can remain irrational much longer than you can remain solvent. Market returns are not distributed normally. A return to "average" (mean reversion) can take a long time. In practice, extreme market phases with several standard deviations occur more often than you can imagine.

What some Martingale enthusiasts also overlook is that they in no way increase the probability of winning with their strategy. All they are doing is postponing when they'll realize their losses. Relying on hope comes at a very high price.

WARNING

The risk/reward ratio (R/R ratio) of the Martingale System is a major cause of concern. If the strategy works, any profits you make will likely be small. Over the long term, however, it's also quite possible that you'll suffer catastrophic losses at irregular intervals.

TIP

The mirror image of the Martingale System states that the only time you would ever double your position size is after a win. This anti-Martingale System, or reverse Martingale, involves halving a trade each time there is a loss and doubling it each time there is a gain. It corresponds to the pyramid trading strategy, which I present in the next section. I call it *brain-compatible* trading.

Throwing good money after bad

Sooner or later, your financial ship is sure to hit the rocks if you continue to follow a strategy of doubling up on losing trades: If the shares you purchased maintain their downward trend and no reversal occurs, your strategy will spin out of control. At some point, you'll be fully invested and no longer able to purchase additional shares. Incapable of any action, you end up freezing like the proverbial deer in the headlights. The position has attained a size that endangers your portfolio. The accrued book losses are enormous, you've lost control, and you start to panic. In this emotionally charged situation, the pressure on you is unbearable, so you sell everything at a huge loss — a sad story familiar to many traders from their own experience.

One particular sad story is probably the best-known example of the devastating consequences of an averaging down strategy: the bankruptcy of the English Barings Bank in 1995, caused by the derivatives trader Nick Leeson. Leeson had aggressively expanded derivative positions that were already trading at a loss. The losses exploded, and the bank had to file for bankruptcy with a total loss of $1.3 billion.

TIP

Always determine the position size first. Buy a third at the entry signal you have defined, purchase according to the price level you previously set, and always remember to set a stop loss. You can then buy more shares if it turns out that your timing was good and the share price is going up. Finally, use a trailing stop to lock in profits. You *must* stick with the trading plan you set up in advance, which determines your entry and exit prices, your position size, and the holding period.

The deeply rooted fight-or-flight survival response in us humans provides an explanation for this throwing-good-money-after-bad behavior. First you fight against the markets and buy additional shares when prices are falling. You want to be right at all costs. Then you freeze in fear because you have used up all your resources and can no longer respond. And then you sell everything in a panic and ruin your portfolio. The result can be a total loss.

The situation always becomes dangerous when your emotions spin out of control. If a winning streak passes and you realize several trading losses in a row, the risk of starting to (unintentionally) fight the markets looms large. The fact is, you're angry as all get-out and you want your money back.

TIP

Chapter 4 has more about the problem of dealing with losing streaks and drawdowns, if you fancy going back a few pages.

And when you've been stopped out several times, your anger might be so severe that you're tempted to force gains at even greater risk. In both cases, you have the unfounded fear that you'll look like a loser. Your self-confidence is shaken because you take the losses personally. Just keep in mind that having experienced a trading loss doesn't mean you're a loser. The two have nothing to do with each other. Losses are part of the trading business. You must protect your self-esteem by dissociating yourself from the self-destructive, delusional belief that you are your trades.

REMEMBER

If you tend to take factually based criticism as a form of personal rejection and your ability to forgive yourself for the errors you make is weak, it might be the result of traumatic experiences in your past that always trigger the same emotional reactions. Consider taking a closer look at what might be triggering you. Chapter 6 has some advice on how to pursue this strategy.

TIP

The stock market is always right. That fact should teach us some humility. The stock market is also unforgiving; hubris and the illusion of control are poor sources for trading advice. Go with the markets, not against them. Think of Don

Quixote's hopeless fight against the windmills. The stock market, like Quixote's windmills, always wins.

Plumbing the Secrets of Success

Traders have the natural urge to buy more when they are losing. Why not just do the opposite and purchase more shares only when you're winning? I know it may be extremely difficult to hold onto winners and not take out the profits immediately; the thought that the course could turn again and your book profits may disappear into thin air makes you nervous. After all, being stuck with a losing trade that was previously making a profit is particularly painful. That is understandable.

However, imagine that the next time you trade a security that is in a stable upward trend you were able to apply the pyramid trading strategy at no great risk to yourself — a strategy where you continue to buy more of the same security and continuously expand your position size. (See Figures 11-1 and 11-2.) Your risk does not increase because you consistently adjust your stop-loss limits by taking advantage of trailing stops.

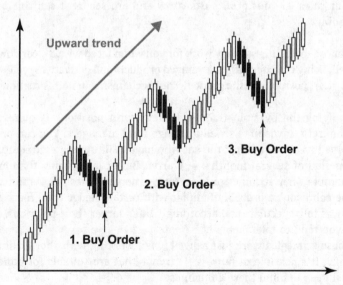

FIGURE 11-1: The pyramid trading strategy in an upward trend with long positions.

REMEMBER In view of your growing position size, you *must* secure your position in order to limit risk. It is crucial that you work with trailing stop-loss limits — in other words, be sure to continuously trail your stop-loss limits in order to keep the risk to your portfolio at a minimum.

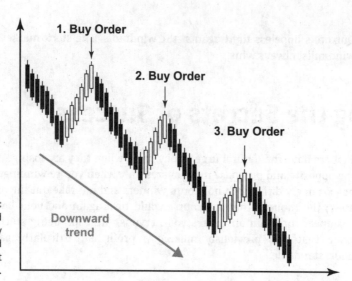

1. Buy Order

2. Buy Order

3. Buy Order

Downward trend

FIGURE 11-2: The pyramid trading strategy in a downward trend with short positions.

Even if you're stopped out on a regular basis and realize small losses, the long-term profit prospects of this scaling strategy are many times greater. You're no longer fighting the markets. You're no longer speculating on counter-movements or trend reversals. You're now following market price action, you're emotionally stable, and you're sparing your nerves. Trading losses are handled according to your rules — your profits can grow and are secure. I call this *brain-compatible* trading.

TIP

You can make this strategy work for you when faced with a clear downward trend as well. Using the appropriate leveraged products and derivatives, you'd be able to build up short positions in the market. The mechanisms in both situations are the same.

Applying the pyramid trading strategy with positions is quite popular among long-term investors as well as hedge fund managers. You can probably think of some investors right off the bat who have built up strategic equity positions over a period of several months — Warren Buffet is probably the most well-known example when it comes to long-term-oriented investors. As for the other side of the coin, you're probably familiar with certain hedge fund managers who, when prices fall, speculate and accordingly build larger short positions.

REMEMBER

These strategies work just as well when working with shorter time frames. Even daily, it's possible to find stable trends that are suitable for building a position. Just keep in mind these guidelines:

>> The trend has to be confirmed and stable.

>> Your trading plan has to include specific entry prices and the maximum position size.

>> Your trading plan has to include trailing stop-loss limits to hedge your position.

>> You had to have previously set the price level at which you'll exit and take your profits with you. (This profit target can be staggered when applicable.)

You'll be unable to apply this particular strategy often, because it takes time to plan the trades and you need the necessary discipline in order to implement the individual steps precisely. But, when the conditions are right, you can make substantial profits without great risk.

REMEMBER

Success is just what you need in order to develop a winning mentality. Your energy now gets to focus on promising setups. "The trend is your friend" is a well-known stock market motto. So let go of all those losing shares and hold on to the winning ones.

Note: The big wins make all the difference when it comes to profitable trading.

When Fear of Loss Makes You Lose Your Mind

The fear of loss is one of the strongest emotions in trading, which is why you'll literally do anything to avoid potential losses. Loss aversion is deeply rooted in the human psyche and has helped us humans survive throughout our evolution. Neurofinancial research provides some exciting insights into the biochemical processes in the brain that occur when losses are imminent or profits beckon.

Looking at prospect theory and loss aversion

The Nobel Prize winner Daniel Kahneman and his colleague Amos Tversky developed their prospect theory in 1979. With their experimental work on decision-making of market participants under uncertainty and risk, both psychologists laid the foundation of behavioral economics and won Kahneman the Nobel Memorial Prize in Economic Sciences in 2002.

Their relevant findings specifically dealing with traders speak to traders' various ways of dealing with risk. According to prospect theory, the phenomenon of loss aversion significantly influences human decision-making behavior. This inevitably leads to cognitive biases.

Think of it this way: As soon as you purchase a security, your next steps will be affected by whether you're making a profit or a loss. Fundamental or technical factors play a subordinate role. You act risk averse when able to realize a small profit, and you behave in a risk-seeking manner when faced with a loss. To be precise, you prefer an insecure higher loss over a secure but lesser loss. You move your stops and may even buy more shares under certain circumstances. "Hope springs eternal," you may say. This hope to recoup your losses is the inner drive that forces you to act unreasonably.

EXAMPLE

In experiments with money, it was shown that most individuals prefer to receive 50 dollars in hand rather than bet on a 50/50 chance of either receiving 100 dollars (great!) or 0 dollars (dismal!). Safety comes first. When you keep the odds, however, but change the punishment and reward, people also change their attitudes toward risk all of a sudden. Most people prefer a 50/50 chance of losing either 100 dollars or 0 dollars than definitely losing 50 dollars. Again, hope springs eternal.

Preventing losses: A closer look at the trader brain

Traditional financial theory assumes that the rational trader processes gains and losses in the intellectual areas of the brain and then makes a decision after weighing the relevant information. The reality is different: Gains and losses are stored in emotional experiential memory. No decisions are made without the participation of the emotional brain areas. If the limbic systems are overactivated, then the intellect remains turned off and you make decisions impulsively based on ingrained reflexes.

Modern brain research provides the explanation for what on the surface seems to be unusual asymmetric risk behavior in trading: The human brain undertakes steps of analysis — steps that belong together from an economic point of view — in quite different areas of the brain. In fact, profits and losses are processed by two entirely different areas of the limbic system, as experiments using brain scanners confirm. At the same time, the risk of loss is weighted much higher than chances of winning.

TECHNICAL
STUFF

Expected profits activate the limbic reward system, the *nucleus accumbens*. The expression of the neural messenger substance dopamine, colloquially known as the happiness or joy hormone, controls the desire for immediate reward. Fear of loss activates the limbic aversion system, the anterior insula — this is one of the areas of the brain responsible for the processing of all types of expected pain. Releasing the stress and anxiety hormones adrenaline and cortisol releases energy reserves and starts the psychic alarm bells ringing. Avoidance of pain is a top priority.

Threats are naturally perceived much more strongly than potential rewards. This makes perfect sense from an evolutionary point of view because underreacting to risk can be fatal. An overreaction would usually be harmless. However, this logic unfortunately doesn't apply to trading. The reflex to avoid loss at all costs only leads to potentially allowing losses to escalate and taking even more risks as a result. It's better to limit losses at an early stage and to realize small losses before greater damage occurs. You're bound to lose your balance faster than you can think when the emotional areas in your brain are activated and take control.

TIP

As a matter of principle, be sure to set a protective stop-loss order that does not exceed your pain tolerance (and makes technical sense) for every trade you make.

The evolutionary urge to quickly lock in your profits can sometimes be daunting. Your performance will suffer. You simply have to achieve bigger profits on a regular basis if you really want to be profitable in trading. (For practical tips on how you can use your winning opportunities, see Chapter 4.)

REMEMBER

Financial losses hurt — that's more than just a metaphor. The part of the brain that processes losses is part of the pain network. Your brain doesn't distinguish between physical and psychological pain. That's why traders don't want to realize losses — under any circumstances.

Dealing with your mental accountant

In trading, you're confronted with your basic instincts. Subconsciously, you place greater weight on potential losses than on potential profits. You assign profits and losses to mental accounts and treat each one differently. (This is referred to as mental accounting). Assigning profits and losses to different accounts prevents them from being assessed equally and leads to all-too-common distortions of the decision-making process.

WARNING

Resist the temptation to book losing positions to what you've labeled your Long-Term Investment mental account. That always happens when you want to sit it out and you refuse to realize book losses. Traders commonly set up what is considered a Play Money mental account where they're happy to lose this money and gamble it away. (Those in the know label this tendency the House Money effect.) Your need to free yourself from any cognitive dissonance is satisfied. Such freedom, of course, has its price. Not only is the risk to your portfolio increased, but it also impacts the return on your portfolio over the long term.

When ancient instincts gain the upper hand

Traders tend to spend more energy preventing losses than generating a profit. From an objective point of view, this is clearly counterproductive, but is understandable in terms of evolutionary history.

In evolutionary terms, being sensitive to loss was more beneficial than being grateful for wins. An overreaction would usually be harmless, whereas insufficient reactions to true risks could prove fatal. The ounce-of-prevention-is-worth-a-pound-of-cure reflex is deeply rooted in all living beings. A strong response to potential hazards forms the core of our basic instinct of self-preservation.

During the greater part of evolutionary development, humans were preoccupied with a struggle for survival — in other words, looking for food, reproducing, and protecting themselves against dangers. Only in the past few centuries have humans begun to use their brains for financial decisions.

REMEMBER

As a trader, you subconsciously give more weight to those factors threatening your portfolio than those that promise a possible profit. The perceived fear of potential losses is much more strongly pronounced than the joy of possible profits. Psychological experiments by Daniel Kahneman and Amos Tversky show that losses hurt twice as much as the pleasure that comes from wins of the same amount.

Here's something to try on your own. Let's assume you've been asked to participate in a bet. Here's what's at stake: How high should the prize be to make you willing to bet 100 dollars? Experiments show that the majority are willing to risk 100 dollars only when the prize is at least 200 dollars. When would you join the game?

Time does not heal all wounds

Losses generate strong emotions and dissonance because you're forced to face the fact that you may have made a wrong decision. Interestingly, your loss aversion changes the further your loss position is from your original purchase price — your reference point, in other words. Incidentally, the same applies to winning positions. Sensitivity reduces in both cases the farther you get away from your reference point. Your winnings and losses close to their purchase price are perceived much more strongly than those that are farther away.

That means it might be much easier to let winning trades run when your position is already clearly ahead. Ideally, you've trailed your stop loss to the purchase price. Therefore your position is risk-free and you can sit back. On the other hand, after some time has passed, you may tend to reevaluate your losing positions.

You decide to wait, subconsciously turning a short-term trade into a long-term investment. This is the high art of mental accounting. Your position is now in a drawer labeled Hope Value or Long-Term Investment, to the detriment of your portfolio. It won't get better with time; you'll just have to learn to live with the pain of the losses that are coming your way.

REMEMBER

How many German retail investors still have Deutsche Telekom shares from the 1996 Telekom IPO as a hope-springs-eternal value in their portfolio? The Germans were supposed to become a nation of shareholders. Two further tranches followed in 1999 and 2000. On March 6, 2000, Telekom shares reached a historical peak of $94.93. Then the Internet bubble burst, and their share prices collapsed by almost 90 percent. The decline of the former "people's share" and the long-standing court proceedings that followed the decline caused lasting harm to German equity culture.

These deeply entrenched patterns of behavior are not helpful for trading. Financial markets operate according to other principles. You either adapt to the markets or you fail.

REMEMBER

You need a different mindset — a winner's mindset, to be more specific. Always use protective stops to keep your losses small and focus your energy on managing your winning trades. Chapter 4 teaches you how.

Losing trades that get out of control cost you a lot of attention and cognitive energy. They also tend to cause opportunity costs if you inconsistently close your losing positions. (*Opportunity costs* are missed winnings that you could have made in the meantime with another trade.) Imagine that you had sold (admittedly, at a high loss) after the T-share bubble burst. With the released capital, you could have made many promising trades and probably would have recouped the loss by today. You must maintain a winning mindset and focus on winning trades.

5
Keeping Bad Behavior in Check

Recognize how irrational and biased most trading behavior actually is

Gain an understanding of how systematic misjudgments, distorted perceptions, and a pronounced herd mentality can have grave financial consequences

Learn how to deal with your ego and with deep-seated fear phenomena when trading

Chapter **12**

Avoiding the Obvious Mistakes

This chapter is all about how easily your judgment can be influenced (in a bad way) and how your (bad) habits can lead you astray. However, you can avoid succumbing to these bad influences and habits by sticking to the rules you've set for yourself as well as to your trading plans. Systematizing trading processes can be a godsend when it comes to preventing harmful influences.

Putting Reference Points in Perspective

If you regularly trade securities on the stock exchange, you know how difficult it can be to deal with losing positions in a rational and non-emotional way. We all tend to measure gains and losses in relation to a specific reference point, which generally ends up being (to no one's surprise) the entry price — the price you purchased the securities for, in other words. The entry price serves as an unintentional psychological anchor. As soon as you enter the market, you start reacting rather touchily, shall we say, to price developments. Your reaction will be particularly sensitive to potential gains and changes near your reference price. Your touchiness levels tend to decrease the more your gains or losses distance themselves from the reference price.

Assume that you're facing a market correction. You instinctively buy more shares. After all, the shares in your portfolio are now cheaper — a bargain, you might say. Your position's purchase price is your psychological anchor and reference point for assessing your approach. If, contrary to expectations, the prices keep falling, you may get caught in a downward spiral. The urge to double up on losing trades is immense. But how far do you want to go? What is your pain threshold? Your risk-bearing capacity? You are in danger of losing control, leaving you at the mercy of the market.

REMEMBER

The stock market is not a supermarket offering regular deals and special offers. It is an auction, where supply and demand determine the price. If the selling pressure is high, the stocks will fall longer and deeper than you could ever imagine. You'll be neither emotionally nor financially able to cope with this situation. You might fall back on the dread averaging down strategy — to your detriment. (For more on the averaging down strategy, see Chapter 11.)

TECHNICAL
STUFF

Various empirical studies on the trading behavior of private investors show that securities held for a longer period in one's portfolio tend to underperform. Profit decreases in proportion with the length of time the stock is held. Someone could conclude from these findings that investors tend to hold on to losing shares for too long, which then serves to decrease a portfolio's profit over the long term. This phenomenon confirms the *disposition effect* — the tendency of investors to quickly sell securities that increase in price and to hold on too long to securities that have fallen in price. (For more on the disposition effect, see Chapter 11.)

Your difficulties as a trader can be traced back directly to your subjective perception — a perception totally dependent on your initial reference point. When a trade ends up in the red, emotions that distort your judgment come into play. Your entire attention is focused on this lone trade. You try to make every price movement plausible. You're no longer able to see the big picture.

REMEMBER

In the end, what really counts is the overall performance of your portfolio — the sum of all trades over a certain period rather than individual trades. Keep your sights on the development of your portfolio as a whole.

TIP

Focus on implementing your trading strategy in accordance with the rules you have set for yourself. Trading losses are the rule, not the exception. Pay attention to limiting your losses early on. Don't waste your energy on trades that are going wrong.

Synchronizing Risk Tolerance

If you think you're aware of your attitude to risk, you're simply fooling yourself. In the heat of the moment, your risk behavior on the stock exchange changes like a weathervane on a windy day without your even noticing it. Depending on whether your trade is winning or losing, you'll become more risk averse or more willing to take on risks. Empirical studies show that the majority of traders go for a riskier strategy and are more willing to buy additional shares when they are in the red. Conversely, when they're winning, they play it safe and exit early. Such behavior is understandable. After all, you don't want to lose your book profits when you're ahead. And you don't want to realize small losses when your position is sliding into the red. By buying more shares — with the consequent reduction of the average purchase price — it might be possible to ward off realizing a loss if the stock bounces back.

It's understandable, but nevertheless counterproductive, because this behavior is clearly harmful when it comes to risk and return. Hope is not a strategy. Letting your risk tolerance depend on where you set your position is a sure way to damage your portfolio performance. More than likely you'll realize wins too early and allow losses to escalate.

Many studies show a further interesting phenomenon. Assume that you have already completed some trades. It turns out that your attitude to risk will now change, depending on whether you have realized a win or a loss. For example:

>> After you have booked a trade with a generous profit, you become more risk averse. You predict the probability of a further winning trade to be lower than it is.

>> Only when the market continues to rise do you gain courage and become willing to take risks again. You overestimate the likelihood of further increasing prices.

>> After you have realized a trade with a loss, your willingness to take risks decreases significantly. If you were willing to take a risk when you were in the red, the realized loss from that experience will cause you to be risk averse and you will hold back on opening further trades.

>> Only after realizing several loss trades do you want to recoup at least part of the losses at the end of the trading day. You will be overly willing to take risk. You want your money back and start to overtrade.

Successful trading means that you are consistent when measuring risk — regardless of the outcome of individual trades. Your risk management encompasses the sum of all trades. The performance of individual trades is irrelevant.

The only thing that counts is the profit you make with your portfolio at the end of the month or year. Take that fact to heart and expand your perspective.

Factoring in the framing effect

Changing your attitude to risk is closely related to the framing effect. The frame of reference in decision-making will change depending on how something is presented.

REMEMBER

The framing effect shows that changing how facts are represented leads to different decisions. Equivalent alternatives are perceived in different ways. This behavior contradicts the traditional theory of rational decision-making. A glass that is half full is always simultaneously half empty. How you choose to define the glass contains a judgment and subconsciously changes your point of view. You no longer make decisions in a non-emotional and rational way.

If a securities position slides into the red, your decision-making framework will change. You'll be more willing to take risks, and, under certain circumstances, you may buy more shares rather than close a position. In this case, behavioral economists speak of loss framing. A potentially higher loss is preferred to a lower but definite loss. When you're in the winning zone, you become risk averse and have the urge to quickly realize winnings. You're now in the gain frame. Sure gains are always favored over higher probable gains.

Your trading decisions are generally influenced by whether the situation requiring a decision is presented in a positive or negative frame. Your risk tolerance varies, depending on whether you're facing unrealized gains or potential losses.

EXAMPLE

In a well-known experiment, the trial participants were given $50. They had two options: Option 1 was the safe choice, where they could keep $20; Option 2 was the speculative option, where the entire sum would be used as a stake in a game of chance. The experiment was carried out in two variants:

>> **Variant 1:** Trial participants were told that they could keep $20.

>> **Variant 2:** Trial participants were told that they had to give up $30.

In the positively formulated frame, the majority decided on the safe choice and kept the $20. In the negatively formulated frame, the majority decided in favor of the risky choice, the game of chance. Even though the results were obviously identical, the way the facts were presented influenced the participants' risk tolerance.

TIP

Practice taking the opposite perspective when trading. For example, just assume that you're in a tricky situation and you therefore find yourself in the red. Your attitude to risk is distorted. Then just imagine that you have a short position instead of a long position. You're now in the gain frame. Pay attention to how your attitude to risk has changed just by completing this thought experiment. Become aware of the differences and thus maintain emotional distance.

In trading, you'll tend to allow the way situations are presented to you when a decision is required on your part influence how you act. Price developments, graphics, and data records can be prepared in slightly different ways so that under certain circumstances you may draw the wrong conclusions. "The only statistics you can trust are those you falsified yourself" is a quote attributed to Winston Churchill. All someone has to do is consciously frame a situation positively or negatively and you're able to trigger a cognitive illusion. The fact is, if we're being objective, you shouldn't allow yourself to be influenced by the different modes of presentation if it doesn't affect the result. But who can be truly objective?

TIP

For more on reframing techniques, see Chapter 7.

Correctly assessing probabilities

Your judgment and objectivity are easily influenced when trading securities. Your attitude to risk changes without your even noticing, depending on which reference points and frames of presentation you cite. To top it all off, traders also find it difficult to assess probabilities. Empirical research shows that market participants systematically assess objective probability of occurrence incorrectly. Depending on whether your position is winning or losing, you'll either overestimate it or underestimate it subjectively. This, in turn, affects your risk assessment, as described in the following two examples. Assume that

>> **Your position is a winner and you tend to want to realize the gains quickly.** In such a situation, you are risk averse. That means you overestimate the probability that the price will fall and underestimate the probability that the price will continue its upward trend.

>> **Your position is in the red and you tend to want to hold on to your losses — and even buy more.** You're willing to take a risk. That means that you're overestimating the probability that the price will recover again and underestimating the probability that the price will continue its downward trend.

When you regularly bet *against* price developments that have a high probability of coming true and bet *for* those with a low probability of coming true, your trading will never be profitable. Your market evaluation and risk assessment are faulty.

Only price pays, so don't trade your emotional state, your opinions. and your predictions. You focus on trading market price action. You've also set the wrong priorities. Your time and attention are wasted on events that rarely occur instead of focusing on high-probability strategies that promise success.

EXAMPLE

Gamblers at the roulette table in the casino tend to put everything on red if black has already been called several times in a row, even though they know that there is no correlation between individual rounds. The odds have not changed — only their framing has.

Managing when images from the past catch up with you

Emotional memories play a significant role when evaluating probabilities. How you estimate the probability of a losing trade may, under some circumstances, be influenced by anxiety-producing images caused by previous bad experiences entering your consciousness. A major trading loss in your past that hasn't been processed and healed can result in a form of trauma — one that will keep on catching up with you when similar situations arise. All it takes is a trigger and the old images are there once more; you are once again taking a ride on an emotional roller-coaster.

TIP

In Chapter 6, I talk about visualizations. You can use them to expunge negative images and replace them with positive ones.

EXAMPLE

The fact that shareholder culture has not established itself in a place like Germany is because many investors suffered traumatic losses after the bursting of the dot-com bubble in 2000 and the collapse of Telekom's "people's share" in the same year. Since then, large sections of the population now view the stock exchange as dubious financial gambling. The old images that trigger fears of substantial losses have been deeply anchored in the collective memory and still hold sway.

So how do images from the past affect you? What is the result?

>> You tend to give events and information occurring today a special weight if similar situations have already occurred in the past.

>> Your imagination influences your risk perception and the way you assess probabilities.

>> You tend to assess as improbable any market movements that you find hard to imagine and you therefore tend to suppress them.

>> Easily retrievable memories of comparable market conditions in the past will tempt you to overestimate certain probabilities and underestimate others.

This is understandable. This is human nature. It's far easier for you to imagine events that have often occurred in the past than those that have not yet happened. Because, often, no connection whatsoever exists between past events and the current situation, this imaginative lack leads to well-known distortions in perception and to errors in judgment. In behavioral economic research, this phenomenon is referred to as availability heuristics.

REMEMBER

Availability heuristics, also known as availability biases, are those mental short-cuts individuals use in order to be able to assess a situation quickly when faced with uncertainty. It influences your judgment, depending on how easily you can recall similar situations requiring a decision from the past.

Estimating probabilities incorrectly is further evidence of how biased and easily influenced you are when trading. Emotions frequently determine your behavior. Depending on where you stand with your a position and what kinds of memories are now coursing through your brain, you may subconsciously lose your objectivity. A big losing trade you had to close painfully will remain present for quite a while. It is the associated feelings of fear tied to those difficulties that prevent informed trading decisions in similar situations in the future.

EXAMPLE

If you tend to follow media reporting on tragic plane crashes, you'll estimate the risk of air crashes as significantly higher than someone who avoids such stories. Because the images are anchored in your memory and can be retrieved at any time, you can imagine frequent crashes much more easily.

Try to maintain an emotional distance to individual trades and focus on the returns for the entire portfolio. When you become aware of the automatic processes going on in your head, you're in a better position to obtain the necessary emotional distance and thus assess the market situation more objectively.

LOTTO FEVER

Do you regularly play the lottery? You're in good company. Millions of people the world over spend money every week for the dream of living the good life. The prospect of big profits is simply too tempting, even if the probability of drawing six correct numbers at the next lottery draw is negligible. To formulate it precisely: The expected value is negative. You're throwing money out of the window every week. It is not rational. Your emotions overrule your mind. But you let it happen because the lottery ticket lets you dream big and because you're quite willing to spend money to keep the dream alive.

(continued)

(continued)

Here's a dose of reality: Imagine a lottery player who smokes two packs of cigarettes a day. The probability of getting seriously sick from the consequences of smoking is 1:10. The probability of winning the lottery is 1:140 million. The fundamental naivete in the lottery player's thinking is based on the fact that this person ignores the laws of probability and assumes that they won't become ill from smoking but has good chances of winning the lottery. Humans as a whole are far too willing to lie to themselves.

Ambiguity aversion: Believing that you can't change the habits of a lifetime

Humans are creatures of habit, or so they say. We have a natural fear of the unknown and thus tend to prefer the known to the unknown. If, when faced with a new situation, we subjectively experience uncertainty, that uncertainty makes us act in an exaggeratedly cautious manner. We intuitively avoid decisions if we do not know how the results will line up in terms of their probability. In the behavioral science jargon in use today, this heuristic is referred to as ambiguity aversion, also known as uncertainty aversion. Ambiguity aversion is basically a subconscious preference for known risks over unknown risks.

To illustrate this idea, think of a roulette table in a casino. Put simply, according to the rules of this particular game of chance, you can place bets on black or red. You know the risk and the probability distribution. The probability for each of the colors is always 50 percent in each round. (For the sake of simplicity, we will ignore the zero.) If you bet on the right color, you get double your money back. If you bet on the wrong color, you lose the bet. That goes on round after round. Nothing changes. (The situation is similar to a coin toss.)

When trading on the stock market, neither the chances nor the amount of the possible gains and losses are known. You're acting in a dynamic environment full of uncertainty with a high potential for stress. The only way to influence the amount of potential gains and losses is to judiciously use stop-loss and take-profit limits. You can't control the rest.

REMEMBER

Humans instinctively avoid situations of ambiguity that are hard to predict. This explains why strong emotions keep getting triggered when trading. You need enormous amounts of self-discipline.

The antipathy toward the unknown also explains why, as a trader, you find it so hard to invest in markets or asset classes you aren't familiar with. You think that you lack the necessary information and knowledge. You fear that you don't know what you need to know and lack control over the situation. Subconsciously, you underestimate the potential for returns. Under certain circumstances, you may be missing out on lucrative trading opportunities. Empirical studies emphasize the negative impact that such fears have on the investment returns of private investor portfolios.

Overcoming home bias

The power of habit limits your investment horizon. Maybe you've already noticed that you tend to trade securities in markets you're already familiar with. Economists refer to this behavior as home bias — a bias confirmed by a large number of studies. The majority of portfolios investigated, for example, displayed a one-sided focus on domestic investments. This is because you tend to know your own home market much better than foreign markets. This gives you confidence and a feeling of control. You believe that you're better able to assess the market's opportunities and risks.

REMEMBER

Routines and habits are tried-and-true survival strategies for the human brain. You get to save cognitive energy and can keep your mind free to tackle other tasks. This strategy may work well in everyday life, but in trading such strategies can have negative consequences.

You have to acknowledge the price you pay for this need to feel secure that lies at the root of the home bias phenomenon. After all, such a one-sided investment approach increases the risk to your portfolio. It also means that you may miss opportunities in other markets. From a theoretical point of view, it's best to diversify your investments, spreading them out on various markets and asset classes that have little correlation with one another. The risk to your portfolio decreases when you're able to compensate for fluctuations. Doing so prevents concentration risks. Diversification has been shown to lead to an increase in expected returns on your portfolio while maintaining the same risk exposure.

EXAMPLE

Looking at the example of Germany, most investors and traders there invest using the DAX — the leading German stock market index. They do so despite the fact that German-listed companies have only a share of just under 4 percent of the world's market capitalization. Germans are thus missing opportunities in other regions of the world. For example, the US share market has been doing significantly better than the structurally weak German stock market. This happens, of course, because of the growth of US technology stocks.

TIP

Take a close look at how much of a homebody you are when it comes to your portfolio. Where are the growth markets and the seminal sectors in other parts of the world? Which markets are undervalued? Citing an alleged lack of information or excessive transaction costs or exchange rate risks is no longer a compelling argument for not including Asian companies, for example, in your portfolio.

The endowment effect: Basing decisions not on what you have but rather on what you can get

Humans have the tendency to value items they own higher than equivalent items they do not own. This empirically proven behavior is known as an endowment bias (also known as divestiture aversion).

EXAMPLE

Daniel Kahneman, the winner of the 2002 Nobel Memorial Prize in economic sciences, carried out a simple experiment with two groups to demonstrate the nature of endowment bias. The first group was given a coffee mug and was tasked with determining a price for which they would sell the cup to the other group. The other group was tasked with naming a price for which they would buy the cup. The price differential was immense. The owners of the cups demanded more than double the price the buyers were willing to pay.

Ownership thinking is not rational because you inevitably overestimate the value of a security you own. Psychologists speak of habituation effects and emotional attachment. In other words, the value of an investment depends on the holding period and to what extent you have emotionally bonded with that investment. This kind of behavior may be justified in everyday life, but sentimentality has no place on the stock exchange or in your portfolio.

TECHNICAL STUFF

Neuroscientific experiments provide a link between endowment bias and loss aversion. You subconsciously demand a higher selling price in order to compensate for the loss of the security. The end result of these subconscious actions is that you keep losers in your portfolio for way too long. You rate the price level you can reasonably expect to receive as unacceptably low. You then confirm the disposition effect by sitting on your losing trades and then storing them away in another mental drawer labeled Long-Term Investment — which is another term for a losing proposition.

TIP

Write down in your trading journal the following statement so that you can always remember it: The current value of stocks in your portfolio does not depend in any way on who owns them or when they were purchased or which price they were purchased at. Leave any of those facts out of your calculations, and trade strictly according to your plan. Before trading, determine your setup — your entry and exit points, position size, holding period, and, above all, your loss containment through protective stop-loss orders.

Status quo bias: Not letting "what is" determine "what will be"

Closely related to endowment bias is the status quo bias: It's the desire, in the immortal words of John Lennon and Paul McCartney, to "let it be." Both behavioral abnormalities indicate a tendency toward a passive attitude. Humans want situations to stay as they are. Under certain circumstances, change means stress, so we prefer the status quo. We like to retain habits that have proven useful.

EXAMPLE

In an experiment designed to test the hypothesis of the status quo effect, trial participants were given the choice to invest an amount they had inherited. If the inheritance consisted of shares from company A, the majority of trial participants preferred to remain invested in security A. If the inheritance consisted of shares from company B, the majority preferred to stick with B shares. The participants who inherited cash showed no preference for either of the shares.

The example shows that investors prefer to preserve existing conditions and have no wish to make changes. The participants saw no opportunity costs associated with their decision — namely, the unrealized wins of alternative investments. Errors caused by inactivity are always easier to accept than errors from activity. Giving up the status quo is perceived as a loss in some ways. And, despite its utter irrationality, traders value this loss higher than the potential wins of alternative investments.

In trading, the status quo effect appears as described here:

>> You hold on for far too long to trading strategies that no longer work.

>> You have become accustomed to a particular trading style and have become inflexible.

>> You're too late when it comes to adapting to changing market conditions.

>> Your loss aversion increases as you hold on to loss positions for too long (the disposition effect).

>> You delay when it comes to making necessary adjustments to your portfolio.

>> You may hold shares in companies you're familiar with for too long, even if the returns are below average.

REMEMBER

The status quo effect means that you frequently respond too late to changing market conditions. In addition, the status quo effect may make other behavioral abnormalities — such as endowment bias, loss aversion, and ambiguity aversion — much worse.

Chapter **13**

Dealing with the Stock Exchange's Collective Misbehavior

In this chapter, I offer you a look at mass psychological phenomena and, more specifically, the (well-documented) herd behavior of market participants — behavior that gets reflected in a variety of ways. One particular benefit of reading this chapter is that you'll learn to recognize, early on, the contagion risks stemming from market sentiment and information overload and then exploit them for your own benefit.

Living the Stone Age Life

One clear result of a trader's reliance on selective perception is that they are influenced by mass sentiment in trading situations. They suppress the results of their own market analysis and prefer to rely on those of others. They are deathly afraid that their assessments may be wrong, and they also assume that others have more (and better) information. If they follow the opinion of the majority and invest accordingly, they may then try to justify this decision by dredging up information designed to confirm their actions. They refuse to acknowledge any information that may indicate they've made an incorrect decision. The goal here is to avoid cognitive dissonance. Such behavioral patterns occur far too often in trading.

In nature, you'll find that animals instinctively herd together. This behavior increases the safety of the individual animal and makes it easier to search for food. The herd instinct is also deeply rooted in us humans, as research by evolutionary psychologists clearly demonstrates. Our ancestors have always come together because they were only able to survive as a group. Pitting yourself against the opinion of the majority was dangerous. Peer pressure requires conformity and behavior that supports the group's goals.

Seeing humans as social beings

Humans are social beings, constantly seeking recognition and confirmation from their chosen group. As such, we humans are marked by certain emotional and behavioral patterns:

>> The feeling of belonging gives us security.

>> Being part of a group is a basic human need.

>> We easily let others lead our behavior.

>> We learn to observe and imitate behaviors from an early age.

>> We look for role models and try to follow their practices.

Psychologists who specialize in how humans learn say that we automatically assume the behavior of the group we identify with and intuitively reject other behaviors.

REMEMBER

This method of learning and of adapting our behavior to match that of the majority has served us well in our evolutionary history, but when it comes to financial markets, these innate behavioral patterns can lead to significant errors — errors with serious consequences. Just keep in mind that other rules and principles prevail on the stock exchange — rules and principles that have nothing to do with our joint evolutionary history.

Herd behavior as a mass psychological financial market phenomenon arises from the fact that investors, when faced with a new situation, are wracked by uncertainty: They can't draw on experience, and they prefer to react to the actions of other market participants and follow their lead. They instinctively act as the masses do because they believe that the masses have better market knowledge. The cause for this behavior has an emotional basis. Two aspects stand out:

>> The fear of being wrong and missing out on profitable trades.

>> The need for security and a sense of belonging.

Because these processes are unconscious ones, our intellect hardly has a chance when trying to counter them with rational arguments. In herds, it's the emotions that dominate, not the intellect. This inability to make one's own decisions and a lack of introspection are typical drivers of asset bubbles in financial markets.

TECHNICAL STUFF

From the point of view of brain research, herd behavior is quite understandable: Anytime one deviates from the majority opinion, the amygdala — which is the limbic system's fear center, so to speak — raises the alarm and increases the emotional pressure to get back in line with group sentiment. Biochemical processes ensure that the bonding hormone oxytocin — the hormone tasked with encouraging an individual's adaptation to majority opinion by facilitating trust and attachment — is released.

Recognizing that it's all in your head

The stock market is all about psychology because market participants are not rational. They trade subjective expectations about an uncertain future. This uncertainty calls up a range of feelings that can cause investors and traders to sometimes act completely irrationally. Emotional responses such as these can trigger more or less extended phases of exaggerated market swings in both positive and negative directions. Speculative bubbles on the one hand, and severe dips or panic on the other, plague the financial markets with disarming frequency. The blame for these extremes can usually be laid squarely at the feet of collective herd behavior. Fear and greed are strong emotions that tempt us to follow markets in an uncritical manner.

TECHNICAL STUFF

Robert Shiller, winner of the 2013 Nobel Prize in economic sciences, says that emotions and bull markets mutually influence each other. This reinforcement effect leads to "irrational exuberance," which is a clear warning sign that markets might be overvalued.

The logic behind such herd behavior is shockingly simple. The actions of market participants become a self-fulfilling prophecy. When the markets rise significantly, everyone wants to jump on the bandwagon. Peer pressure turns you into a mindless follower and you end up a victim of the boom. That's what happened with the dot-com bubble of the 1990s. When emotions gain the upper hand, market fundamentals or valuations obviously no longer play a role. When the speculative bubble bursts, everyone turns into lemmings, resorting to panic selling in falling markets. Whoever hesitates when all the others flee is trampled by others. In such a panic, people blindly sell off their shares in order to save at least part of their assets.

André Kostolany said that mass psychological reactions in the stock market are like a theatre audience: "One yawns, and in next to no time everyone yawns. One of them coughs, and the whole hall immediately coughs."

The great disillusionment comes later, when the rational mind is turned back on and you realize that you have become the victim of your basic instincts and highly contagious emotions.

Numerous studies show that the vast majority of private investors regularly fall into evolutionary traps. They buy when the market reaches the end of its upswing and sell when it reaches its lowest point. This sentiment-driven buy-high-sell-low strategy repeats itself in all stock market cycles and has been statistically confirmed. This is why market jargon often refers, somewhat disparagingly, to private investors as *dumb money* and to the institutional investors as *smart money*.

REMEMBER

Certain exceptions prove the rule of Private Investor = Dumb Money. It seems that private investors did everything right after the COVID-19 crash of March 2020: They multiplied their trading activities. In the United States alone, more than a few million brokerage accounts have been opened since the start of the crash. Retail traders speculated with significant leverage on a rapid recovery — and won big. The big investment firms were caught off guard and were forced to close their open short positions and liquidate the hedges at progressively higher prices, thereby triggering a short squeeze. Sometimes the dumb money is smarter, after all.

Following the trend

Sir Isaac Newton's first law of motion, which states that a body at rest tends to remain at rest and that a body in motion tends to remain in motion, also has an effect on financial markets as a mass psychological phenomenon. The thought processes and decision-making processes of the masses changes slowly. If the vast majority of market participants have gotten used to a trend, it takes an unusually long time for a trend reversal to occur. This delay results in a certain amount of inertia within the complex market system.

Market participants quickly get used to the fact that share price dips during a bull market present buying opportunities. After several strong trading days, we're quite happy to enter the market and allow ourselves to get carried away by the herd. The fear that we might be missing something is great. After a severe market correction, we react quite differently. It no longer seems like such a good idea to use rock-bottom prices as an excuse for entering the market.

From an objective point of view, the risks definitely outweigh the opportunities when it comes to entering the market in the first case, and the opportunities outweigh the risks of an entry in the latter case. Studies confirm this phenomenon. However, our evolutionary conditioning plays a trick on us here, robbing us of our objectivity.

WARNING

The mentality of buying the dips doesn't work when longterm trends are broken and we enter bear market territory.

TIP

Always ask yourself the following question: Have the market conditions fundamentally changed? Is the upward trend broken? In which time frame? When you realize that you can utilize your own feelings as a counter-indicator, just do the opposite of what your emotions are prompting you to do. That way, you distance yourself from the crowd and you might be able to anticipate early the next market move.

You can see collective herd behavior in private as well as professional investors. Both are naturally sluggish and like to follow trends. When everybody agrees on market trends — average market participants as well as experts — what actually ends up happening often turns out quite differently. A popularly cited explanation tells us that investors always like to speak about something positively when they are fully invested in that something. They have (understandably) an interest in seeing prices continue to rise. However, it seems that demand is lacking and there are no additional buyers. That means prices could fall. Investors like to speak negatively about the market when they're not invested. As always, they're afraid of missing a potential rise in share prices. At some point, they'll jump on the bandwagon after it's moving, along with the other members of the herd.

TIP

Pay close attention to the market mood. With lots of self-discipline, you'll be able to recognize your opportunities and take advantage of them.

Knowing when herd behavior is actually rational

The financial markets are a great place to observe mass psychological phenomena. Deeply rooted patterns of human behavior that seem sensible in many areas of life are immediately punished on the stock exchange. If you aren't careful when trading and you subconsciously adapt to majority opinion, you're sure to fall into an evolutionary trap.

Should you always consciously act counter to what the majority is doing? Not necessarily. After all, herd instincts on the stock exchange aren't fundamentally irrational. In certain market situations, conscious herd behavior can be rational. Behavioral economists at the University of Mannheim have clearly demonstrated as much in a 2001 study based on their research.

You can describe herd instincts on the stock market as rational when the behavior is based on price-relevant information that has made necessary the reevaluation of the market or an individual security.

Herd behavior in one direction or another is always irrational if no new price-relevant figures, data, or facts are being used as the basis for a buy or sell decision.

Imagine the following situation: The reporting season has just begun. The listed companies report their results for the last quarter and provide a forecast for expected developments in the current fiscal year. The analysts' earnings estimates are high, and the market participants' expectations are high as well. This is reflected in the increasing prices.

All seems fine and dandy, but then the financial sector surprises everyone with a series of profit warnings. The forecast for the current fiscal year is significantly gloomy. What follows is a sell-off and a correction of the now overvalued financial stocks. The correction is rational as long as stock prices reflect the new information. Investors behave rationally when they continue to sell in accordance with majority opinion until the sector has reached a fair valuation level.

It's generally sensible to close a loss position as quickly as possible, as painful as that may be.

Sitting on your losses when market conditions have deteriorated is not a clever strategy. You lose your ability to act, you risk further losses, and you miss out on potentially profitable opportunities in other sectors of the market. Most of all, you end up damaging the return on your portfolio.

Of course, when rosy forecasts prove correct, herd behavior can be equally rational. If the financial sector exceeds market expectations, it generally leads to a buying spree and a reassessment of the sector. As an investor, it makes sense to buy along with the majority of investors until the new information has been priced in.

If you suffer a 50 percent loss with your investments following a collapse on the stock exchange, you'll need a 100 percent return on investment in order to recover the losses and get back to where you were before the collapse. Take a look at Chapter 4 for more information about the importance of risk management tools.

Collective restraint when it comes to buying can also be a sign of rational herd behavior. For example, when important economic figures are pending for publication or when market participants are expecting a decision on interest rates at an upcoming meeting of the central bank, restraint is called for. The effects on markets of such news can be considerable. In view of the existing uncertainty, it can be sensible to wait for the results along with the majority of your fellow traders. Anything else would be just high-risk speculation.

The asymmetric distribution of actionable information between market participants plays an important role in the question of whether herd behavior can be rational. Not everyone has access to the same information. This creates uncertainty. When selling pressure in the market is strong and trading volume is clearly increasing, it can be rational for individual investors to quickly withdraw from the market.

This herd behavior is based on the assumption that the market has an informational advantage. You'll feel safer if you sell alongside everyone else, even if you're convinced that the market sell-off is excessive. You'll join in when you notice that everyone else wants to sell. The downward spiral has started. No one wants to be the last person holding the bag when panic takes hold of investors. When trading, as in most areas of life, the devil takes the hindmost.

REMEMBER

Protecting your trading account should be your utmost priority. If you've reached the loss tolerance threshold you set for yourself as part of your predefined set of trading rules, you must sell along with everybody else. Capital preservation secures your survival in volatile markets.

Caution: Contagion Ahead!

Psychologists have extensively researched the phenomenon of *emotional contagion*, where the observed behavior of one individual leads to the reflexive production of the same behavior by others. Positive and negative feelings are unwittingly conveyed via facial expressions, gestures, and body language and lead to the affective imitation of the person being observed. Empathy and compassion are characteristics that are necessary for survival — characteristics that humans have acquired over the course of evolution. We allow ourselves to be carried away by other people's feelings. (Feelings of fear can be quite contagious, as you've probably experienced.)

TECHNICAL
STUFF

Gustave Le Bon, the founder of mass psychology, explains clearly, in his 1895 study *The Crowd: A Study of the Popular Mind,* how emotional contagion among the masses works. When present, emotional contagion awakens a high level of connectedness and works to subordinate individual interests. The simplest of emotions dominate. Opinions, assumptions, and rumors bubble up, goad each other on, and work to form a collective belief.

The mood on the stock market constantly leads to emotional contagions. For example:

>> Positive moods and expectations of market participants generally lead to rising prices.

>> A pessimistic mood among investors leads to falling prices.

>> If everyone is euphoric on the stock market, we are happy to allow ourselves to get carried away.

>> If, on the other hand, fear is spreading, it will get us too.

Given such feelings, it should come as no surprise that you run the risk of making trading decisions at precisely the wrong time.

The reason the risk of contagion exists is that the true value of a share is never known. Today's stock market prices reflect the different expectations of the market participants about an uncertain future. The opinions and analyses about the market mutually influence each other and lead to contagion effects. The feeling of uncertainty favors *information cascades* — situations where you make a decision based on the observation of others without regard to your own, private information. You suspect that others know more, so you surrender to majority opinion and ignore your own market assessment.

REMEMBER

In the early days of the stock market, when traders were making direct exchanges on the parquet floor, traders made regular emotional outbursts. Stress, chaos, and lots of yelling were part of everyday life on the trading floor. Fear and euphoria lay side by side. Emotions ran high, but it was also possible to tamp down emotions by being in direct contact with others. In modern computer-based trading, however, such direct contact between market participants is lacking. The risk of contagion has not been averted by any means.

The increasing proportion of automatic trading programs frequently makes price movements erratic. The unwieldy, anonymous masses of various actors on the stock exchange make you feel unsafe when you're trading. This means the risk of contagion is particularly great.

Insecurity about price changes and the fear of missing the right entry or exit point can lead to falling behind and chasing after the market and the prices. You react in a particularly sensitive way.

If a sufficient number of market participants trade while caught in the same mood, it can quickly lead to irrational exuberance. If everybody buys and the prices rise, it's contagious. The market knows more and is always right, you think. You're infected and you buy blindly, along with the masses. The fear of losses in falling markets is even more contagious. You sell along with the masses, without reflecting on what you're doing.

TECHNICAL STUFF

A particularly fatal form of contagion in the financial markets is the bank run. It refers to a stampede of customers to their bank where they have deposits that they want to withdraw as quickly as possible, regardless of whether they have a valid reason to do so: If there is any doubt regarding the solvency of a bank, it creates a crisis of confidence. It's rational for individual bank customers to want to withdraw their money as fast as possible and not be last in the queue. The fear of losing money leads to a self-fulfilling prophecy. The contagion effect creates the risk that all customers fear: The bank goes bankrupt. Domino effects in the entire banking market can occur at any time. (Economic history is filled with many examples of just this phenomenon.)

"Your deposits are safe!" At the height of the financial crisis in 2008, German chancellor Angela Merkel and her finance minister wanted to reassure German retail investors with this promise. Her words were enough to halt a rush of citizens determined to withdraw their deposits held by the banks. The risk of contagion was averted. The far-reaching promises rebuilt lost confidence.

FOMO: The great fear of missing out

In the English-speaking world, FOMO, or *fear of missing out*, is a well-known and often-used acronym for a form of social concern and anxiety. It is the fear of missing an important event or circumstance. Psychologists use this phrase to refer to a compulsive worry of no longer being up to date and, under certain circumstances, of missing out on important events. This phenomenon has been reinforced by social media, with social anxiety disorders sometimes being the result.

The acronym FOMO has also become common parlance in financial markets. The media likes to use the term *FOMO trade* as a way of referring to a more complex phenomenon. When markets reach new heights, the investors who aren't invested fear missing out on the bull market. A new, all-time high is a clear indicator of FOMO trades. The pressure of being left behind becomes unbearable. You buy because you want to belong and because you fear being left standing in the lurch, staring after the rising market. It feels so much better to be with the herd, even if your intellect knows you're acting irrationally. It's when you have protected yourself against falling stock prices or have built up short positions or aren't invested at all that you come under pressure to act. Pessimists then buy in a booming market against their will and against their better judgment. This compulsive herd mentality often leads to market exaggerations or even speculative bubbles.

In a bear market, on the other hand, investors tend to go from fear of missing out to fear of holding on — from FOMO to FOHO, so to speak. No investor wants to be the last one to get into booming markets. And no investor wants to be the last one to get out of collapsing markets.

REMEMBER

Professional investors can also be caught making FOMO trades. The performance and competitive pressures in the investment industry make FOMO trades hard to resist. When markets rise more than expected and investment managers have incorrectly positioned themselves, they may have to cover short positions and buy even more shares contrary to their strategy, regardless of the price. Otherwise, the investment manager will be expected to explain to their clients at the next investment committee meeting why they missed their benchmark. The fear of being significantly behind the benchmark is somewhat cynically referred to as FOMU, or fear of massively underperforming. For individual fund managers, it's basically more rational to steer toward a cliff along with the masses rather than try to stand alone against the market and be trampled by the herd. That's because, if customers pull out their money and investment funds experience massive outflows, their own career is at stake. When seen in this light, professional investors are also pushed by the markets. They have to chase after every rally, only to have to flee when the next correction comes round.

TINA: There is no alternative

When no alternative investment opportunities are available, it's known, appropriately enough, as TINA (*there is no alternative*). This principle was trumpeted by former British prime minister Margaret Thatcher, who used it to underscore her contention that alternatives to her government's economic policies didn't exist. "There is no alternative" was the polemical hyperbole.

In later phases of a bull market, it's often said that there could be no alternative to further investing in equity markets. In the zero-interest-rate environment of recent years, other asset classes produced hardly *any* returns, so overweighting equities was easy to justify. No other fundamental reasons were ever put forward to justify this reliance on the stock market. In accordance with the TINA effect, market participants buy shares only because they supposedly have choice but to buy risky stocks. Market dips are defined reactively as a favorable buying opportunity, in line with a buy-the-dip mentality. A bubble occurs, where the valuation of the markets is decoupled from the real economy. When bond yields rise, market sentiment can change rapidly and TINA is dead.

REMEMBER

In trading, don't let the TINA effect turn you into a victim. The most important criterion for any trading decision lies in a thoroughgoing fundamental and technical analysis. There are always alternatives. It's always better, for example, to have a high cash position in your portfolio than to end up in a stock market collapse being overweighted in stocks.

REMEMBER

FOMO trades, TINA effects, and reactive buy-the-dip strategies are all hallmarks of speculative bubbles that inevitably will be corrected. Protect your portfolio with sensible diversification of risk.

Dealing with Information Overload

The flood of news in the modern information age is overwhelming. When you trade on financial markets, you're overwhelmed by more or less relevant information every second — never forget that this is how the media makes its money. Headlines and reality often diverge. The media wants to arouse emotions, not provide objective information. And don't forget that humans, by nature, pay more attention to negative information than may be necessary. Humans are naturally biased and tend toward distortions in perception. Be clear about this: Your fundamental and technical analysis of the markets is always subjective, error-prone, and dependent on your mental and physical condition.

Serious or not? Separating the wheat from the chaff

It isn't easy separating wheat from the chaff. It's often hard to make out the truth or the origin of many messages. Press agencies release news that spreads to media channels like wildfire. A big order, a technological innovation, or a new business field will be picked up by many media sources and packaged as an exciting story. The variation and repetition of already known information can have a trend-strengthening effect.

NOISE: THE SOUND OF LEAVES IN THE FOREST

The Nobel Prize winner Daniel Kahneman assumes that decision-making processes are unreliable and error-prone. Market participants can all too easily be influenced by irrelevant factors, whether they're emotional states or external circumstances — or both. Kahneman refers to these disturbance factors as *noise* — that is to say, *noise that only serves to distract*. The random variability in decision-making processes (chance variability of judgments) is not to be confused with distortions in perception (biases). A bias has a pattern and a tendency in a certain direction. For example, you consistently see indicators only for downside risks. That is a bias. Noise is random, unpredictable, and it impairs accuracy. That is why it's so important to identify noise and shut it out. Concentrate on the essential decision-making parameters in trading. Less is more. Avoid sensory overload in the multimedia information age.

For individual investors, it's often hard to recognize similar stories that, instead of being independent of each other, in fact only originate from a single source. Small cause, big effect, you might say. The connection between cause and effect is not linear but is exponential. This inevitably leads to irrational market reactions when assessing and pricing in the impact of the news. When, for example, two traders discuss the upside potential of a stock, it can happen that both of them base their judgment on the analysis and recommendation of the same study. Without knowing that their estimates are not independent of each other, the study will be counted twice (double counting), and in so doing, this lends too great a weight in the opinion-forming process of both traders.

Facing the tabloid syndrome

The media landscape has changed dramatically. In earlier times, you could find reliable information via the print media. The financial press were often opinion makers who set trends. And, when the supermarket tabloids reported on the stock exchange, experienced traders would view them with suspicion. For a long time, there was no better counter-indicator. Empirical studies showed that, if tabloid newspapers were celebrating unlimited profit opportunities on the stock exchange, then the end of the bull market wasn't far away. Similarly, the next upturn wasn't far away if the tabloids were speculating a bear market that would last many years. Investors referred to these media exaggerations as *tabloid newspaper syndrome*.

REMEMBER

Journalists display their own herding behavior. Even if there are fewer and fewer opinion leaders in the media landscape in the digital age, you can still discern a recognizable pattern in the dissemination of news: A well-known medium provides direction, and the flock of journalists follow blindly, copying the story in a variety of ways.

Fighting the contagion of recurring messages

The democratization of access to information via generally accessible digital media reinforces movements in either a positive or negative direction. Continuously repetitive messages are the order of the day. The problem is that market participants are too easily influenced by media reporting. Behavioral economists at the University of Bonn have been able to prove in experiments that humans tend to see recurring messages as more credible and to attach great importance to them.

In the case of positive information, you'll end up being too optimistic, and in the case of negative information, you'll be too pessimistic. The effects on your behavior in trading are dramatic, economists claim. You'll regularly overestimate the upside potential and fuel the bubble with further purchases. Or you miss favorable entry opportunities because you're feeling excessively negative. You remain on the seller side and fuel the downturn in the markets.

George Akerlof and Robert Shiller, both winners of the Nobel Memorial Prize in economic sciences, analyzed the phenomenon of the spread of recurring messages and stories in their research. They concluded that the recurrence of similar stories in social networks can distort opinions so much that it leads to irrational bubbles and sharp corrections in the markets.

Experiments by the Bonn researchers confirmed the analyses by Akerlof and Shiller. Recurring news leads to misjudgments by market participants. These self-reinforcing effects can affect entire markets and trigger exaggeratedly strong or weak market phases.

Media reporting often follows price developments and not vice versa. "It is not the news that make the prices, but the price action makes the news!" warned Andre Kostolany. When the markets unexpectedly move in one direction, the reasons for that movement come later. Usually, there is no rational explanation or causal relationship. The media are expected to supply an explanation, or a "story." That is their business. Beware of false conclusions.

Robert Shiller is convinced that market participants are unable to independently process new developments. The actors on the financial markets observe each other and look for orientation. First, they must agree on an interpretation of the new events. Often, the triggers are fear-producing images or unpredictable consequences. Once an avalanche starts rolling, it can no longer be stopped. The herd mentality of investors then suddenly leads to a highly contagious panic reaction.

Don't forget that the explanations of market movements are based on old valuation criteria and on knowledge gained from looking backward to the past. You use what you already know as a point of reference. If developments take place that don't match your existing criteria, you suffer from cognitive dissonance, which leads directly to

» Blocking out useful information and suppressing what you don't want to hear

» Ignoring the facts

You make the world fit your preconceived beliefs. You subconsciously assume a return to normal (known as mean reversion).

Because the media make a lot of money doing so, they are committed to stirring up fear and panic on the one hand and euphoria and greed on the other. Don't forget this fact when you're assessing information for your trading decisions.

Search out just a few serious and reliable sources of information and stick to them. You don't need more than that.

Discovering Slowness

Dynamic and complex financial markets require high levels of attentiveness and fast reactions when you're trading. Unfortunately, the human psyche is not up to the task. When new, price-relevant information arrives, you'll find it hard to quickly adapt your market assessment.

Living with conservatism

When faced with market developments, you're going to react particularly slowly if the information contradicts your expectations. In behavioral economics, this empirically proven phenomenon is known as *conservatism*. "There are always more reasons to wait than to act" is conservatism's motto.

You'll also react particularly slowly to information and data that is complex or difficult to understand. You may in fact prefer to overlook it. By contrast, you'll perceive news connected to pictures and gripping scenarios more strongly. The human brain loves stories with lots of imagery.

In economic theory, the idea that financial markets are efficient has dominated for a long time. Supposedly, all existing information is already fully reflected in share prices. That means, according to the *market efficiency hypothesis*, no investor can continuously generate above-average returns. So much for the theory. The reality is different.

Gauging the profit announcement drift

Share prices often react with a time delay to any news that deviate from the expectations of market participants. Such delayed price adjustments contradict the theory of the efficient market, but such adjustments have been confirmed over and over again through price developments after company numbers are published.

>> If a listed company reports better-than-expected results, the stock price will outperform the market and rise above average for weeks.

>> Results that are worse than expected may lead to further losses for several weeks.

Obviously, the repricing of the stock only occurs gradually over a period of up to 60 trading days, as numerous studies have shown. In financial market research, this statistically demonstrable phenomenon is known as *post-earnings-announcement drift,* or *PEAD.*

Private investors react surprisingly conservatively and cautiously. Their motto? "Time will tell." Changes in attitude take time. The reason is that expectations are based on assessments from the past, and the real numbers are incorporated in future earnings estimates only after some delay.

Even the big professional investors need time. First off, the earnings estimates are adjusted and the upside potential is determined. As investment companies often build up big positions in single stocks, it takes time to build up or dismantle these positions on the market. That's why investment managers use financial derivatives to hedge their portfolio — *overlay strategies,* to use the current jargon.

Moving massive investment sums is relatively slow. This explains the time delay for markets reacting to price-relevant news. That gives you, as a trader, the opportunity to position yourself at an early stage in the market. When companies have surprisingly good or bad results, the profit announcement drift often occurs. For several weeks, stock prices move continuously in one direction.

TIP

Take advantage of profit announcement drift and enter with a long or short position until the current share price reflects the new fundamental value of the company.

Turning the tables and taking advantage of your opportunities

Irrational price developments and speculative bubbles also offer opportunities to medium- to long-term investors. After all, every price distortion gets corrected sooner or later. The fundamentals still determine the long-term value of the stock. That's why you focus on real knowledge-based information and sober analyses. Less is more. You are unable to either process or verify the flood of information that overwhelms you via the online portals. Your decisions will not improve — quite the contrary. Many studies confirm this statement.

Fifteen thousand shareholders were interviewed as part of a somewhat older study at Rheinisch–Westfälische Technische Hochschule Aachen/Aachen University. The result? The vast majority assigned a very high level of importance to the information level of investment decisions. However, the reality is sobering: The decision-making process of most investors is characterized by mental and emotional biases, distorted perception, and selective information processing. And herd behavior.

You have an opportunity to participate successfully in the stock market even without huge amounts of expertise. All you need to do is pay attention to the psychology of the markets and your own emotionally conditioned thinking traps. Do you blindly follow majority opinion because you're uncertain and afraid that others know more than you? Does majority opinion cause the market to be exaggerated in one direction or the other? Does the media coverage fuel the market movements with their reports?

Always take a closer look. Consistently following a well-thought-out trading plan will provide you with a secure, stable base. Calmly check whether reasonable grounds exist for a market movement. Don't trade as long as you're feeling uncertain.

Chapter **14**

Getting a Better Grip on Your Trading Ego

This chapter is all about our fundamental weaknesses as human beings. Our egos, for example, are our greatest enemies when it comes to trading — and thus require special attention. You'll find out how to recognize (and learn from) mistakes without impacting your self-esteem. Regular self-reflection and the meticulous keeping of a trading journal are essential parts of this process.

Dismantling the Myth of Learning from Your Mistakes

"We learn from our mistakes" is a common enough phrase. It's based on the (unproven) assumption that humans learn from mistakes made in the past. Supposedly, mistakes are valuable experiences that allow us to be better in the future. At least that's the theory.

TECHNICAL STUFF

Psychology makes a distinction between good and bad errors. Good mistakes are constructive because they drive the learning process forward. Bad mistakes are destructive because no error analysis takes place afterward, which means we end up repeating the errors.

Psychologists and neuroscientists seem to agree with the German poet and lyricist Friedrich Rückert:

'From damage comes wisdom!'

All wise people say

Damage enough have I suffered,

Yet I am still a fool today.

This poem aptly describes the stark reality of the human learning process — or, to put it more bluntly, the reality that *no* learning takes place. This is especially true of financial markets, where a willingness to learn from mistakes is not often found. Studies show that market participants don't learn much from their mistakes, because they fail to recognize them as such.

Any error analysis, root cause analysis, or search for alternative strategies requires a certain amount of insight. However, such insight is usually nonexistent. When people make trading mistakes, they often don't even want to accept that any mistakes have taken place. They subconsciously apply a whole arsenal of mental tricks in order to reduce the cognitive dissonance arising from the possibility that they have (heaven forbid!) made a poor decision. That means they twist reality until it suits their beliefs. This is the case even when mistakes occur because of minor instances of negligence or inattention — mistakes that could easily have been corrected, in other words. Most traders have the necessary know-how it takes to avoid such errors — and serious strategic errors based on false conclusions are the exception here. Know-how, then, is not the issue. What is really missing is the ability to gain fundamental insights on the one hand and to acknowledge and recognize one's own mistakes on the other.

So, what could account for these missing abilities? Here's what comes to mind:

>> The illusion of control

>> The attribution of any success solely to your (supposedly extraordinary) talents

>> Hindsight bias

>> Overconfidence bias

>> Optimism bias

The next few sections of this chapter examine in greater detail each of these barriers to learning.

The Illusion of Control: Not Having the Handle on Things You Think You Have

You're firmly convinced that you have everything under control. When you make a sloppy mistake now and then, you initially refuse to let it unsettle you. You may even tell yourself, in your devil-may-care way, that everything will turn out okay — after all, everything has always gone well before. As a matter of fact, many traders believe they have some influence over the markets. Armed with this arrogant attitude, you end up underestimating the probability of making a bad trade or you subconsciously accept the risk of losing big. Traders often mistake randomness for control. Behind this reckless behavior is the feeling that you're good at assessing and controlling the markets. The thing is, you may not be that great at assessing the market, and it's certainly the case that no one on Earth can control it. Markets are based on probabilities; nobody can predict the outcome of any movement in stocks with complete accuracy.

You overestimate your abilities and, as a result, are suffering from what behavioral economists refer to as the illusion of control. This particular mental bias promotes perceptual distortions and prevents you from learning from your mistakes.

The illusion of control is reinforced if the following statements are true:

>> In the past, your seemingly safe forecasts have proven to be correct and you thus have experienced no major losses from mistakes you might have made.

>> You're especially well versed when it comes to one particular market, which has led to increased self-confidence on your part and a feeling that you're in control of your surroundings.

EXAMPLE

It has been a few years, but you might remember how stock exchange transactions used to be made: You submitted a securities order at your custodian bank, which was then executed by a broker on the stock exchange. You then received the execution on the next day. This process has changed dramatically. Today, in the age of electronic trading, you can directly and autonomously trade in real time. It's all in your hands. This suggests, however, that you have greater influence and control than is actually the case.

Thinking That the World Dances to Your Tune

Our self-esteem can easily be shaken when we engage in trading. That's why we're always looking for confirmation and recognition and suppressing errors and weaknesses. Don't you also get the sense that every win confirms your amazing abilities? Don't you also assign any and all losses to adverse market conditions or simple bad luck? It's always beyond your control and the market's fault when a trade goes wrong. (It's a martyr complex all the way.) All such thoughts and attitudes are your attempts to protect your ego.

What you're dealing with here is a particular heuristic and common emotional bias that behavioral psychologists refer to as errors of *self-attribution* or *self-enhancement*. Attributing successes to your own abilities and blaming failures on others prevents you from recognizing your own shortcomings. By making choices based on overconfidence in your own skills you eliminate any chance that you'd actually learn from your mistakes. In fact, self-attribution further strengthens the overestimation of one's own trading abilities. You take all the credit for your success and believe that you're much better at trading than is actually the case.

This behavioral pattern can have a significant impact on the rate of return on your portfolio, as described in these examples:

>> Under certain circumstances, you take higher risks because you overestimate your skills and underestimate random movements in the market.

>> You neglect risk diversification in your portfolio because you overweight individual securities you're confident about to an excessive degree.

>> You trade excessively *(overtrade)* because you suffer under an illusion of control and believe that you can influence the market.

Distinguishing between ability and luck

How can you recognize and avoid self-attribution errors? First of all, you need to question the reasons for your trading decisions so that you can fully understand them. The best way to do so is with the help of a trading journal, where you document everything in writing. (For more on keeping a trading journal, see Chapter 5.) James Montier, the well-known American market strategist, recommends asking yourself the following four questions:

- » Were you right for the right reasons (claiming skill), and were you able to make a profit?

- » Did you make profit for all the wrong reasons (luck, random profit that shouldn't fool you)?

- » Can you determine that your losses occurred for all the right reasons (bad luck, or the fact that rule-based implementation of your trading strategy will always mean some trading losses)?

- » Did you sustain losses because of the wrong reasons (your own mistakes or your own breaking of the rules)?

It is crucial that you recognize the answers to these two questions:

- » When were your profits caused by your trading expertise?

- » When were you just lucky?

When you understand where your weaknesses lie and what mistakes you have made, the learning process can begin. It's all a question of learning from mistakes through the insights you have gained. After you have achieved that, you're on your way to becoming a successful trader.

Taking on the humble trader role

The German writer Theodor Fontane famously said, "Between pride and humility there is a third element that is a part of life, and that is courage." Any truly successful trader has internalized humility and doesn't take themselves too seriously. They recognize and accept the market mechanisms and trade accordingly. This takes courage. After all, you have no influence on the market, and market price action is much more random than you can imagine.

Living with Hindsight Bias

One additional obstacle that makes it difficult to learn from mistakes in trading involves *hindsight bias*, a psychological phenomenon that can negatively affect your trading decisions. Hindsight bias is based on the idea that you tend to retroactively estimate the probability of an occurrence of a market movement much higher in hindsight than when the event was actually occurring. Looking back at the market event, you are convinced you could have predicted the outcome before it actually happened. This is not surprising. You usually feel smarter after the fact, and it is certainly easy to explain a market slump in hindsight because (obviously) there were enough signs to clue in an intelligent person like yourself. In hindsight, you subconsciously begin to see the slump as predictable.

The advantages of hindsight are obvious. Because you now know what actually happened, you're suddenly able to see quite clearly all the reasons that spoke in favor of the slump occurring — and to ignore all the signs that spoke against such a slump happening. You revise the probability of an outcome after the fact. The thing is, you couldn't have known any of it when you initially had to make your assessment. After the slump, you're no longer able to empathize with the situation you were in when you first assessed the market. You underestimate the degree of uncertainty you were faced with at that time. The (current) knowledge of an event eliminates any (past) uncertainty, and you automatically come to one conclusion or another — all with the benefit of hindsight. This may cause overconfidence in your ability to accurately predict future market developments.

The outbreak of the global financial crisis in 2007 provides a striking example of hindsight bias. In hindsight, experts deemed the crisis as both inevitable and predictable. From their current perspective, everybody supposedly knew exactly what was coming. And, knowing what would happen, we fail to carefully review the reasons for the outcome. And yet, curiously enough, no one drew any conclusions about the consequences of the looming crisis.

The fact is, hardly anybody got the particulars of the crisis correct. In fact, critical voices who tried to warn about the coming danger were seen as paranoid. There was a general lack of introspection into the mistakes that were being made. If financial crises or bubbles were easy to spot as they occurred, they could have been avoided altogether.

Examining the specifics of hindsight bias

Hindsight bias is one of the major cognitive distortions: You overestimate your ability to determine probabilities. Applying this heuristic when trading results in your belief that you're in a better position than anyone else to predict future market movements. Those who know the outcome of a past event systematically overestimate their abilities to forecast future events. They lack each and every form of introspection; they fail to learn from their mistakes and are lulled in a false sense of security. Under certain circumstances, they may accept greater risks than they can tolerate. With the illusion of control, they allow the next market move to take them by surprise. But they always have a logical explanation for their actions — after the horse has left the barn.

TECHNICAL
STUFF

From an evolutionary point of view, hindsight bias makes sense. In order to survive, our ancestors needed to constantly be able to make decisions and take action. For that to happen, one needed self-confidence and the courage to make predictions. Mistakes may have been fatal for the individual but were advantageous for the development of mankind.

Dealing properly with past trading errors

The psychologist Nathaniel Branden once said, "The first step toward change is awareness." That sounds like a long learning process. It is. The first step is to recognize that you have made a trading error.

TIP

Take out your trading journal and write about the following questions in detail:

>> What were the arguments against your trading decision at that time?

>> What spoke in favor of it?

>> Which positive or negative signs did you recognize, and which ones didn't you see?

>> What forces could have led to a different market movement?

Confronting both sides of a decision forces you to make a more objective and realistic assessment of the market situation. This creates the necessary emotional distance that you require to recognize your trading errors.

Reining in Overconfidence Bias

Humans naturally have the tendency to systematically overestimate their own abilities and skills (overconfidence bias). This effect belongs to one of the cognitive biases, which can play a substantial role in trading decisions. Here, you overestimate your abilities in seemingly simple and well-known market situations. Interestingly, you tend to underestimate your abilities in complex and unknown situations.

WARNING

Many traders mistakenly think it's a good strategy to trade according to their personal convictions. The idea here is that, if you're convinced of a trading idea (high conviction trade), you should then enter a position at high risk. This is, of course, a fallacy. People tend to take unnecessary risks when their overconfidence is at its highest. Experience shows that people quickly lose their emotional balance when things go wrong. The problem with overconfident traders is that they tend to overtrade and fail to appropriately diversify their portfolios.

The perception of your own competence, in turn, influences your attitude toward ambiguity. Assume that you know your domestic stock market particularly well. You feel confident and competent. You're willing to recklessly invest in unknown domestic shares without knowing the risk or probable returns. In this case, your overconfidence potentially outweighs any concerns a more sensible person might have about the excessive risks you may be taking on.

Your ambiguity aversion always prevails when you don't sufficiently trust your own market assessment and abilities. This typically happens in foreign markets and unknown asset classes. You intuitively stay away from these and prefer to stick with what you know.

Handling Optimism Bias

Humans are optimistic by nature. We regularly assess future prospects as better than they actually are. This particular willingness to take risks, show courage, and demonstrate drive has shaped human development to this very day. It makes it easier for anyone to deal with stress and setbacks, because they're able to look ahead with confidence. People by nature have the tendency to overestimate the probability of positive events and underestimate the probability of negative events that can happen to them.

To no one's surprise, this unrealistic optimistic disposition is reflected in trading and financial markets as well. Studies show that *optimism bias* leads people to see positive market developments as significantly more probable than negative ones. This is confirmed by statistics on positions of market participants over time.

Optimism bias has a further effect in that most traders automatically assume that negative developments will affect only the portfolios of others and not their own. The implicit assumption is that they aren't affected by losses as frequently as others. They believe that they are better informed and act recklessly only under certain circumstances. They underestimate the risks and overestimate their abilities.

EXAMPLE

A great number of empirical studies explore how individuals draw false conclusions based on misplaced optimism. In a well-known experiment, students were asked to assess their risk of disease in comparison to the group average. Naturally, the majority of respondents judged their own risk to be below average. That is a contradiction because the average of the group couldn't all be at an under-average risk. You surely know the conviction of most car drivers — they insist that they drive better than average. In addition to being evidence of a poor grasp on mathematics, this too is a sign of unrealistic optimism.

REMEMBER

A healthy dose of optimism makes life easier. If you want to achieve something in life, you must trust your abilities. In that way, overconfidence can be motivating. You keep going and remain capable of action. You grow from defeats. Successful companies have also failed in the past. However, what may work in your day-to-day employment is not a good trading strategy. You don't want to lose money on the stock market. Failing means total loss and can frequently lead to financial ruin. Picking yourself up and starting all over again will no longer be an option. That's why you should be aware of any possible cognitive distortions that can trigger optimism bias. Be on the lookout for these conditions:

>> Overconfidence and giving in to the illusion of control

>> Neglecting risk diversification by focusing on a few familiar securities (concentration risk)

>> Having a one-sided focus on domestic investments (home bias)

>> Excessive confidence in positive media coverage

You may not even notice a tendency to be overconfident and overly optimistic when it comes to your trading habits. A trading journal can help open your eyes and gain self-knowledge.

TIP

Be sure to document the arguments and assessments that have led to your trading decisions. When you compare these records with reality, you can recognize the magnitude of the effects of all these distorting biases. Only then can you learn from your mistakes. With that out of the way, your next step should be to make a list of counter-arguments to your opinion when planning your next trade. This creates the emotional distance you need in order to make more objective and conscious decisions.

Chapter 15

Fear: Your Constant Trading Companion

This chapter deals with the strongest of all human emotions: fear. Fear is everywhere and frequently crops up in trading. Although feeling fearful is extremely unpleasant, it's crucial that you understand the source of your deep-rooted fears and face them head-on. That way, you'll see how to deal constructively with errors in trading instead of falling victim to regret and self-pity. If you use the techniques outlined here to avoid the evolutionary fear trap, you'll be able to maintain the emotional equilibrium you'll need to trade successfully.

Trading fears arise from a whole array of various thoughts in your mind and can cause emotional as well as physical reactions. If the markets take over control of you, you've already lost. You're emotionally vulnerable and you can quickly lose your balance. Change your thoughts and your reactions to them will also change, allowing you to behave differently.

TIP

In this context, affirmations can help you develop more constructive ways of thinking. For more on affirmations, check out Chapter 6.

There's a subtle difference between generalized anxiety and specific fear. This difference also makes its presence known in trading environments. *Anxiety* is an abstract, generalized feeling that arises in situations we humans see as threatening. *Fear,* on the other hand, refers to the specific reaction of the psyche to an actual danger or threat. From an evolutionary point of view, fear is necessary for survival because any human triggered by fear will immediately take defensive measures against threats. (You may know it as the *fight-or-flight mechanism*.) Fear and anxiety are primary emotions that trigger identical biochemical processes in the body. Conversationally, the two terms tend to be used interchangeably in common parlance.

Deep-rooted anxiety may come to light when you're trading, with the result that, for example, you're suddenly afraid that you aren't trading with the right trading system or you find yourself repeatedly looking for excuses not to open a position. Maybe in the past you suffered a series of losses that proved traumatic. With every new trade, you fear yet another staggering loss.

REMEMBER

In line with the conversational tone of this book, I use *fear* and *anxiety* interchangeably.

Reckoning with the Dominance of Emotions

Emotions play a major role in all trading decisions, so much so that emotions easily prevail in times of crisis. Market swings are often quite violent, frequently random, and usually not rational. Such volatility can easily knock you off balance, especially when you're in the red or you have missed out on some big opportunities. In both cases, you face the risk that you will lose your emotional balance and react impulsively, leading to a loss of control as well as to poor decision-making.

When it comes to the stock market, you can always find countless experts and brokers who try to explain an emotional topic using rational arguments. Even the solutions they recommend are mostly technical in nature, ranging from improved trading platforms to new sophisticated trading strategies. The truth is, however, that such technical solutions never work because they fail to address the human factor — the fact that humans, with their emotional outbursts, will always be the weak link in the chain. Systems and strategies lull people into a false sense of security — a security that does not (and never will) exist in volatile markets. Your inner uncertainty remains. Even exercises to improve self-discipline are insufficient. You cannot simply suppress your emotions over the long term. The only way to escape the evolutionary trap is to learn how to consciously deal with your emotions.

EXAMPLE

Imagine walking on a balance beam that is lying safely on the ground. "No problem," you think, as you stroll along in a totally relaxed fashion. Now imagine that the same balance beam has been suspended between two trees at a dizzying height. The tension rises as you shake in your boots at the thought of taking a single misstep.

You can easily trade free of emotion when you're trading on a demo account. As soon as you're trading with your own money, your emotions can overwhelm you.

Your discipline dissolves into thin air when basic human instincts, like fear and panic, come into play. Fear is the dominant emotion that arises when you're experiencing a roller-coaster of emotions with your trades. Nobody is spared from fear in trading. Fear, despair, rage, and anger trigger anxiety, which is why the challenges associated with trading have always been on the emotional level. Trading platforms and systems are important but do not determine your success.

TECHNICAL STUFF

The basic instinct of fear was the ultimate survival advantage in human evolution. Whoever quickly reacted to dangers would survive and pass on their genes. There was no time for rational considerations. Our genetically-based fear disposition has the function of sharpening our senses so that we can protect ourselves. In this sense, fear is a defense mechanism. When danger pops up, the automatic fight-or-flight response is triggered within fractions of a second. Fear is the strongest human emotion and eludes volitional control.

Fear is basically a biologically meaningful emotional reaction to an external threat or hazard. However, when the fears are related to your trading day (where — let's face it — you face no immediate and grave threat to your life), psychologists speak of baseless `groundless` anxiety.

THE EMOTIONAL STRESS AXIS

Strong emotions always lead to physical reactions. Negative emotions, such as anxiety or panic, usually make themselves known in the form of heart palpitations, increased blood pressure, muscle tension, shivering, or sweating. Neural circuits are responsible for sending stress signals to a region of the brain that controls the body's motor functions. The sympathetic nervous system is activated and prepares the body for archaic fight-or-flight situations. This biochemical pathway is proof of the brain-body connection. This natural stress response, preparing the body for action, developed over the course of our evolutionary development and hasn't changed much to this day. These processes are incompatible with the requirements of trading.

REMEMBER

Fear has a protective function and is designed to shield humans from physical and emotional risks. Trading is an emotional minefield that goes against our very nature because profits and painful losses are a natural part of the business in equal measures. This can be a stressful challenge for your self-confidence and self-esteem. (You can find techniques for strengthening your self-esteem and self-confidence in Chapter 6.)

Recognizing How Your Trading Fears Affect You

From an objective point of view, you have no reason to be anxious when trading. You've calculated your risk before making any trades and you know for a fact that losses are a perfectly normal part of trading life. Your intellect nods along approvingly, but your emotions follow a completely different script.

Generalized anxiety is the order of the day when it comes to trading, because you will always face uncertainty. You're working with probabilities and you have no control over potential gains or losses. The market may suddenly turn against you at any moment. You can only control your trading outcome to a certain extent with stop-loss and take-profit limits.

When trading, you always have to deal with your subliminal fear of making mistakes, failing completely, or simply losing control. Mistakes are painful and cost money — a lot of money, under certain circumstances. Your brain is incapable of correctly estimating the risks of loss and is permanently on alert. With your excessive need for control and your perfectionist tendencies, you try to keep your latent fears at bay — mostly in vain. Trading anxiety kills your confidence and makes you feel worthless.

Fear can be triggered very quickly and show up in trading in many ways:

>> You're afraid you won't find the right entry point.

>> You're afraid of missing lucrative trading opportunities or trends.

>> You're afraid of your setups being stopped out prematurely.

>> You're afraid of realizing small losses.

>> You're afraid of losing any book profits you might have gained.

>> You've experienced a series of losses and you're paralyzed by fear.

>> You're afraid of having to take responsibility for your mistakes.

>> You're afraid of failing when it comes to trading — and of failure in general.

>> You're afraid you'll use the wrong trading system when trading.

REMEMBER

When trading on the stock exchange, fear is the main reason that novice traders fail after just a short time. Brokers disparagingly call them *quarter customers* because most of them have to close their trading accounts within a few months — their first quarter, in other words.

Discarding beliefs that stand in your way

Sometimes, it's the deep-seated, limiting beliefs that subconsciously sabotage you in trading — beliefs inherited, for example, from parents or teachers who influenced you at an early age. Even if these experiences happened many years ago, they will have shaped your view of the world. One consequence of such deep-seated belief systems might be that you regard trading success as such with some distaste. This can play out in many different ways:

>> You don't allow yourself to be successful because part of you secretly believes that money is the root of all evil.

>> You don't allow yourself to be successful because trading is supposedly a slacker's way of earning easy money — it's not a lifestyle gained by doing difficult, honest, or serious work.

>> You're afraid that you're not ready for success because you were told early on that you were a loser and would never amount to much.

REMEMBER

Limiting belief systems and the fear of failure are ubiquitous — they're also among the biggest obstacles when it comes to achieving any kind of personal success. If you see yourself here, you should seek professional help in order to process these subconscious traps that only serve to sabotage you.

TIP

If you really and truly want to let go of your limiting beliefs, take a look at the self-coaching techniques I describe in Chapter 6. These can be quite helpful when it comes to overcoming fear and moving beyond limiting beliefs.

Dealing with defensive reactions caused by fear

In trading, fear triggers automatic defensive reactions, resulting in irrational behavior patterns like these:

>> You sell your winners too early.

>> You move your stop-loss limits and hang on to your losers for too long.

>> You're often unable to act or you're undisciplined.

>> You tend toward uncontrolled emotional actions.

>> You hesitate, wasting good opportunities and missing good entries.

>> You change your trading system and rules far too often.

REMEMBER

Fear is a strong emotion that fulfills an important protective function in your life. Fear arises in the deeper emotional areas of the brain. The *amygdala*, the fear center of the brain, takes care of the distribution of the stress hormones, adrenalin and cortisol, which fuel your body's corresponding defense reactions. When it comes to this particular process, your intellect is essentially switched off.

Developing strategies for crisis situations

Over the course of your life, you have developed a number of different strategies to cope with crisis situations you've faced. For the most part, you're completely unaware of the kinds of behavioral patterns you have internalized. How could it be otherwise? When you're in a state of anxiety, stress hormones ensure that you don't have to think — you're on autopilot. You've adopted tunnel vision as you stare down the danger confronting you.

Depending on your predisposition and personality structure, the neurotic processing of anxiety and stress states when trading occurs mostly in line with one of the following patterns:

>> **Fight mode**: You trade hectically, mindlessly, and much too often (compulsive staccato trading, in other words).

>> **Frozen in shock**: You're incapable of action and you stare at the markets like a deer in headlights.

>> **Flight mode**: You look away and turn off the computer because you don't want the losses to be real. (Out of sight, out of mind.)

>> **Panic mode**: You can no longer endure the pressure, so you sell everything, no matter the price. You just want to abandon the market as soon as you can.

TIP

You can counter the fear of losing control by staying active and trading small positions. For example, you might sell part of your loss positions or respond using a series of small, narrowly limited counter-positions. The trick is to remain capable of acting. Action soothes you and helps you regain your lost self-confidence.

Fear is always your partner when trading. Basically, you definitely have something to fear, and that is fear itself. This can lead to anxiety-ridden expectations and a fear that seems to be self-fulfilling.

Avoiding self-fulfilling prophecies

In trading, unexpected things always happen. You can't control the markets. Price movements are unpredictable. If you don't believe in your own success in trading, you'll unintentionally act in such a way that ensures success will always be out of reach — a vicious circle of mental blocks and self-sabotage. You're no longer able to access your competencies and you have given up before you even start, because you're afraid that you will be unable to fulfill your own expectations. Psychologists speak of a direct link (a feedback loop, in other words) between expectations and behavior. That's the theory of a self-fulfilling prophecy in a nutshell. This quote from Henry Ford sums up the idea admirably: "Whether you think you can, or you think you can't — you're right." Your thinking has a great influence on your ultimate success or failure.

Fear arises whenever you feel unprepared for a particular situation. If the anxiety you're experiencing solidifies into a permanent pattern, you need to stop trading and seek professional advice. After all, fear is the biggest obstacle to success.

But it doesn't need to come that far. With a bit of distance, you can learn to recognize where your fear is coming from, what its function is, and how your fear expresses itself.

REMEMBER

The good news is that this particular vicious circle can be broken. You can in fact overcome your trading fears. Just keep in mind that it's not a simple exercise. To quote Henry Ford again, "There are more people who surrender than those who fail."

Finding Your Way Out of the Fear Trap

The basic human genetic setup no longer suits the requirements of the digital era we live in today. The dangers, for the most part, are not life threatening. The basic instinct of fear as a protective mechanism against external hazards is unsuitable for your success on, say, complex financial markets.

REMEMBER

You *must* recognize and understand your trading anxiety. Fear leads to stress, loss of control, and poor decision-making. Fear poisons the mind.

Successful trading requires emotional balance. You can maintain it through a variety of measures:

>> Stress reduction through physical activity

>> Understanding your fear and putting it in the proper context

>> Self-reflection: Face your fear!

>> Correctly assessing consequences

>> Thinking in terms of success

>> Creating a sense of community

The next few sections examine each of these measures in greater detail.

Reducing stress through physical activity

The kinds of hazards someone faces in the trading world are of a rather abstract nature, and they require reactions other than fight-or-flight. Anxiety triggers the release of stress hormones and turns your body into the equivalent of a high-tension wire. Over the long term, this situation is harmful to your health because this type of stress level leads to the shutdown of important body functions. This tension, however, can be relieved by a program of physical activity. When trading, you're mostly sitting motionless in front of your various screens. Your state of stress continues and becomes chronic if the stress hormones aren't broken down. The consequences are feelings of being overwhelmed, anxiety, and panic attacks. In times of crisis on the stock exchange, the result is a massive and chronic stress response.

TIP

Physical activity is necessary to break down the stress hormones. Do some exercise, go for a walk, make sure you move your body and get a change of scenery. And don't forget to take regular breaks when trading. For example, do a few stretches every hour in order to compensate for sitting stock-still in front of the computer.

The human brain checks incoming information in terms of its physical effects. Fear and stress reactions are initially physical and humans are inherently programmed for activity. That's why movement and relaxation exercises are highly effective. Psychological tension and physical activity are incompatible; activity dissolves psychological tension and automatically relaxes you. As a result, your fear diminishes.

REMEMBER

Trading is one of the more stressful professions, simply because you're confronted with unforeseen events and potential losses over and over again. Now, you can't

A STOCK MARKET CRASH AS A CORTISOL SHOCK

The neuroscientist and former head trader at Deutsche Bank in New York, John Coates, quite impressively demonstrates the health consequences that high volatility and market slumps may have for market participants. Traders don't neutrally process information like a computer does; rather, they do so in an emotional and physical way. The brain-body axis ensures the immediate distribution of the stress hormones adrenalin and cortisol. The body is automatically prepared for action and physical activity. However, the expected physical discharge of tension doesn't take place because you're staring at a screen, motionless. The stress state becomes chronic with incalculable consequences for your health. In experiments, Coates was able to prove that traders become strikingly risk-averse when they're under chronic stress and were susceptible to panic selling with "the herd." Looked at that way, a stock market crash stands revealed as a cortisol shock.

prevent stress hormones from being released, but you can ensure that the stress hormones get broken down again. For that to happen, you need to have the right mindset — a focused mental state when you're trading that includes a commitment that you'll take the time for physical activity.

Regularity and structure are important psychological factors. When you're stressed, it's important to have proven processes and routines. They give you a foundation and orientation in times of trouble and prevent the dreaded tunnel vision from taking over. Stabilizing patterns and solid structures keep you from losing your nerve. In that way, you remain disciplined and have a clear head for making trading decisions that are well-thought-out.

TIP

Introduce solid structures into your trading day. Plan your daily schedule in advance and keep to it, day after day. These rituals serve as anchors that will help keep you grounded.

COMPULSIVE ACTS

You must not lose your nerve when the markets spiral out of control. If you lose control, your fear systems take the command — with sometimes disastrous consequences. In this context, psychologists speak of recurrent compulsive behaviors that are in fact merely attempts to deal with the fear.

Uncertainty and fear repeatedly lead to acting blindly, merely because they offer the appearance of being in control. Action calms the nerves at a superficial level — the irrational panic buying of food and toilet paper in crisis times are visible examples. Compulsive washing is another typical example of such structuring compulsions.

Putting your fears in the proper context

Your fear isn't the result of the supposed dangers of the stock market — they are the result of what you have learned to see as dangerous over the course of your life. That's quite a different kettle of fish. It's always your subjective opinion of the market that reigns supreme, because your convictions and your beliefs determine your trading patterns. Violent market swings trigger fear and terror in many traders while they cause others to reach their peak performance.

Be clear about the fact that fear always involves a processing system that relies on data rooted in the past. Whatever you believe that might pose a danger, and therefore triggers fear in you, can mostly likely be traced to bad experiences you've had. If, for example, you experienced a painful series of losses in the past, it takes only a single trigger to awaken the old fears you had stored away. Your emotional memory instinctively tries to bring these old experiences into the present, in the mistaken belief that the present situation will result in the reoccurrence of the same losses from the past. These emotional memories thus serve to impact your ability to trade successfully in the present day.

Every trader has stored away behavioral patterns that end up being triggered by fear — this is normal. Stop for a moment and carefully assess the current situation to see whether you really and truly have grounds for this fear. If you're afraid that you'll sustain heavy losses, check your trading setup. Make sure you set the stop-loss limits for each position in such a way that they don't exceed your maximum loss tolerance.

The truth is, we humans always dredge up fears from the past and bring them back into the present, even when such fears have nothing to do with the current market situation. Such fears nevertheless work to sabotage any hope for an objective inner trading attitude that's appropriate for current circumstances. Losses that have been insufficiently processed in the past always catch up with you. You lack the right mindset, which means you'll be unable to control or suppress your stored fear reflexes. Such reflexes inevitably come to the surface when you come under pressure.

Violent market swings are often only the external triggers for inner fear linked to past negative experiences. Many traders subconsciously insist on a strategy of attempting to assert some kind of external control on markets rather than do the necessary work of clearing their minds of the residues of past traumas. Markets, however, cannot be, and never will be, controlled. Fighting the markets is always hopeless. Basically, you end up fighting against yourself because you're afraid of facing your own fears.

The sections in Chapter 6 dealing with self-coaching outline a number of mental strategies for coping with stress and anxiety.

Practicing self-reflection and facing your fears

We humans all carry with us harmful burdens from our past to some extent. We *all* suffer from the consequences of these burdens, despite the fact that we often don't even know the origin of these emotions. Suppressing fears and letting sleeping dogs lie is usually the strategy we subconsciously apply.

A better strategy is to consciously face our fear. The way out of fear is to push through it. Start by recognizing the patterns and then ask yourself these questions:

>> Where does this fear come from?

>> When does fear rise to the surface, and in which situations?

>> What images and memories are evoked?

>> What, precisely, happens to me? How shall I respond?

>> What effect does my anxiety have on my trading success?

>> How does my fear relate to the current market situation?

>> What conscious or subconscious purpose might these fears fulfil?

Here's something straight out of the psychologists' bag of tricks: Face your fear! By that, I mean that you should consciously recognize your fear and speak to it. It doesn't matter how you go about it. If you feel like it, get angry. Say to yourself: "I see you. You messed up my market entry, but next time I'll be more careful!" An inner dialogue such as this one automatically creates emotional distance. You expand your perspective rather than fall into the tunnel vision trap. The trick is to escape the emotion so that you can feel relief. Your head is free again.

Basically, it's all about taking the observer role and consciously thinking about what happens to you when you enter a state of fear. Observe without judgment, and grapple constructively with your emotional states. The regular confrontation with your fear is a good exercise that will, over time, contribute to a form of desensitization.

REMEMBER

Your fear is a processing pattern from the past, not a meaningful response to the present.

Rather than reflexively push away your fear, you can learn to accept it as something that a) belongs to the past and b) is designed to protect you against future errors. This self-protection mechanism is the part of your fear that you should always appreciate because that part serves as a helpful warning signal for similar situations in the future. When you have grasped this fact, you can take the next step and decouple from your current trading situation those fears originating from your past.

TIP

As soon as you feel fear, immediately stop trading. Only when you have created the necessary inner distance to markets and your positions should you feel free to act again.

In this context, short meditation sessions and breathing exercises can help you

>> Regain an inner distance to trading

>> Remove the effect that fear may have over you

>> Free you from ever feeling at the mercy of fear

>> Regain emotional balance and control

When you have achieved all this, you have managed to acquire the right mindset for successful trading.

TIP

If you can't get anywhere with this form of self-reflection, or if it's hard for you to face your fears on your own, please seek professional assistance. After all, fear is the biggest obstacle to your success in trading.

Correctly assessing consequences

Generalized Uncertain fears serve to paralyze you when trading. However, what you're afraid of hasn't occurred yet. Fear about future events is playing havoc with your imagination. Try to specify exactly what the consequences of your actions will be. Ask yourself these questions:

>> What could happen?

>> How realistic or likely are the consequences?

>> How badly can my misjudgment affect my portfolio? Or, in other words, how big might my trading losses be?

When you ask yourself these questions, you quickly discover how nonspecific many of your fears can be and how little they may have to do with your actual current situation. From the perspective of a neutral observer, you'll be not only better able to realistically assess the consequences of your trading decisions but also in a better position to recognize anxiety-producing thought patterns.

TIP

Ask a trader colleague to provide an external assessment of your actions. Exchanges with like-minded people can help calm your nerves.

Thinking in terms of success

When you're in a state of fear, you become disconnected from your basic competencies. A discrepancy now exists between your desire to be a successful trader and your current condition, ruled as it is by your fear of mistakes, losses, and failure. You can blast through this blockage by collecting and visualizing your previous trading successes. More specifically, you can

>> Remember successful strategies and how you profited as a result of your trade

>> Remember the feelings of happiness associated with the winning trade

>> Imagine the later opportunities and potential for profit you can have with your strategies

>> Try to imagine, using as much detail as possible, the good feelings your success will bring you

Focus on the positive, and counter any and all vague predictions of failure with actual, proven patterns of success. In doing so, you'll become more aware of your successes and strengths. By already putting yourself in the emotional state you want, you anticipate trading success and regain access to your competencies. After all, you *can* trade successfully. You have demonstrated as much on several occasions! That's what's called a winner's mindset.

TECHNICAL
STUFF

The human brain doesn't distinguish between actual success stories and the success stories you imagine. In both cases, reward centers in the brain release *dopamine*, the happiness hormone, strengthening your self-confidence and increasing your motivation. For more on this topic, see Chapter 6.

TIP

If you regularly suffer from trading fears, write them all down in a success journal! Set aside time every day to note everything you did right — every last positive experience, every profitable trade, and every emotion accompanying a success. Maybe you will recognize patterns of success. (More on that in Chapter 5.) I'm certain you'll feel more confident. Visualizing your successes and then documenting them in writing helps you focus on your competencies instead of foregrounding the negative. You won't find a better way to protect yourself against emerging fears.

Creating a sense of community

Humans aren't naturally lone wolves — they're actually quite social beings. In evolutionary history, it was always an advantage to be part of a group. Our ancestors were unable to survive on their own.

A healthy social environment also gives us stability, recognition, and security. Trading, however, is an uncommonly lonely occupation, where most traders sit alone the whole day in front of computer screens and talk to themselves. The inner dialogue can be brutal at times. You're never as harsh to anyone as you are to yourself, which makes you prone to self-doubt and feelings of fear. Anxiety researchers point out that fear is almost always the direct result of a lack of a sense of community.

Among your circle of friends and acquaintances, you'll rarely find people who empathize with your moods, let alone understand what it is that you actually do in front of all those screens. Trader forums and group chats are no substitute for a true interpersonal dialogue.

So, with whom can you discuss and develop trading ideas? Regular exchanges with like-minded traders are irreplaceable. You feel understood and you get a chance to be mutually supportive, both technically and mentally. This creates a sense of community and gives everyone involved strength and discipline. You can hold the mirror up to each other and develop together. It's helpful when someone says, "Hey, maybe today you should stop trading and secure your profits" or "You're fighting against the markets in an attempt to recoup losses — that's sure to go wrong."

To find out more about the benefits of real and virtual networks, see Chapter 5.

Look for a trader coach trained in psychology as a sparring partner, and then regularly maintain contact with that individual in person, by phone, or by chat. The dialogue you establish will enable you to learn how to know yourself better and in that way leave behind subconscious anxieties. Do that and you'll be well on your way to becoming a successful trader.

Forcing individuals to sit in front of screens all day without making a move would be called cruel and unusual punishment if it were accorded to convicted criminals — cruel to the body as well as to the mind. Trading is, by all accounts, a massive physical and mental burden — one that is foreign to our very nature.

That's why regular physical activity as a way to counteract the effects of such burdens is so important, as is the need to maintain one's emotional distance when it comes to markets.

The Fear of Feeling Regret

"Repentance is an insight that arrives too late to be of any use" is a quote attributed to the Austrian physician Ernst von Feuchtersleben. Humans instinctively strive not to make decisions they might regret afterward. We usually only see that we've made a mistake after the fact. When regret does set in, it usually hits us hard emotionally. Suddenly we realize that we did everything wrong. "If only I had known . . .", you soberly think. But now it's too late. This drive to avoid regret and remorse at all costs is immense, and it distorts our decision-making behavior.

Knowing what to do when facing regret

Trading errors are the order of the day. Even the best trading strategies won't protect you against bad trades. The problem is that your trader psyche can't deal with mistakes and subconsciously wants to avoid unpleasant feelings of remorse.

Such examples of what is called regret aversion in behavioral economics occur in trading when

> >> You have to admit that you've made a bad trading decision
> >> You subsequently realize that you missed making the right trading decision

It's not the market that's responsible for any trading losses you experience or profits you let slip away. It's you. You're personally responsible. So, when bad things happen, you have major regrets. You blame yourself, convinced that you were either too hesitant or that you somehow overlooked something.

EXAMPLE

After completing a thorough market analysis, you decide to buy a certain technology stock. Your timing is great, and the share price goes up from $50 to $60 in a short time. You're satisfied. Now the share price stagnates at a high level. You start to get nervous because some analysts have corrected their forecasts downward for the industry. Prices begin to fall and you quickly decide to sell.

A few days later, a takeover bid occurs and the price explodes, rising to $100. You rage away, regretting the earlier sale. You promise not to sell next time, even if this turns out to be a wrong decision in retrospect.

As this example shows, you tend to value missed winnings higher than the relief that comes from avoiding losses. You prefer to hold a losing position rather than run the risk of exiting a winning position too early and missing out on a further increase in share prices. Your desire to avoid feelings of regret is often stronger than the subconscious desire to realize profits quickly. The aversion to regret can sometimes be overpowering. This, of course, runs counter to all reason.

Obeying before the fact

The crucial point to remember is that regret aversion is so strongly conditioned in you that it unintentionally influences and distorts your future decisions. In other words, when it comes to placing your trades, you'll always take into account the feeling of regret that you may feel if you find out you have made a wrong decision. You'll always compare your actual trades with all the alternative trades you might have made at the time of the decision. For example, you'd wrack your brains in self-reproach, telling yourself that if you had only chosen the long entry instead of opening a short position at the day's low, you'd have made a killing.

Naturally, this kind of self-reproach has consequences. After all, your brain is allergic to negative emotions. Regret and remorse trigger dissonance, which you've been trained to avoid at all costs.

Let's face it: You refuse to admit you made a poor trading decision. This avoidance strategy in trading results in the following irrational thought and behavior patterns, sometimes called escalation of commitment:

>> You mentally create fictitious mental accounts where you evaluate your missed gains and all the losses you supposedly could have avoided.

>> You hold on to your winning positions for far too long and miss out on opportunities for realizing gains.

>> You hold on to losing positions for far too long because you're afraid that prices might rise again after you closed the position.

>> You tend toward herd behavior because you believe you can limit future regret if you follow the crowd for protection — meaning that you won't be left standing alone with your bad decision.

Avoiding feelings of regret will lead to irrational and inappropriate trading decisions. You want to protect yourself from the disappointment of making bad judgments in the future. In order to justify this behavior, you borrow from evolution's bag of tricks. That way, you free yourself from cognitive dissonance and your ego is once again calm. Your calm is undisturbed, despite the fact that your trading performance probably suffers because you've chosen to close your eyes and you've also proven to be unwilling to develop any further.

REMEMBER

Regret aversion is a strong emotion that can a) quickly knock you off balance and b) impact your trading performance over the long term. When regret comes into play, the disposition effect — the one that causes you to take out profits too early — is temporarily suppressed.

The fear of regret also explains why it's so difficult for many traders to keep a trading journal. The documentation and subsequent monitoring of your trades force you to face your mistakes and weaknesses. This is certainly an unpleasant task, but it's absolutely necessary if you're in any way serious about your future development.

TIP

Regretting your trading decisions is never helpful. It focuses on the past rather than on the future. The fact is, there's simply no way you go back in time and reverse your bad trades. Be courageous, be honest with yourself, and direct your attention to learning to continually improve your trading.

Seeing why traders prefer to do nothing

You'll notice that, given the choice, you prefer to regret something you did rather than something you didn't do when it comes to trading. A winning trade you closed too early will annoy you much more than a losing trade you let run. It's an interesting observation because humans tend to subconsciously tolerate errors resulting from negligence better than mistakes resulting from a conscious action. Keeping a position and doing nothing is easier than making an active decision and acting accordingly. This behavior anomaly is closely linked with the status quo effect. (For more on the status quo effect, see Chapter 12.)

To see how the status quo effect plays out, imagine the following: Trader A has a position in Apple shares and is thinking about switching to Microsoft shares. He decides against it. In hindsight, he realizes that he missed out on profits totaling $2,000 because he failed to act in time. Trader B has a position in Microsoft shares and decides to switch the position to Apple stock. In doing so, he also misses out on profits of $2,000. Both traders are angry about failing to realize the same amount of winnings. However, experiments show that the emotional response is quite different. Trader B regrets his actions considerably more than Trader A — the trader who did nothing. It's living proof that we humans prefer to cling to the status quo and avoid change.

You should never underestimate the fear of making mistakes, a fear that is particularly evident if you have made a series of bad trades. Emerging self-doubt affects your ability to act, which means that you hardly dare to take risks. Regret aversion paralyzes you.

DIVIDEND STOCKS

Studies show that private investors prefer stocks with dividend payments. There's more involved here than merely a desire for secure holdings:

- On the one hand, annual payments serve as justification for longer holding periods.

- On the other hand, annual distributions can help reduce regret if you could have achieved higher gains by investing in other stocks (or dividends as consolation for missed profits, one might say.)

TIP

As long as you correctly implement your setups, you should never allow yourself to be swayed by a series of bad trades. Put some emotional distance between yourself and the markets for a while. Use the time off to research opportunities for when you return to the markets in a more emotionally balanced state of mind.

It's paradoxical (because it's contrary to prior observations) that as time goes by, and with sufficient emotional distance, you tend to regret what you didn't do much more than what you did. Seen in the bright light of day, you don't understand why you lacked the courage to take action, even when such actions sometimes turn out to have been mistakes. You wasted many opportunities and wish that you had decided differently. Failure to carry out trades for fear of making mistakes is the one mistake you'll probably regret the most.

REMEMBER

Pity the trader who has nothing to regret — after all, they can't develop. You can't change the past, but you can learn from it.

6

The Parts of Ten

Chapter **16**

Ten Psychological Traps to Avoid When Trading

In this chapter, I present you with a list of ten psychological traps to avoid when trading — a list you should always keep in mind whenever you have anything to do with the stock market. By no means exhaustive, this list focuses on a small selection of the potential dangers you might face simply because psychological pitfalls are sometimes highly individualized and depend to a great extent on one's character, abilities, personal strengths, and personal weaknesses. (Addressing each instance is beyond the scope of this book.)

Dismissing Demo Accounts Out of Hand

Beginners are often impatient and tend to overestimate their abilities. They rush in, open trading accounts, and listen avidly as their brokers encourage them to get started trading right away. Beginners are generally greedy, and the dream of earning easy money makes them cocky. Fools rush in where angels fear to tread, and the inevitable occurs: The psychological trap snaps shut and they end up having to pay out a lot of money for lessons learned.

That's why experienced traders truly appreciate their demo accounts. With paper trading, you get a chance to test your strategies while patiently practicing your various processes and setups. By adopting paper trading, beginners can gain valuable experience by trying out different markets, different financial instruments, and different time frames with no financial risk. With a few dry runs in simulation mode, you can determine the right trading style for your personality.

TIP

Every pilot spends hundreds of hours in flight simulators in order to internalize techniques they have to be able to retrieve automatically in case of emergencies — trading simulations serve the same purpose.

Insisting On Flying by the Seat of Your Pants

You can understand why many traders want to remain flexible and trust their gut instincts when trading. Such desires will inevitably lead them down the garden path, however, because trusting your gut turns you into a toy that the market can play with as it messes with your emotions and exploits your genetic predispositions. Experience shows that if you have no proven trading strategies, clear processes, and a fixed set of rules, you will fail. Managing your money intelligently, as well as the risks to your money, is also a must. Without a plan in hand and without the proper money and risk management, you'll trade blindly, opening yourself up for yet another emotional trap to snap shut on you.

TIP

A select few experienced traders have, over the years, managed to learn the art of intuitive pattern recognition. They've developed a sixth sense when it comes to markets, and they rely on their gut instinct in a manner that is both well-thought-out and controlled.

Letting Your Ego Rule the Roost

Your ego can sometimes be rather an unpleasant type to have hanging around when you're trading. It refuses to accept the fact that cognitive dissonance exists, so it tries to smooth out the dissonance by coming up with excuses for everything. Your ego forces you to suppress and rationalize all manner of unpleasantries that contradict your own convictions. Because it's difficult to reconcile your ego with incorrect assessments, you fall victim to yet another psychological trap. When it comes to trading, dogmatism is quite a serious character flaw. The market is always right — even when you feel unfairly treated. That's something you simply have to learn to accept.

TIP

Successful traders have internalized their humility and remember not to take themselves too seriously. They follow the markets and take a piece from every suitable pie that comes their way. They trade the patterns they see, not their beliefs or hopes.

Believing That Goals Are for Wimps

Only those who know their destination find their way, said the legendary Chinese philosopher, Lao Tzu. Have you defined your trading goals? Do you know what time frame is practical for achieving them? What are your expectations? If you can't answer these questions, you'll end up falling into the next psychological trap. Without goals, you lack the motivation and mental strength necessary to survive difficult trading periods.

TIP

Prepare a proper business plan for your trading business with short-, medium-, and long-term planning goals as well as profit-and-loss accounting. You should know what you'll have left over after deducting all costs and taxes.

Attempting to Bat 1000

If you believe that you have to win 100 percent of the time, your downfall is inevitable. This particular psychological trap will snap shut on you in the shortest possible time. Losses are part of the nature of the trading business. Even with the best will in the world, there's no way you can avoid regular losses, even if you have an above-average hit rate. Consistent loss limitation combined with capital protection is the only sensible strategy. Never trade without protective stops.

TIP

Trade only with the money you can spare — never with the money you need for your livelihood. Sticking to this rule will protect your nerves.

Indulging in Revenge Trading

Okay, you're angry about an unexpected trading loss and you desperately want to get your money back. You feel like a victim. Anger and rage, however, only cause you to violate your rules, rendering you incapable of waiting for the correct entry signals, so you impulsively make too many trades.

That, in a nutshell, is revenge trading. You lose your emotional balance and the emotional trap snaps shut.

Never let tunnel vision take over. If you feel it happening, take a break. Physical exercise and relaxation techniques can help you clear your head.

Overtrading

Overtrading is often the result of revenge trading. You want to get your lost money back, so you place one order after the other in a manner that is both hectic and impulsive. You break all the rules and end up in a downward spiral. The combination of anger, overconfidence, and greed lead to the emotional trap snapping shut. You've lost control and you will (possibly) end the day with unnecessarily high losses.

Be like a hunter in a tree stand — on the lookout and patiently awaiting the correct entry signals. This should be the only strategy guiding your trade frequency. If other forces are pushing you, it's time to take a break.

Doubling Down to Recover Losing Trades

Let's say you're behind with a position and understandably annoyed. You have exactly three options when it comes to responding:

>> **Close the position or let yourself be stopped out according to your rules.**

This is brain-compatible trading. You accept the loss and move on to search for new entry opportunities in the market.

>> **Hold the position, remove the stop-loss limit, and hope its price will reverse.**

> Wishful thinking isn't a particularly effective strategy — you might miss out on better trades.

> » **Increase your risk and add more into a losing trade, in the hope that you will recover initial losses with the next small rebound.**

> You move against the trend with an inflated position. Hoping for a reversal, you are essentially attempting to time the market.

The last strategy on this list is very risky but popular with traders and often works. But woe betide ye if the market doesn't play ball and your losses careen out of control. "Don't give up on losing trades," you might think. This is the evolutionary deep rooted fight-or-flight response. Your psychological trap alarm bells should be ringing, because you now may be fully invested and dependent on a desired reversal that may not come. You've lost control and you're incapable of action. The trend continues to move against you. The stock does not turn around, leading to substantial losses. Stress and anxiety are the inevitable consequences. The psychological pressure is too intense to bear and you close the position at a huge loss. Your trading account may even be exhausted.

The doubling down trading strategy is the main reason that traders fail. It is riding the tiger. Your trader psychology isn't prepared for the emotional pressure if it goes wrong.

TIP

Learn to accept small losses and focus your attention on the next winning opportunity.

Failing the Marshmallow Test

Experts tend to recommend that you limit your losses and let your profits run, but that's easier said than done. Bad experiences with losses make many traders forget that wins need to be managed professionally. Otherwise, the next psychological trap snaps shut. This trap originates in our evolutionary development, related as it is to our biologically driven desire for immediate reward. This deep-rooted reflex leads to the fact that traders usually take profits too early. If you don't manage to let your profits run, you won't be profitable with your trading over the long term.

TIP

Set clear profit targets for each trade, and when clear trends are apparent, pyramid your way to profits. This is brain-compatible trading at its finest. (For more on pyramiding as an investment strategy, see Chapter 11.)

Being (Unnecessarily) Contrarian

The old stock exchange proverb "The trend is your friend" seems to have fallen on deaf ears for many traders. It seems that it's quite popular to go against the prevailing trend. This is based on the hope of perfectly timing a turning point or trend reversal, which essentially means desperately searching for signals that may initiate a turn. (If you find that you're always saying to yourself, "The market should start correcting itself right around now," you're probably in a heap of trouble.)

This way of thinking may be a natural reflex, but it's no trading strategy. The market isn't interested in what you hope or believe. You build positions with the overall market trend in mind. Sailing against the wind requires an elaborate zigzag course. The psychological burden is correspondingly huge. The psychological trap snaps shut again. You will rarely succeed if your strategy relies on perfect timing — the resulting losses may burden you emotionally.

TIP

Resist the urge to build up long positions in falling markets and short positions in rising markets. You'll never find the perfect entry point. Go with the market, not against it. Your psyche will thank you for it. The only things that take off against the wind are airplanes.

Chapter **17**

Ten Success Secrets of Mentally Superior Traders

n this chapter, I show you the top ten secrets of success that characterize the work of mentally superior traders. If you follow the approaches listed here, practically nothing can stand in the way of your becoming a successful trader.

Gaining the Right Inner Attitude to Trading

If you're a successful trader, you've come to understand that trading is

» A business that works according to certain rules defined by the market

» An ongoing personal learning and development process

» An area where you have to maintain an emotional distance from your trading positions and focus instead on your strategy and setups and on signals from the markets

Adopting a Process-Oriented Trading Approach

Success means that you understand the importance of processes and that you have

» Set up your trading processes and systematized your trading

» Acted solely according to your tested and proven strategies

» Applied a fixed set of rules with setups that you've tested in a simulated environment so that these rules determine entries and exits, position sizes, and holding periods

» Ensured that your systems and processes are flexible as you continuously develop these elements and adapt them to market requirements

Prioritizing the Protection of the Capital in Your Trading Account

If you don't preserve capital and prevent loss in your portfolio, you can't be successful, so you need to

» Develop a money- and risk-management system to protect your portfolio

» Avoid concentration risk and establish an upper limit for the maximum size of single positions

» Determine a risk measure for the maximum loss amount you can tolerate per day or week

» Limit losing streaks (though you cannot prevent them) in accordance with your portfolio risk

» Stop trading immediately when you reach your defined loss threshold

» Adapt your strategy and setups where necessary (only after you've completed an error analysis) and regain a balanced emotional state as you start trading again

Carrying Out the Necessary Mental Loss Management

Successful traders know that it's all in your head, so you

» Recognize that losses have nothing to do with you or your ability but are instead part of the trading business — a business you're actively managing according to risk levels

» Truly accept losses and see them as a learning opportunity — rather than taking them personally and identifying with them. (You are not your trades.)

» See individual losses only in the context of your entire portfolio and the profitability of the day or week

» Refuse to hold on to losing trades, because you are unafraid of having to realize small losses

Exercising Mental Opportunity Management

Successful traders build their success on recognizing opportunities such as these:

» Focusing on the profits and goals you want to achieve

» Defining a profit target for each trade

» Following market price action and avoid trading against trends

» Choosing big-profit opportunities and, wherever possible, applying the pyramid strategy, as described in Chapter 11

Staying Humble

If you're a successful trader, you know that humility is a virtue and that you

» Internalize the imperative that you will never listen to your ego when it comes to the stock exchange

>> Humility in place of dogmatism is the only attitude that promises success

>> Accept the fact that markets are not fair, are not equitable, and never care about your feelings

Taking Responsibility

If you're a successful trader, you talk the talk and walk the walk, which means that you

>> Internalize the concept that you alone are responsible for your success or failure

>> Always refrain from blaming the markets, the broker, the trading platform or software, or any other adverse circumstances for your mistakes

>> Concentrate on improving your systems and setups

>> Ensure that you have the mental strength and emotional stability necessary for successful trading

Keeping a Trading Journal

Successful traders write it all down. Follow these suggestions:

>> Use your trading journal to analyze mistakes, carry out some self-reflection, and chart your personal and professional development.

>> Analyze your entries in the journal to identify subconscious patterns of thought and behavior that may be blocking your success.

>> Recognize the trading journal as an excellent coaching tool.

Finding Your Personal Trading Style

Successful traders know that no two successful traders are alike. To enhance your uniqueness, you

>> Successfully assess your own character traits and skills

>> Use simulated environments to determine the right trading style for you

>> Trade using only those market niches, financial instruments, and time frames where your strengths come to the fore and you have a distinct trading edge

Maintaining the Balance between Cognition and Emotion

When you're a successful trader, you know that balance is the key to maintaining your mental edge in trading:

>> You trade only in a state of psychological and physical stability.

>> You realize that you're fully cognitively capable only when you're in an emotionally balanced state.

>> You use relaxation exercises and mental techniques to restore the balance between cognition and emotion.

Chapter **18**

Ten Guiding Principles for the Perfect Trading Day

n this chapter, I show you what a perfect trading day looks like in practice. You have armed yourself if the following statements apply to you:

» You have prepared yourself thoroughly — technically as well as mentally.

» You know that a positive mindset makes it possible for you to profit from your professional expertise.

» You have worked out a plan for the day — one with concrete guidelines and goals.

» You know which trading style is best suited for your personality.

» You're an expert in your particular market niche — you play to your strengths and thus create a trading edge for yourself.

- » Your trading is based on what you do best.

- » You have successfully tested your trading strategy using your demo account, and you have determined that it's replicable. In other words, you have determined that your strategy regularly yields more profits than losses in all kinds of market conditions.

- » You know exactly when you will enter into a trade — and when you won't.

- » You have a solid set of rules to work from, and their parameters are unambiguous.

REMEMBER

You have internalized your routines and your process because you're convinced that you are doing the right thing.

Every trading day becomes a positive learning experience because you're concentrating on your strengths and implementing your trading plans in a consistent fashion. The point is not to win every day — but rather to optimize your processes and to strengthen your self-confidence when it comes to your own competencies.

- » You have learned to accept small losses, and you're able to focus your attention on future profit opportunities.

- » You react to market changes and not to individual trade losses. Losses have nothing to do with your abilities, but rather must be seen as just part of the trading business — a business whose risks you're in a position to systematically manage.

- » You concentrate on the profitability of your entire portfolio.

The decisive factor for your further development as a trader lies in deciding that improving your trading processes is more important to you than reaching your profit targets. You can formulate and control your process goals; you have no control whether you'll achieve your profit targets.

REMEMBER

Concentrate on those aspects you can control: your processes and the rules-based implementation of your tested trading strategy. By focusing on these matters, you can be successful.

Your profits depend on factors that are completely unpredictable, including arbitrary and random market movements — factors that are completely beyond your control.

REMEMBER

For you, trading is a permanent learning process that serves to further your own, personal development. Keep a trading journal; be responsible for your own development.

Planning Out the Technical Aspects of the Day

The day begins with taking stock (no pun intended) and thoroughly analyzing the markets:

>> You draw the right conclusions from the results and lessons of the previous day and determine which steps would improve your performance.

>> You analyze the market that will be the focus of your trading day today, and you develop concrete trading ideas.

>> You look for and evaluate other approaches and other perspectives that might provide counterarguments to your own trading ideas. (You play the devil's advocate, in other words.)

>> In your market evaluation, you take into account fundamental and technical indicators, relevant newsfeeds, and the analyses of those select few experts you follow.

>> You discuss your trading ideas with members of your trading community, experienced colleagues, or a mentor, and you incorporate their feedback into your planning.

REMEMBER

The market points the way. You observe, analyze, and follow market movements when the probability of success is clear. Using your setups, you carve out a profitable piece from the patterns you recognize.

Planning for Unexpected Scenarios

You expect the unexpected — and plan accordingly:

>> You work with scenario analyses in order to train your stress resilience as well as to keep a handle on risks to your portfolio.

>> You have identified the influencing factors and triggers that set unexpected developments in motion.

>> You have prepared yourself for both best case scenarios and worst case scenarios because, emotionally speaking, you've already played out both scenarios in your head and strategically calculated all possible outcomes.

>> Market turmoil fails to endanger your emotional balance, because your clear thinking has made it possible for you to come up with a set of contingency plans.

REMEMBER

Think the unthinkable. Leave behind established thought patterns as you take into account (as part of your trading strategy) those black swan market events — those completely unanticipated occurrences that are difficult to even imagine and that can completely upend the market. Portfolio protection must be your top priority.

Managing Risks Beforehand

Risk management is a central feature of your approach to day-to-day trading:

>> You know those low-risk market phases and times of day when you usually trade at your best. You precisely time when you plan on beginning the trading day and when you will end it.

>> Your trading frequency — the number of trades you plan to make in a given period, in other words — is determined solely by the quality of your strategy's entry signals.

>> You have determined the maximum daily loss you can experience while still protecting your trading account. When you have reached that limit, you immediately cease trading for that day.

>> You have set realistic profit targets for the day. When you have reached your target, you cease trading in order to protect your profits.

REMEMBER

Trading is a business, and, like any business, you have to plan and manage your trading with an eye toward the risk/return ratio, just as any CEO of a large company must do.

Filtering Relevant Information

You know which resources are relevant for your trading strategy:

>> You keep information overload at bay because you understand that knowing more doesn't automatically lead to better performance.

>> You understand that having more information only serves to distract you, fails to lead to a better understanding of the market, and often produces a false sense of control and self-confidence.

>> You sidestep the stress that comes with the daily flood of information by concentrating solely on those sources of information and factors that are relevant to your trading plan.

>> You make use of those few serious and reliable sources of information that actually provide added value. By doing so, you're able to distance yourself not only from the unreflective herd mentality of the masses but also from succumbing to the dreaded FOMO trade. (For more on FOMO trades — trades driven by your *fear of missing out* — see Chapter 13.)

>> You do the necessary research to determine whether there are verifiable reasons for a particular market movement or the development merely stems from media hype and herd enthusiasm.

>> You have become an expert in your particular market niche and you regularly compare notes with other traders who are active in the same field.

WARNING

It's unrealistic to assume that you can somehow gain an informational edge when it comes to inefficient markets. You can hardly avoid biases, herd behavior, and far-from-reliable rules of thumb when you're under stress, all of which inevitably lead to bad trading decisions.

Being Mentally Prepared

Good mental preparation ensures that you're focused and that you begin your trading day with a positive mindset:

>> You ensure that you won't be disturbed in your work environment, by removing possible distractions. The idea is to stay focused on your work.

>> You start your trading day with relaxation exercises and breathing techniques that work to develop your ability to concentrate and your self-discipline.

>> You use affirmations, visualizations, anchors, or reframing techniques from the self-coaching toolbox (see Chapters 6–8) to prepare for a successful trading day. A positive mindset makes you psychically more resilient and directs your attention to the success factors of your trading approach.

>> You have achieved a state of emotional balance and remain calm. You're now in a position to attentively follow the markets and your trades in a relaxed state as a fully neutral observer.

> » You define your daily targets as processes and not as absolute financial indicators. The point is to trade in a manner that is rules-based and controlled.

> » You focus your attention every day on what you can do to become a better trader.

TIP

Power comes from inner peace. Learn to master your trading day with the serenity and mindfulness of a Buddhist monk.

Keeping Your Parameters in Mind

You have conscientiously and thoroughly prepared every trade you plan to make, so you have

> » Considered market trends, technical indicators, and the volatility of the markets when preparing your trading setups

> » Observed the markets and waited patiently for your particular entry signals before acting

> » Determined the position size of your planned trade and decided whether you should enter the market all-in on one entry or gradually scale into the planned position size when the appropriate entry signals sound (scaling method)

> » Determined the specific time frames you are planning to trade, by determining the holding period of your positions before entering the market

> » Set a realistic risk/return ratio as well as a corresponding initial stop-loss and take-profit limit for each trade

> » Ensured that your risk of loss for every single position never exceeds more than 1 to 2 percent of your portfolio

> » Immediately exited a position when you have either reached your take-profit target or your time limit

REMEMBER

Plan every single trade. Trade solely according to plan and not in accordance with your beliefs or hopes.

Managing Ongoing Trades Professionally

You follow your open positions attentively so that you can respond appropriately to relevant market changes:

- » You adopt the role of neutral observer as you attentively follow your open positions and market developments. You maintain the necessary emotional distance.

- » You embody a disciplined mindset toward losing trades. You do not identify with the outcome of a single trade. At the end of the day, all that matters is the sum of all your trades.

- » You intervene in an ongoing trade only when the market environment and the associated probabilities of success have changed substantially.

- » In certain justifiable cases, you keep risk management in mind as you manage positions that are in the red, by incrementally closing out a percentage of your position — *scaling out,* in other words.

- » If your position runs up a profit, you reduce your risk in well-justified situations by securing your profits and cashing in.

- » Or you make a position that's in the black risk-free by setting the original stop loss in line with the original purchase price for the position — a *trailing* stop loss, in other words.

- » If it's clear that a stable market trend is set to continue, you can take advantage of the pyramid strategy and successively increase the size of the position currently in the black. You protect gains and you manage your portfolio risk by trailing the stop loss orders after each additional purchase.

WARNING

The active position management of ongoing trades is an art, not a science. To succeed at it, you need a great deal of experience as well as self-discipline. If you're a beginner, I strongly recommend that you do not intervene in an ongoing trade. Act in accordance with your original, planned setups.

Controlling Your Emotions in Advance

You want to stay, calm, cool, and collected when trading. That's why it's vital to consistently tackle, early on, your need for balance:

- » You regularly take short breaks and "recharge your batteries." You avoid the dangers of tunnel vision and maintain an emotional distance to the markets.

- » You use breathing techniques and relaxation exercises to develop your psychic resiliency.

- » Emotional stress and psychic tensions dissolve when you take part in physical activity. Physical movement breaks down the stress hormones your body produces.

- » You repeat a few short affirmations or visualizations to develop your mental strength.

- » You analyze, interrogate, and reflect upon those thought and behavior patterns of yours that seem to stand out.

- » You synchronize your physical and psychic states and orient yourself so that you're in a position to achieve your daily goals.

REMEMBER

Neuroscientific studies show that only those people whose body and spirit are in a balanced state are capable of using their cognitive abilities efficiently. Only then do they have full access to their logico–analytical intellectual capacity and to their intuition.

Evaluating Your Trading Day

A technical analysis of your trading day lets you take stock of your current situation. Evaluating your trades shows you which parts of your strategy and setups can be improved on:

- » You analyze each trade to determine which actions were correctly carried out and which actions failed. What could have been done better? Do you want to assign yourself any "homework" as part of your further trading education?

- » You recognize — after the fact and benefitting from the necessary distance — any chart patterns or formations that, in the hustle-and-bustle of your daily grind, you managed to overlook.

- » If you had to book too many trading losses, you ask yourself whether market conditions have changed, thus necessitating a change in your trading strategy and setups. Then you ask what exactly you could have done better.

- » Pay special attention to the balance of your own analyses. You're just as likely to learn from your mistakes as from your successes. Build up your strengths and stay motivated. Concentrate on those decisions that have worked well for you.

- » Analyses and evaluations can help you determine whether the profits you've made or the losses you've sustained occurred in accordance with your trading rules you had set for yourself or occurred against those rules. If your profits came from breaking the rules, they came to you purely by chance and are thus in no way indicative of your superior trading abilities.

REMEMBER

Markets are dynamic and change constantly — and you change along with them in that you further develop your strategies and setups every day. That approach is asking a lot from you, including a great deal of flexibility and a willingness to learn.

Learning from Your Mistakes and Developing Further

The different, quite varied techniques of self-coaching can help you recognize your weak points while also helping you develop further:

>> Writing out an evaluation at the end of your trading day trains your inner observer and keeps your ego in check. You ask yourself the correct (and often uncomfortable) questions because you want to develop further.

>> You improve your ability to recognize both explicit and implicit patterns. You learn how to interrupt harmful emotional patterns and replace them with helpful, solution-oriented behaviors.

>> You ask yourself whether there are any noticeable behavior patterns, negative self-talk, physical reactions, or recurring emotional reaction patterns that reveal themselves in certain situations, and you determine what triggers these reactions.

>> You use the self-coaching techniques I discuss in Chapters 6–8 of this book to dissolve negative thought and behavior patterns and replace them with positive ones.

>> You calculate the concrete costs of your harmful patterns of behavior — your missed profits as well as the losses you've suffered, in other words. This transparency is instructive and motivates you to counter such behavior early on if it makes another appearance.

>> The trading results of the day hold up a mirror to you and work to ensure that you don't fall victim to any form of self-deception. You and you alone are responsible for your results.

>> You have a mentor, a trading coach, or an experienced trader colleague to whom you can give an account of your actions at the end of the day. You lay your cards — your emotional states and conditions as well as the financial results of the trading day — on the table.

THE PATH IS THE GOAL

Nobody is perfect. You probably won't often experience the perfect trading day. Even in your regular life, that perfect day is a rare occurrence. What's decisive in this respect is that you strike out on your journey and that you treat every day as a learning opportunity. You alone determine your own personal developmental process. Be patient and don't put yourself under too much pressure. With the right mindset you can overcome setbacks and the obstacles in your way. As long as you're moving in the right direction, you'll be able to continue developing, step-by-step. The ten guiding principles in this chapter for the perfect trading day can give you a sense of what the real deal is when it comes to trading.

REMEMBER

The follow-up you do at the end of your trading day is your best preparation for the day to come. Don't frivolously throw away these learning opportunities. Your daily analyses can help you continuously improve your trading. Successful trading is a permanent developmental process.

Index

A

abdominal breathing, 136–137
ability
  compared with luck, 218–219
  in performance formula, 52
acceptance
  of emotions as a source of information, 32–34
  in five-phases model, 125
  of weaknesses, 46–47
accountability report, 104
acknowledging risks of storytelling, 160–161
active position management, 80–81
admitting failure, 169
adrenaline, 24, 230
affirmations, 129–132, 133
Akerlof, George, 211
alternate nostril breathing, 138
ambiguity aversion, 194
American Psychological Association
  The Road to Resilience guide, 32
amygdala, 230
analysis
  error, 216
  market, 21–22
  psychological, 91–93
  root cause, 216
  self-analysis, 21–22
  technical, 42–43, 91, 259
analytical logical powers of thought, 15
anchoring, 142–146
anger and rage phase, in five-phases model, 124
answering scaling questions, 92–93
anterior insula, 180
anti-Martingale System, 175
anxiety
  about, 139–140
  baseless groundless, 227
  breathing techniques for, 137–138
  compared with fear, 225–226
  harmonizing body and mind, 140–146

techniques for coping with, 139–149
  working with images in your mind, 146–149
aptitude, gauging, 52–60
asking questions, 134
assessing
  aptitude, 52–60
  consequences, 236–237
  probabilities, 191–192
  profit announcement drift, 212–213
  trading day, 264–265
attitude, inner, 251
autogenic training, 110
availability biases, 193
availability heuristics, 193
averaging down strategy
  about, 248–249
  deploying, 174–175
avoiding
  cognitive dissonance, 170
  mistakes, 187–197
  psychological traps, 245–250
  self-fulfilling prophecies, 231
  stress traps, 23–27
  tunnel vision, 102–105

B

back test, 40
balancing
  cognition and emotion, 255
  opportunities, 66–68
bank run, 207
bargaining phase, in five-phases model, 125
barriers to entry, 39
baseless groundless anxiety, 227
behavioral patterns
  creating successful, 96–97
  recognizing issues causing, 93–94
  replacing harmful, 94–95
  typical human, 14–15
best case scenario, 29

About the Author

Roland Ullrich, born and raised in Cologne, Germany, worked for 20 years for investment banks in Frankfurt, London, and New York, specializing in institutional equities. He was active on Wall Street for five years. In his most recent position, he was responsible for the global equities business of a Frankfurt-based global bank. For the past 12 years, Roland has been advising institutional and retail investors and traders, writing regularly for the financial press, giving lectures, and conducting seminars on the topics of trading psychology and brain-compatible stock trading and investment strategies.

Roland, who studied economics at the University of Bonn in Germany and completed his degree in 1990, is a holder of the right to use the Chartered Financial Analyst (CFA®) designation awarded in 2000 in New York. He has certifications as a systemic hypnotherapy consultant and coach (Milton Erickson Institute Heidelberg) and as a personality and competence trainer (MSA, KODE). In addition, he is a business coach for systemic structural constellations in enterprises (SySt Institute, Munich) and an NLP Coach (kikidan Institute, Berlin).

He is the proud father of four adult sons and lives in Frankfurt am Main, Germany.

Dedication

To Stefan, Florian, Andreas, Sebastian, Tana, and Udur. I love you all dearly. Thanks for always being my inspiration and support team.

Author's Acknowledgments

Thanks to everyone who made the translation of my German book possible, in particular Paul Levesque and Becky Whitney.

Publisher's Acknowledgments

Acquisitions Editor: Tracy Boggier

Senior Project Editor: Paul Levesque

Copy Editor: Becky Whitney

Production Editor: Magesh Elangovan

Cover Image: © Beautyimage/Shutterstock.com